LA FAMILLE DERIAZ

Five Generations
of Swiss Photographers

With a preface
by Charles-Henri Favrod

EDITION STEMMLE
SCHAFFHAUSEN · ZÜRICH · FRANKFURT/M · DÜSSELDORF

The International Center of Photography's presentation of "La Famille Deriaz: Five Generations of Swiss Photographers" is a new chapter of an older fairy tale. It all began in the early fifties with a young Swiss photographer, Werner Bischof, and his wonderful, laughing-eyed bride, Rosellina Bischof. They were much in love and Rosellina was ready to give birth to their second child when disaster struck. Werner and my brother, Robert Capa, were killed in pursuit of their work, Werner in Peru in a mountain car accident, and Bob in Indochina with the then retreating French army.

Since then, Rosellina and I collaborated on many levels to keep the work of these two men in the public view. Our efforts eventually led to the establishment of the Foundation of Photography in Switzerland and ICP in New York City. There were numerous exchanges of exhibits between us and photography gained substantial recognition in our countries and beyond for Werner and Bob and many others.

Rosellina died two years ago at the same time as the Musée de l'Elysée opened in Lausanne, an institution dedicated to photography.

The Director of the Musée de l'Elysée, Charles-Henri Favrod, presented a Deriaz exhibition in 1979 and called our attention to this remarkable Swiss family, whose five generations in Baulmes virtually embrace the 150 years since photography's invention.

The showing of "La Famille Deriaz" at ICP/MIDTOWN would not have been possible without the tireless efforts and cooperation of Armand Deriaz, the fourth of the "Five Generations", and the curatorial acumen and organizational talents of Trudy Wilner Stack, ICP/MIDTOWN Gallery Coordinator. We at ICP are delighted and honored to present the work of this unique Swiss family as a grateful memorial to Rosellina and Werner Bischof, whose lives and devotion have advanced photography and understanding.

Cornell Capa
Founder and Director, ICP
New York, June 1988

Contents

La Famille Deriaz

Charles-Henri Favrod
Director Musée de l'Elysée, Lausanne

Located at the foot of the Jura mountains, Baulmes is one of the oldest towns in the Swiss canton of Vaud. Prehistoric artifacts dating from the Stone Age have been found there in a mountain cave called "la cave à Barbareau." The medieval map known as "la Table de Peutinger" shows the Roman road that led from Lausanne to Orbe and Pontarlier passing through Baulmes along the gorges of the Covantannaz river. The local people still call this difficult passage "Caesar's Road". The forests near Baulmes are dense and wood has always been an important resource. At one time there were even wood furnaces for smelting iron. Later, at the end of the 19th century, a lime and cement factory was built at Clées, where the power of the Orbe river could be harnessed.

The names of the middle class families of Baulmes are Cachemaille, Collet, Eternod, Demelais, Perusset, Pillevuit, Ravussin and, of course, Deriaz. Local history records the name of Jean-Pierre Deriaz, botanist and philosopher, who in 1778 detailed a universal handwriting method in the oddly titled book *The Palace of Sixty-four Windows.* Also noted is François Deriaz, an officer in the French army and cited in the Spanish and Russian campaigns; he was later a colonel during the Restoration, then Inspector General of the militias of Vaud.

Alphonse Deriaz, his great nephew, was born in Baulmes on May 16, 1827. He was the oldest son of François-Louis, known as Boret, and Louise-Fanchette Deriaz, née Collet; his parents maintained a small farm and a hotel called l'Hôtel de France. From an early age, Alphonse was a distant family member, leaving home as a young man, he went first to England where he worked as a domestic servant in a manor house in Surrey. In Southwark on September 21, 1851, he married Caroline-Louise Lehmann, the daughter of Swiss innkeepers. But she died in childbirth shortly afterward. Tradition has it that the husband, inconsolable, then went to Australia to seek his fortune and to forget. Certain is that his younger brother Louis, known as Gaucher (born on May 3, 1830), obtained a goldmining concession in New Zealand. Louis went there in 1867 along with his cousin Louis Pillevuit and Théodore Mabille, both of them also natives of Baulmes. The Vaudois community, thus, seems to have had a calling for adventure and far away places. Although Alphonse Deriaz did not find gold in Melbourne, he did discover the darkroom. After leaving Australia, he explored the United States of the pre-Civil War era. From San Francisco to New York, he was able to witness photography's sudden and universal popularity. Later, in London, he learned to use calotype and collodion processes, or paper and glass plate negatives. In 1860 he went to Paris, where he worked with Claude Félix Abel Niépce de Saint-Victor, a pioneer whose uncle was the inventor of photography.

Alphonse Deriaz worked on projects for the Historical Monuments Commission which, at Mérimée's initiative, was making an inventory of all buildings deemed worthy of note. Thus from 1865, we have original photographs taken by Deriaz of châteaus and churches in the Aisne, Indre-et-Loire, and Seine-et-Marne provinces.

It was in Paris that Alphonse met his first cousin Nanette-Sophie, ten years his senior and the daughter of Jacques-François and Suzette Deriaz (Suzette's maiden name was Deriaz also). The interrelationships between the families seem as dense as their traditions were imposing: despite his taste for long distance travel, Alphonse would marry Nanette-Sophie in Baulmes on April 25, 1852.

The Franco-Prussian War led to his return to Switzerland. He established himself as a professional photographer in the town of Morges at 15 Central Street, and very soon orders for portraits were coming in. But he did not confine himself to his studio; upon request he often travelled to the surrounding towns and countryside. It was during one of these trips in Bière on August 18, 1873 that his son Armand was born, while Alphonse was photographing the artillerymen stationed there.

This only son would be the pride and joy of Alphonse Deriaz. Armand was very bright, eager to learn, and an excellent student. He studied Latin and Greek at School, and learned English from his father. His mother, who had worked at the court of one of Austria's noble families, taught him German. Armand also learned the rudiments of photography, all the more readily now that Alphonse, without altogether abandoning the difficult collodion technique, had begun to take snapshots with gelatin silver plates. The father's dream was that his son become a pastor. But Alphonse's sudden death of a cerebral hemorrhage on October 3, 1889 was to alter this proposed course.

In order to keep the family business going, his widow tried to foster an association with the Genevan photographer Henri Cornu, who, like her late husband had done, collaborated with Staub and Kuhn, publishers of Swiss panoramas. Sadly, her attempt failed. The newspaper *Feuille d'avis de Morges* of December 28, 1889 announces the sale, "for a low price", of all of Alphonse's negative plates. Few people were interested (fortunately for us, otherwise we would know nothing of Alphonse Deriaz and his work), but Armand was to master the situation with energy and decisiveness.

He was only sixteen and his father's death had been a terrible blow. A page from a notebook has been found in which he mourned, in English, "I am joyless. My father is dead. I am unhappy, dull, the dullest of all men in the world. My father, my dear father..."

He thought it best to leave Morges with his mother and settle in the Hôtel de France, the spacious family residence in Baulmes. The hotel now housed several new activities; worshippers from the Free Church and meetings of the Blue Cross now assembled in the former drinking hall, and there was room for the studio, equipment and archives, backdrops and accessories in the out buildings.

In order to master his father's trade, Armand worked assiduously at photographic technique. He subscribed to the first professional journals, bought books on photography, and answered an advertisement from a photographer in Pontarlier, France who was looking for an assistant. As was typical of that time, he got there on his own, bundled belongings over his shoulder, by travelling through the Joux forest at the height of a terrible winter, despite a frostbitten foot.

Post cards officially came into existence in Switzerland on October 1, 1870, but for more than twenty years they had no illustrations. Armand Deriaz understood immediately the potential of the post card for the dissemination of photographic images. This potential was even greater now that the calotype had finally made the reproduction of post cards satisfactory and easy. As soon as he had returned from his apprenticeship in France, Armand began to systematically photograph the entire region surrounding the Jura, from Orbe to Yverdon, from la Sarraz to Grandson. At the top of le Chasseron mountain, he was the first to experiment with Auguste Vautier-Dufour's telephoto lens. The instrument was three meters long and weighed forty kilos. Armand was to use the telephoto more extensively when the innovations of the astronomer Schaer provided a more manageable, rapid and precise lens.

Armand Deriaz published panoramas of absolutely exceptional quality for the period. From the first days of the new century, his post cards reproduced images of life: not only landscapes, but work in the fields and forest, climbs to mountain pastures, soldiers conducting drills, children at school, women at the fountain, the marketplace, athletic events or the champion of the shooting competition. When he photographed these, or for example each stage of the construction of the railroad, both the Vallorbe and the Sainte-Croix lines, or the laborious laying of foundations for the lime and cement factory, he was reporting, recording history.

With his heavy equipment, he climbed the peaks indefatigably, always seeking a better perspective; he missed nothing in the towns and villages scattered in the plain, nor among the alpine chalets surrounded by magnificent, ancient fir trees. In 1912 he proceeded to inventory the most beautiful trees in the canton for the Vaudois Forestry Society. We are thus indebted to him for documenting the small-leaved Marchissy linden tree, the Coppet elm, the Gresalleys ash trees, the great Leysin spruce and the sycomore maple of la Murée. Attentive to both objects and people, this wise and simple man devoted himself to recording a world that, as he was well aware, was fast disappearing. His photos offer a remarkable account of the changes that took place over the first thirty years of the century, years that were decisive for the region.

On March 27, 1914, Armand Deriaz married Elise Cachemaille. Since both the groom's mother and the bride's father had died recently, the ceremony in Baulmes was austere. But on their honeymoon the couple enjoyed the radiance of the Côte d'Azur; their trip from Marseille to Monaco is recorded in a handsome photograph album. On February 16, 1915 they had a son, named Alphonse after the grandfather who had founded the Deriaz dynasty. From a very young age Alphonse II learned the secrets of timing poses and developing, how to handle cameras, and the subtleties of the photographer's eye. When his father's vision deteriorated to the point of near blindness, Alphonse was to accompany him on all his travels and help him in the laboratory.

Armand Deriaz died on May 19, 1932. The newspaper *Journal d'Yverdon* printed a fitting obituary notice: "Since circumstances prevented him from participating in public life, he devoted himself all the more to his private circle. Those who had the privilege of knowing him well remember an affable and benevolent man with a pleasant conversational manner and a discerning mind. Through photography he was able to make his town and his region beloved by strangers, and even succeeded in revealing the canton's charms to his fellow Vaudois."

When his father died, Alphonse was only seventeen years old. Although he had wanted to become a mathematician, he now planned to take over the studio. He left Baulmes in order to pursue photography studies in Vienna and Berlin. Through this training he achieved impressive technical mastery which, upon his return home, enabled him to advance the development of the photograph publishing enterprise. His dynamism was evident in all domains. Just as his father had taken advantage of the automobile in order to take pictures that were completely novel for his time, so Alphonse was among the first to make use of the airplane in producing photographs of the mountains from a completely new and dizzying angle, as well as his aerial views of the villages and towns of the Vaudois region. This method of surveying the canton gave him a unique familiarity with its topography; even today he knows each peak and valley intimately.

He was a post card expert. He pursued the collaborative relationships his father had initiated with Olivieri from Nanterre, Perrochet-Matile from Chaux-de-Fonds, Messaz from Montreux, Finzi from Lugano, printing post cards using the calotype process, then the most efficient way to print on spooled paper. And, in 1933, Alphonse Deriaz took on the challenge of color with Vontobel from Zurich: this involved taking black and white negatives, reproducing them by photolithography, and printing them in eleven successive colors. His era allied a respect for tradition with the innovations of chemical experimentation and research. Paraphenylene diamide turned the photographers' fingers brown, magnesium exploded in their faces, and the plates and cameras were still very heavy, making any attempt to take pictures outdoors into a cumbersome expedition. But already photography had become a familiar, even necessary, part of life. Identification cards became obligatory during World War II, and the entire population of Baulmes filed through the small Deriaz studio in the Hôtel de France. It took one franc and five minutes to have your picture taken.

On September 10, 1938, Alphonse Deriaz married Marguerite Deriaz who, despite her name, was no direct relation. They took their honeymoon under the heavy sky of the Munich accords – to the Côte d'Azur like Alphonse's parents. Then came the mobilization of troops in the Jura along the Franco-Swiss border, and thus new difficulties after the years of economic crisis.

Their family grew: they had a daughter and then, in 1942, their first son, who was born patriotically on August 1, a Swiss national holiday, and named Armand after his grandfather. Young Armand faithfully perpetuated the family tradition by beginning to learn photography almost at the same time he was learning to walk. After having completed his training at the School of Photography in Vevey, he discovered photojournalism, travelling and reporting in such diverse places as Senegal and the Caucasus, Jordan and Northern Ireland, as well as his own Switzerland, where he concentrates on traditional festivals and political demonstrations.

In 1969, Armand Deriaz was awarded the Federal Scholarship for Applied Arts for the third time. That same year saw the birth of his son, whom he did not name Alphonse, as tradition would have required, but Lionel. While still a child, Lionel declared emphatically that he would never be a photographer. But he had not reckoned with the force of destiny. Photography got the better of him, and the fifth generation has now come to the fore. Already, at the age of eighteen, Lionel is printing from the glass plate negatives of the Deriaz dynasty with sensitivity and skill.

There you have it. Over more than a century, this family has observed and recorded places, people and events with an unshakable loyalty. Five generations of artisans, as dedicated as they were modest, travelled the long road from collodion to gelatin silver prints, from glass plate negatives to rolls of 35 millimeter film, from gum bichromate to the color carbro print, and from photolithography to the instant color image, not to mention pioneering the use of cameras and lenses of all weights and sizes.

The virtue of photography is that it can make time stand still and thus can offer a reply to Job's anguished question: "When I am no longer, who will look upon me?" It is through photography that these five generations of the Deriaz family have become representatives of the continuity of life. They expose their worlds, both literally and figuratively, to our gaze, which in turn brings their gaze back to life and makes them our contemporaries.

Translated by Judith Malone

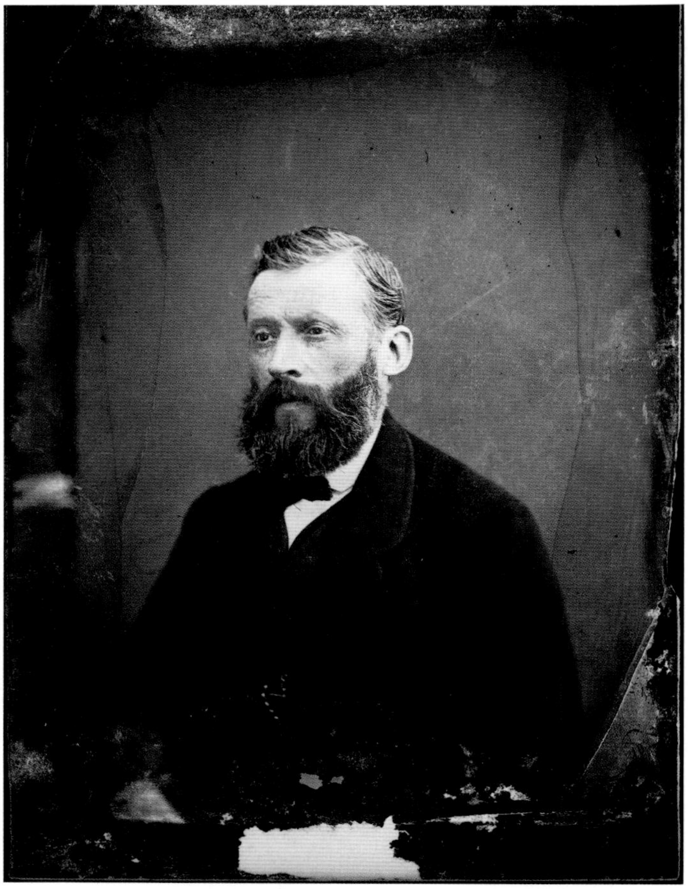

Alphonse Deriaz I

Born on May 16, 1827. As soon as he was old enough to leave home, he travelled to England, Australia, and the United States, and it was through these travels that he discovered photography and began to learn its techniques.

In 1860 he went to France, worked with Niépce de Saint-Victor and undertook projects for the Historical Monuments Commission.

The Franco-Prussian War caused him to return to Switzerland and he subsequently opened a photography studio in Morges. There, photographing local festivals and ceremonies, individuals and groups, he chronicled daily life and notable community events.

He died on October 3, 1889.

Self-portrait, 1875.

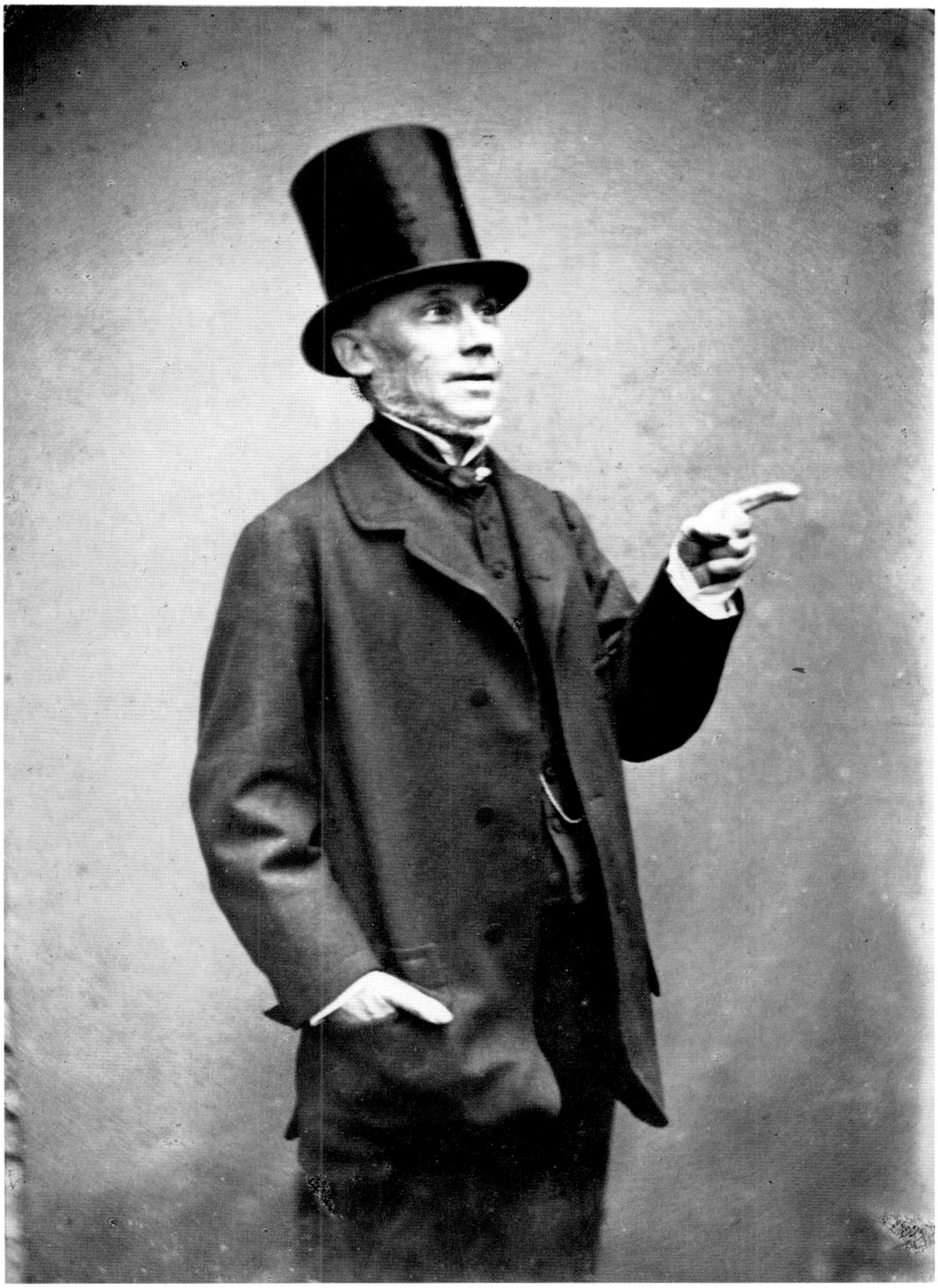

Morges. Distinguished citizen, 1871.

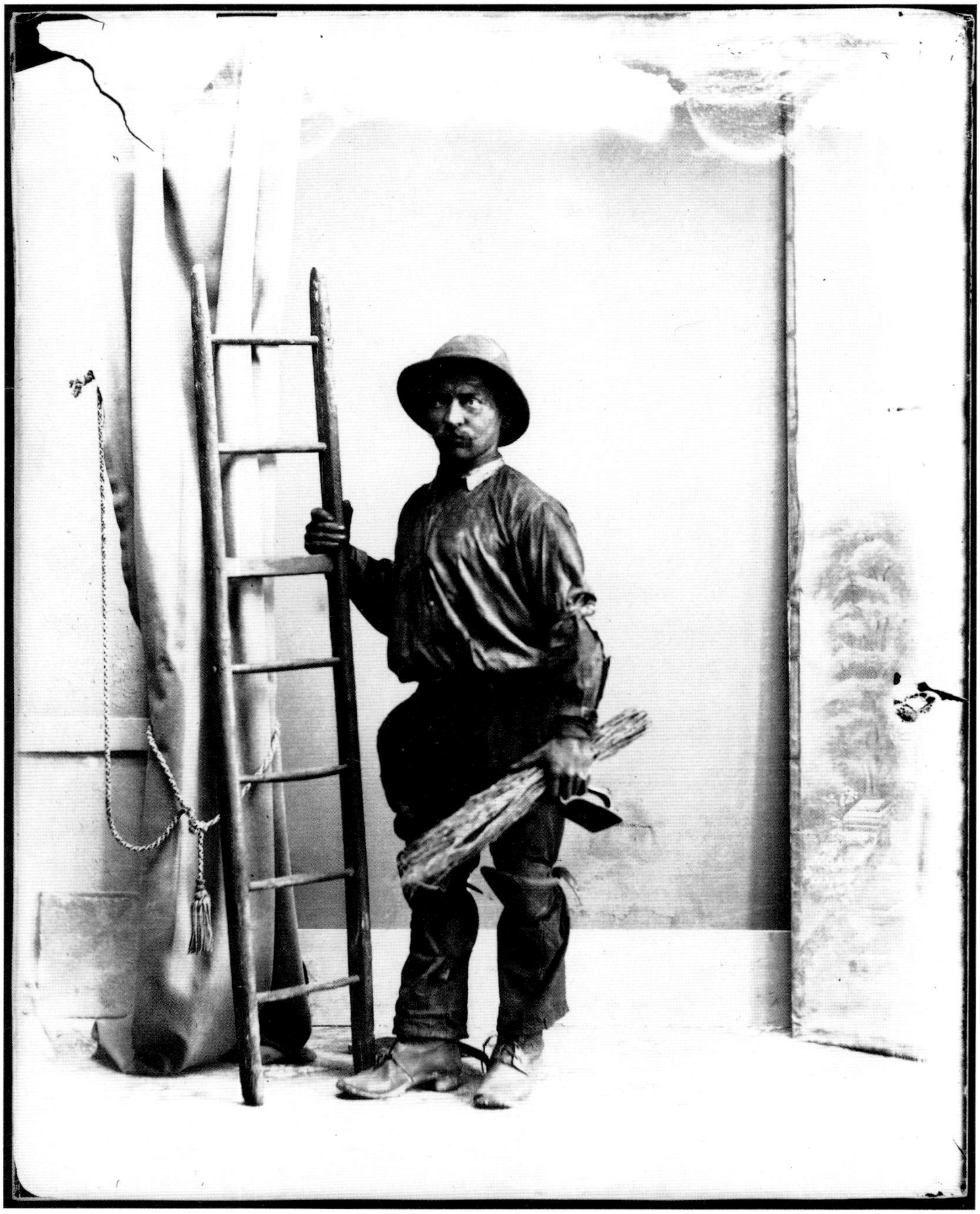

Morges. Chimney-sweep, 1874.

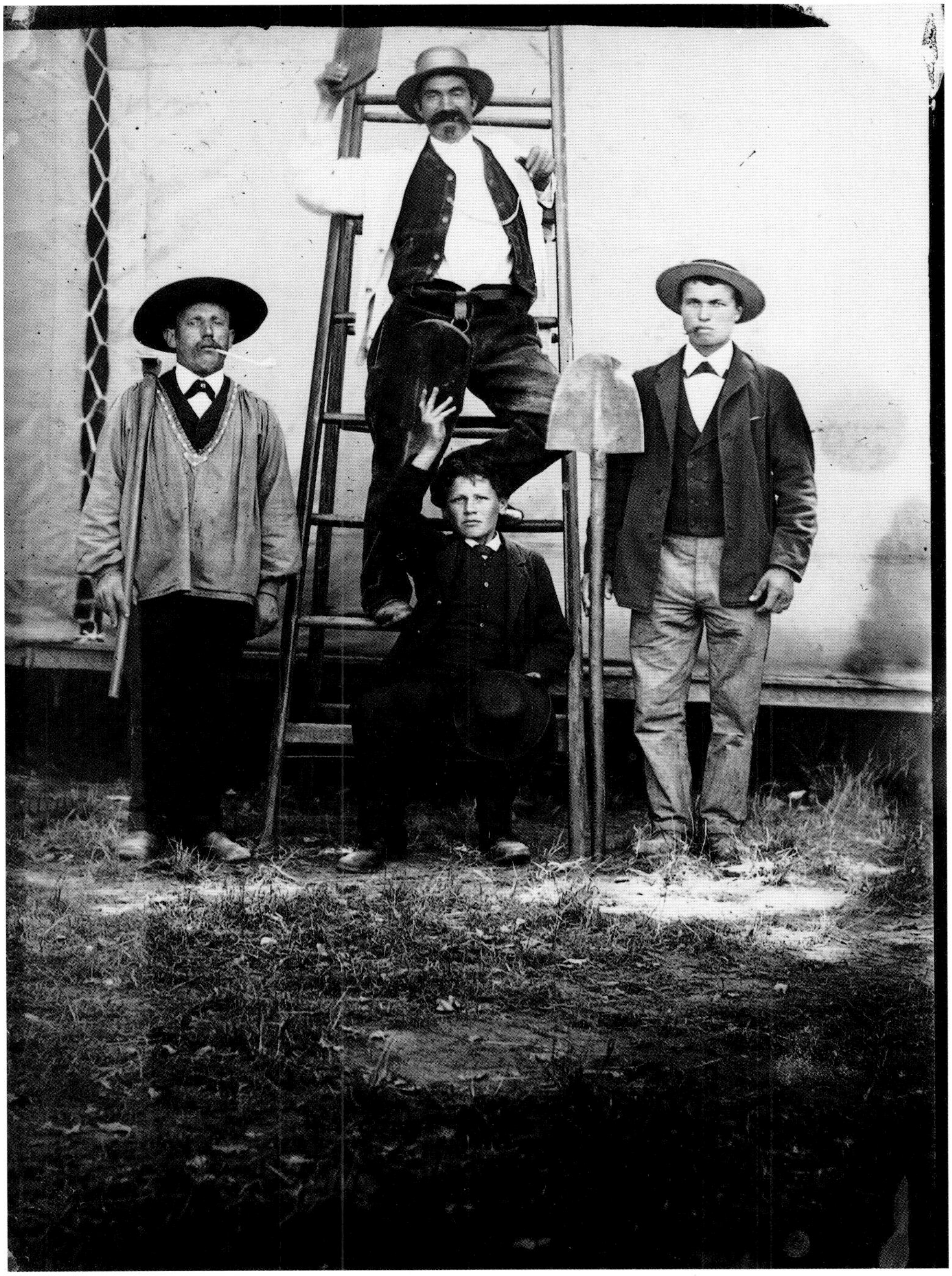

Morges. Roofers, 1873.

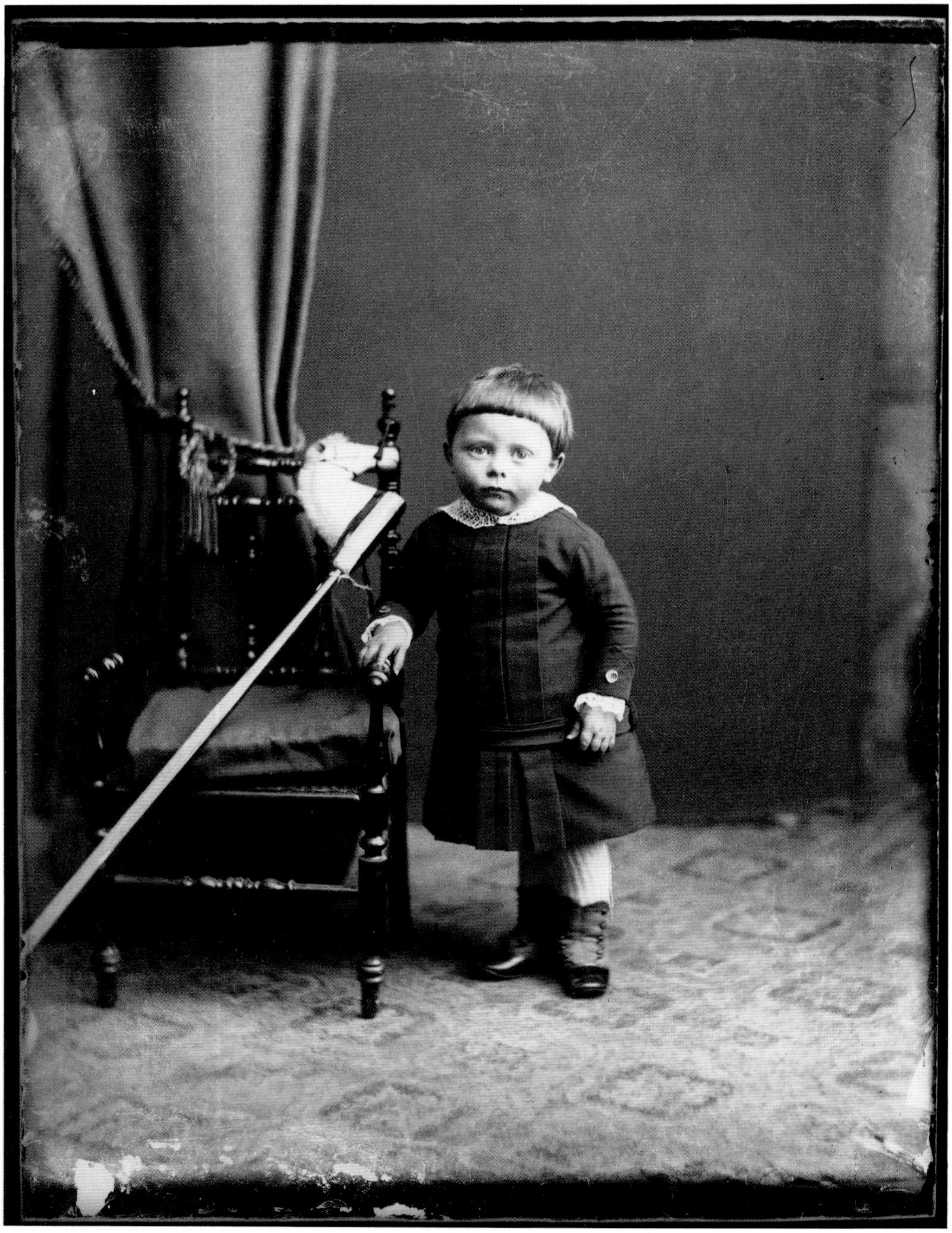

Morges. Studio portrait, 1873.

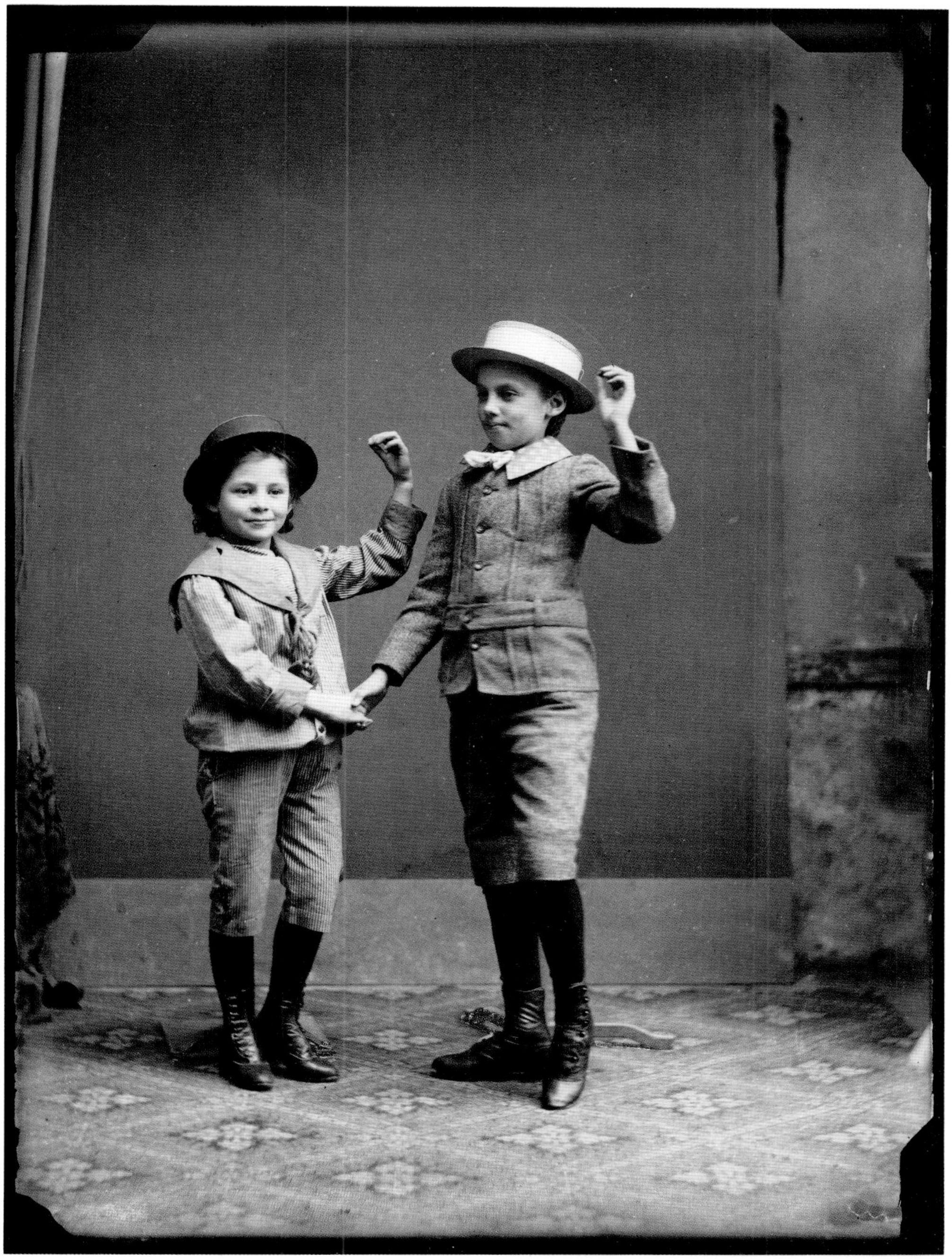

Morges. Jig, 1873.

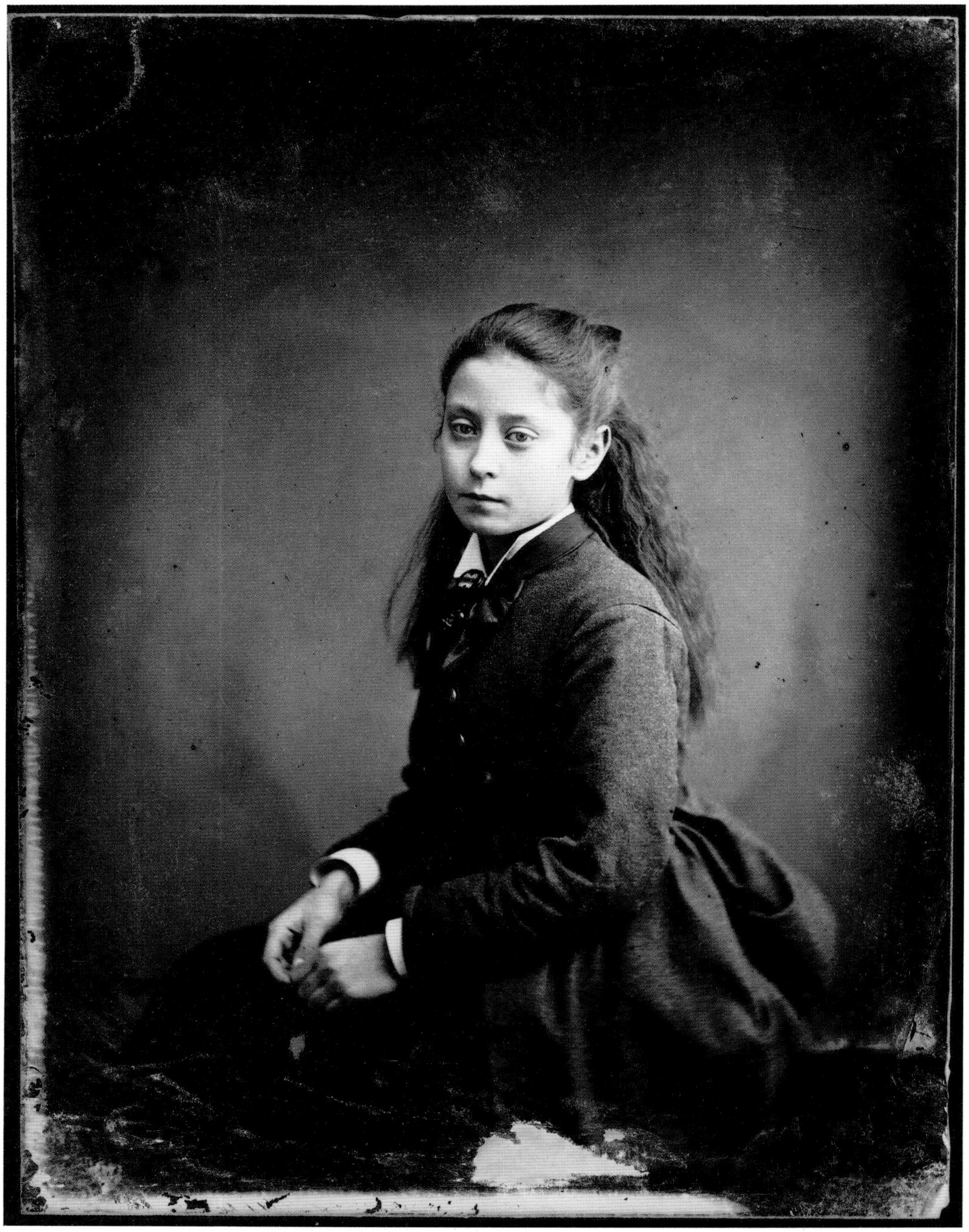

Morges. Studio portrait, 1872.

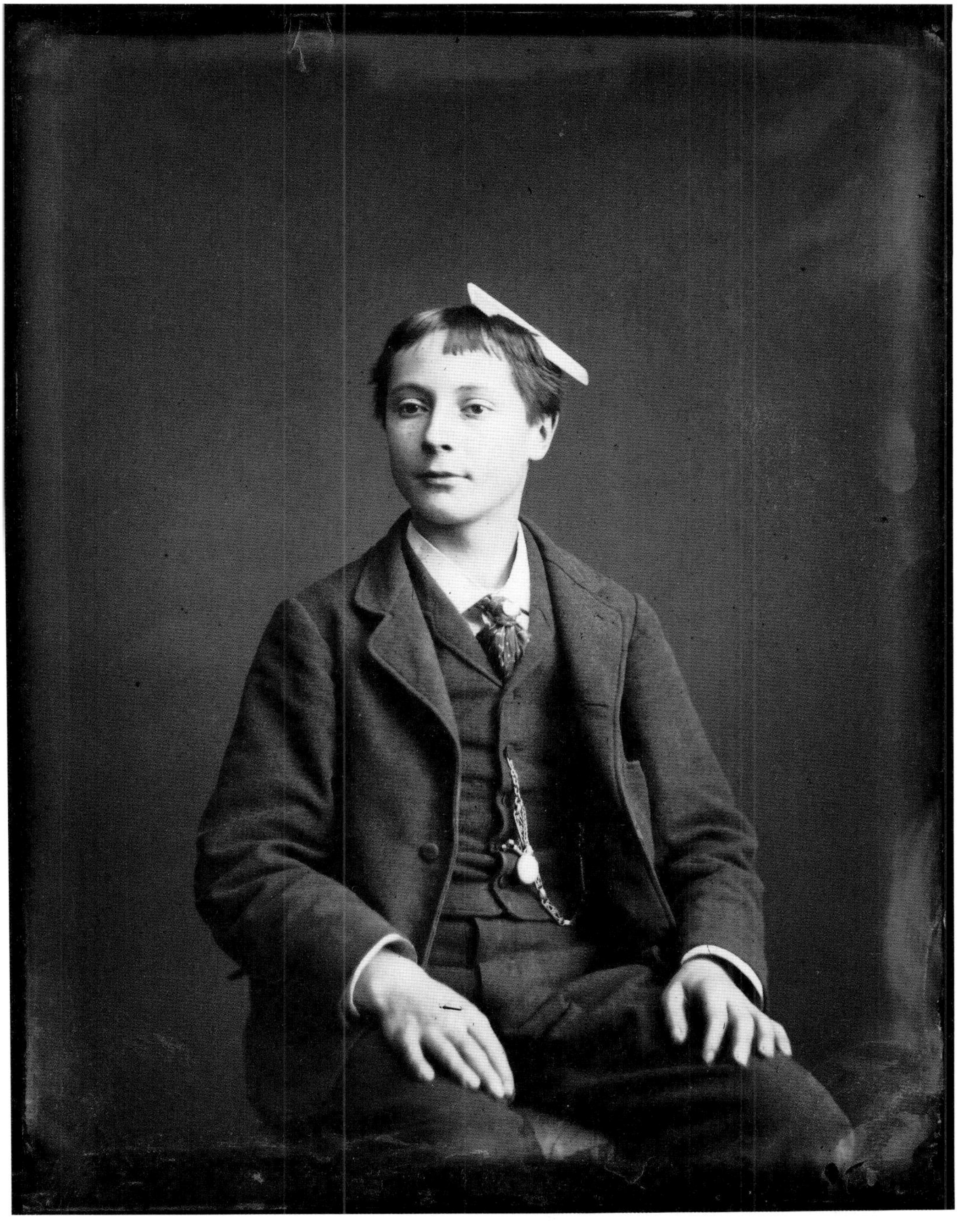

Morges. Studio portrait, 1872.

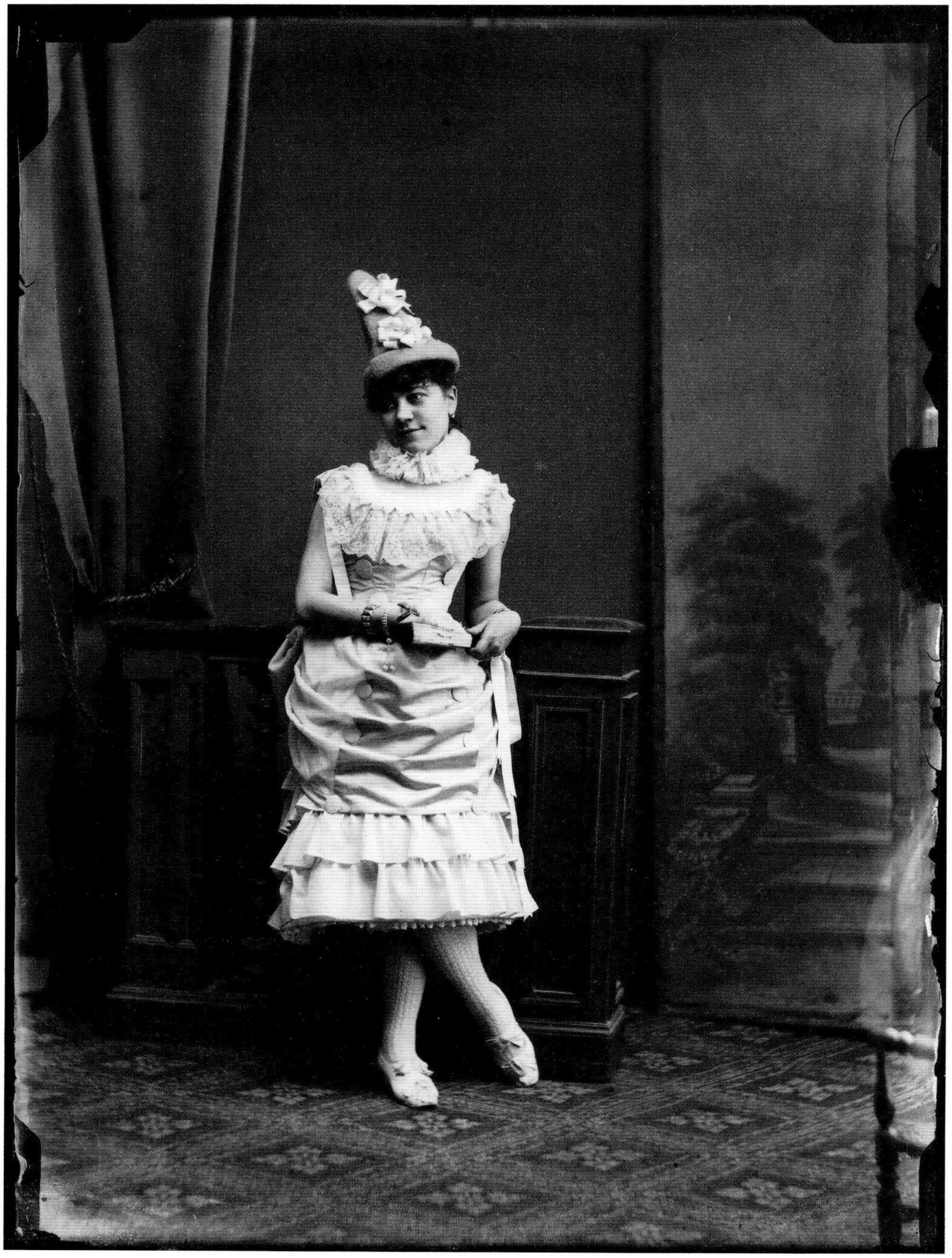

Morges. Colombine, 1872.

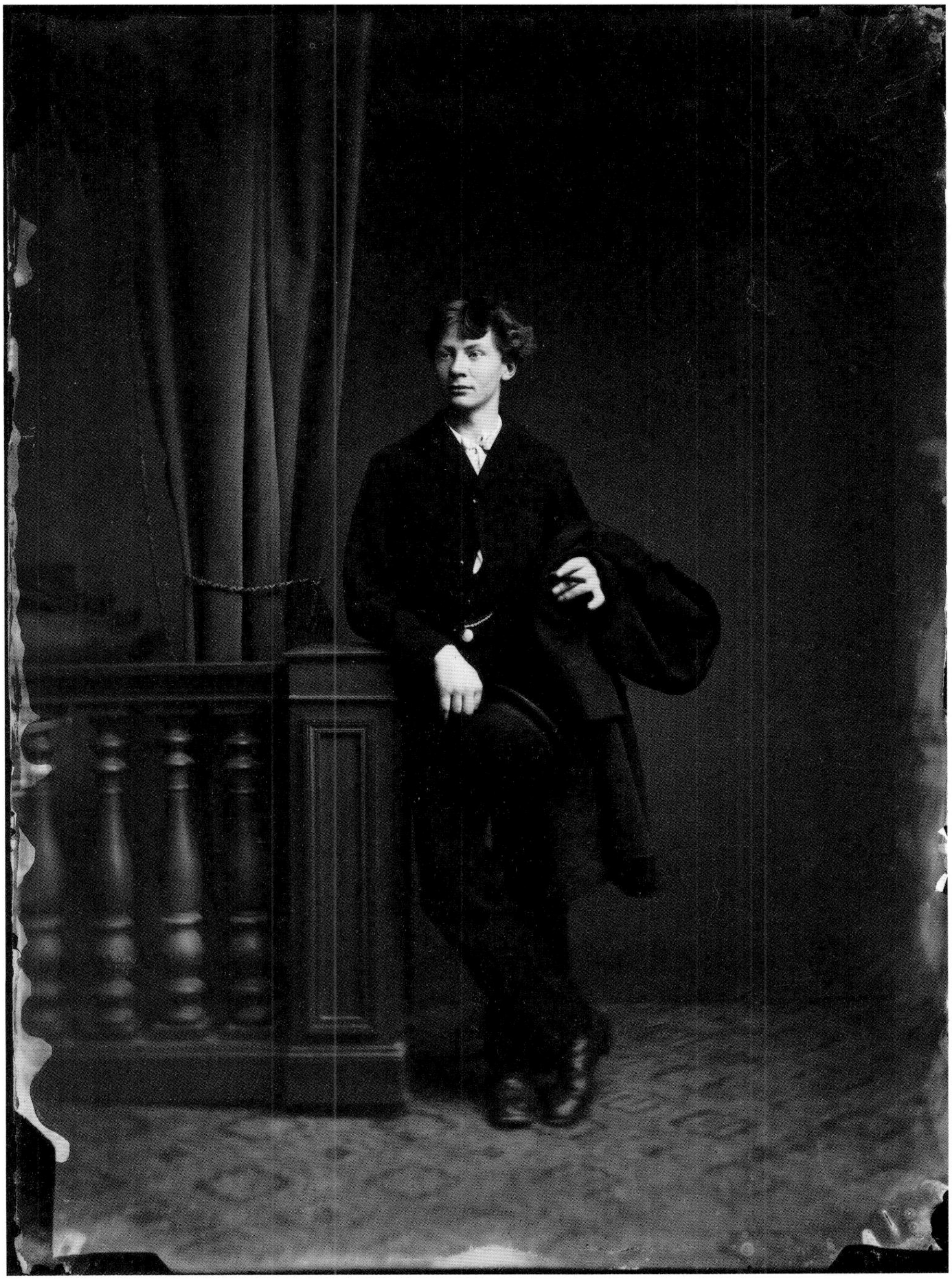

Morges. Studio portrait, 1872.

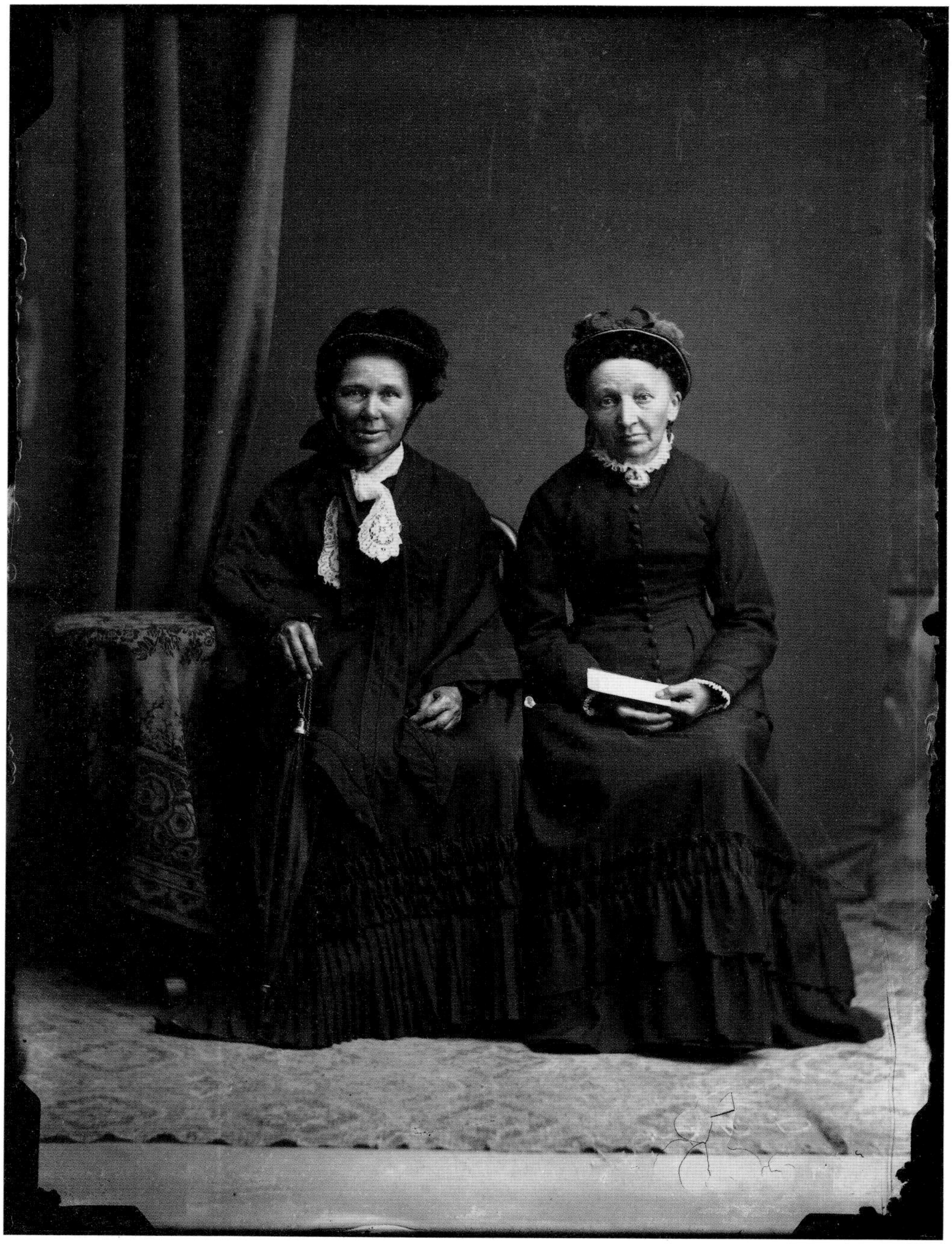

Morges. Studio portrait, c. 1873.

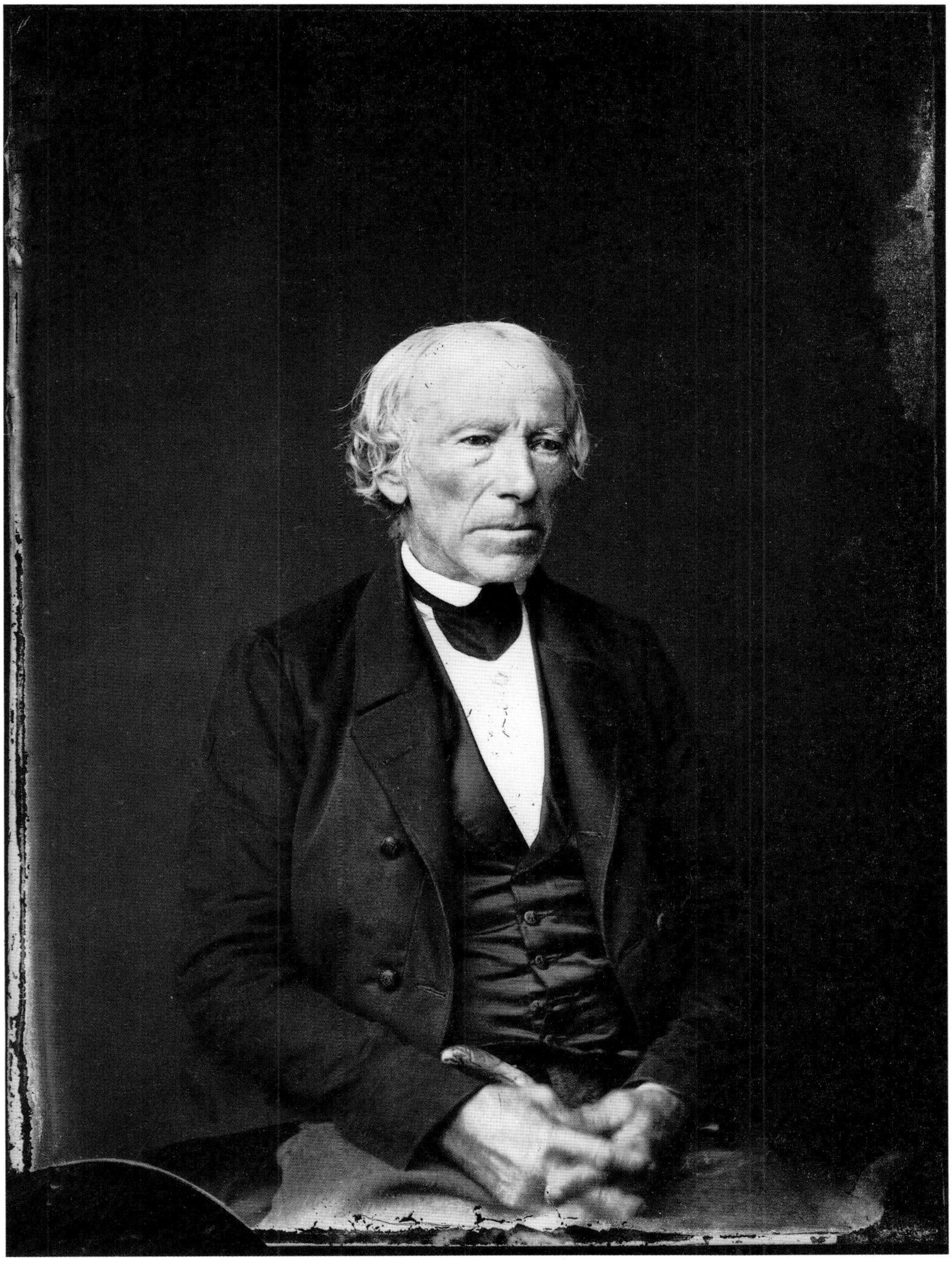

Morges. Studio portrait, c. 1873.

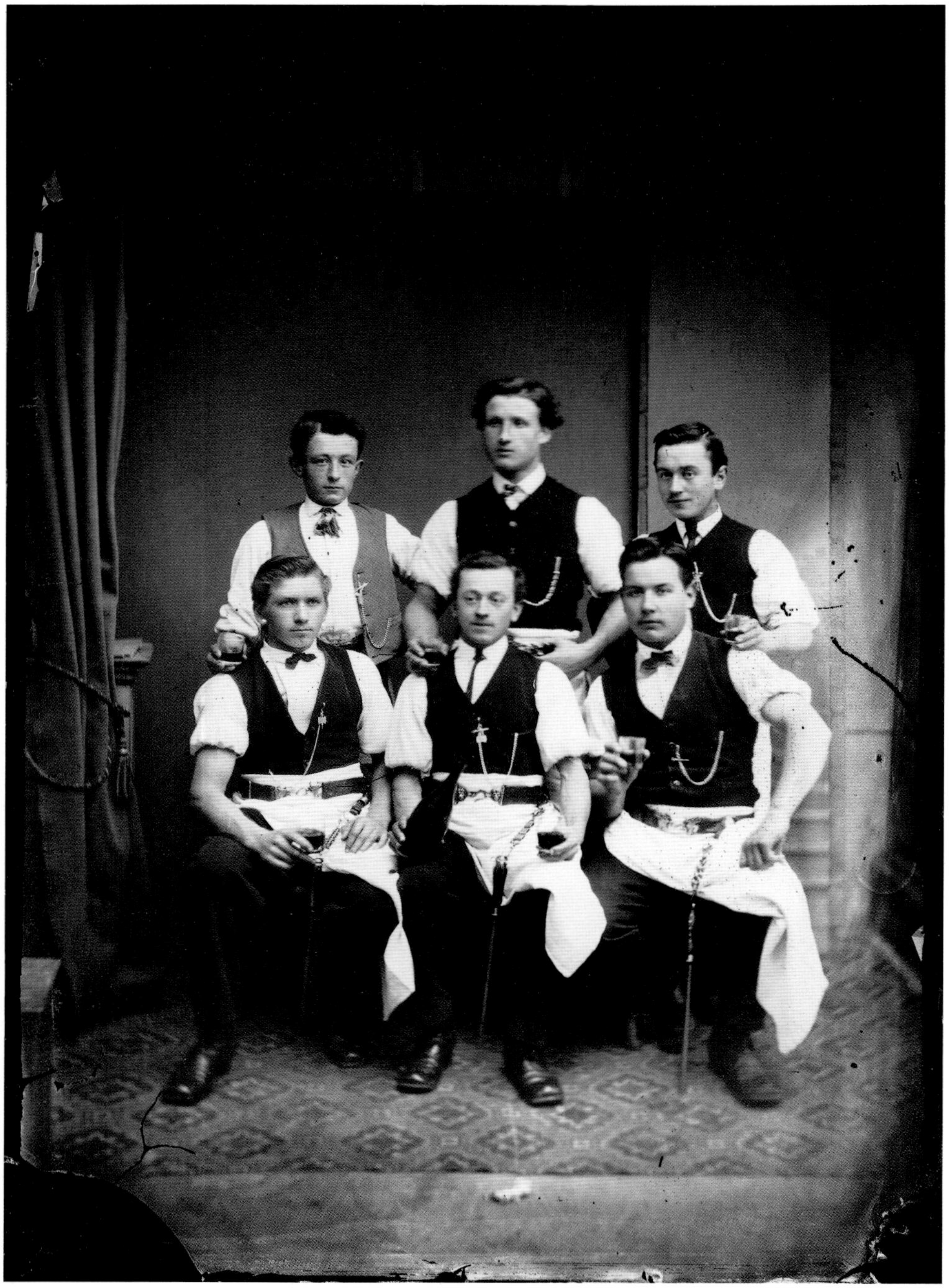

Morges. Butchers, 1876.

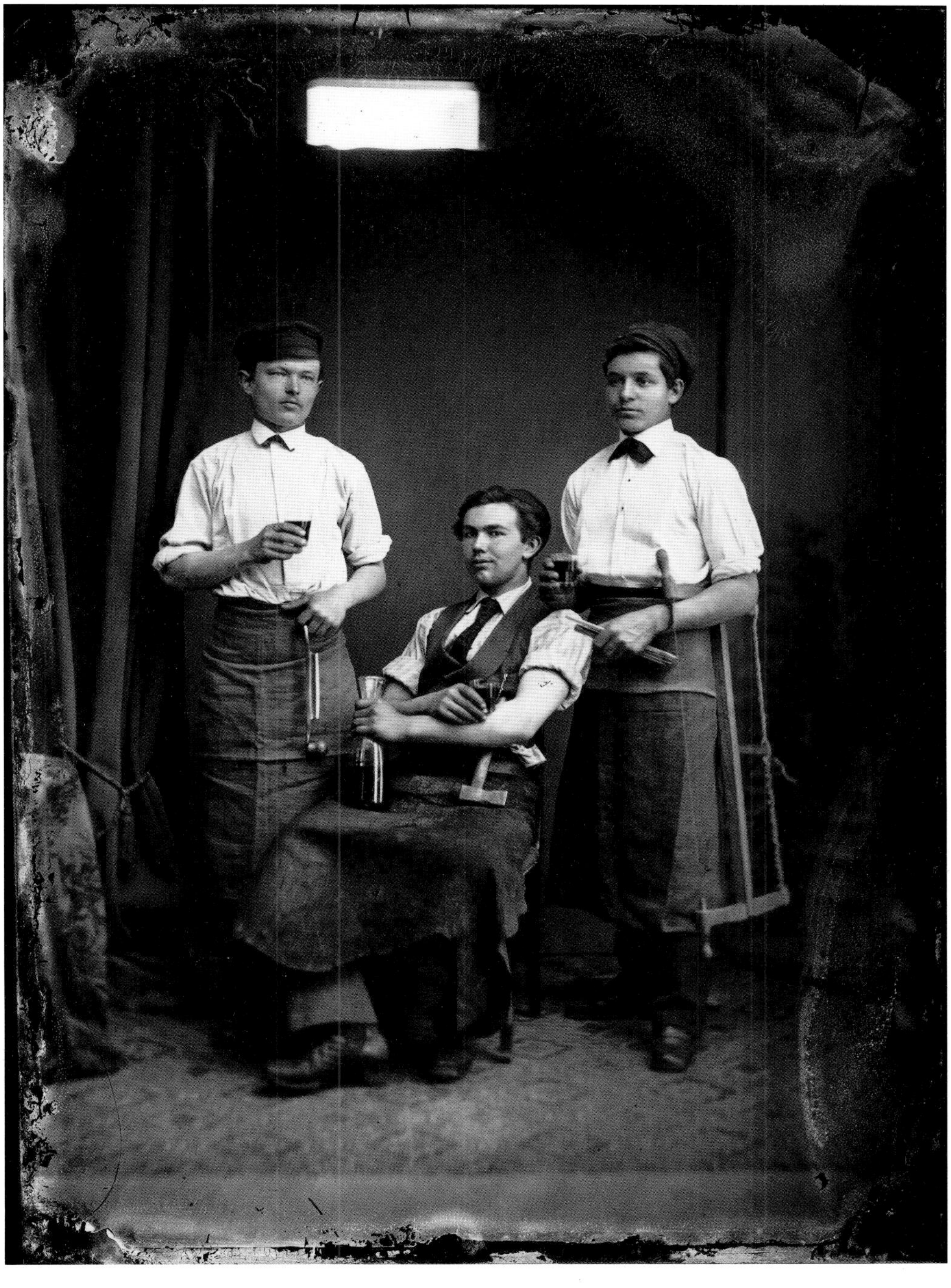

Morges. Carpenters, 1881.

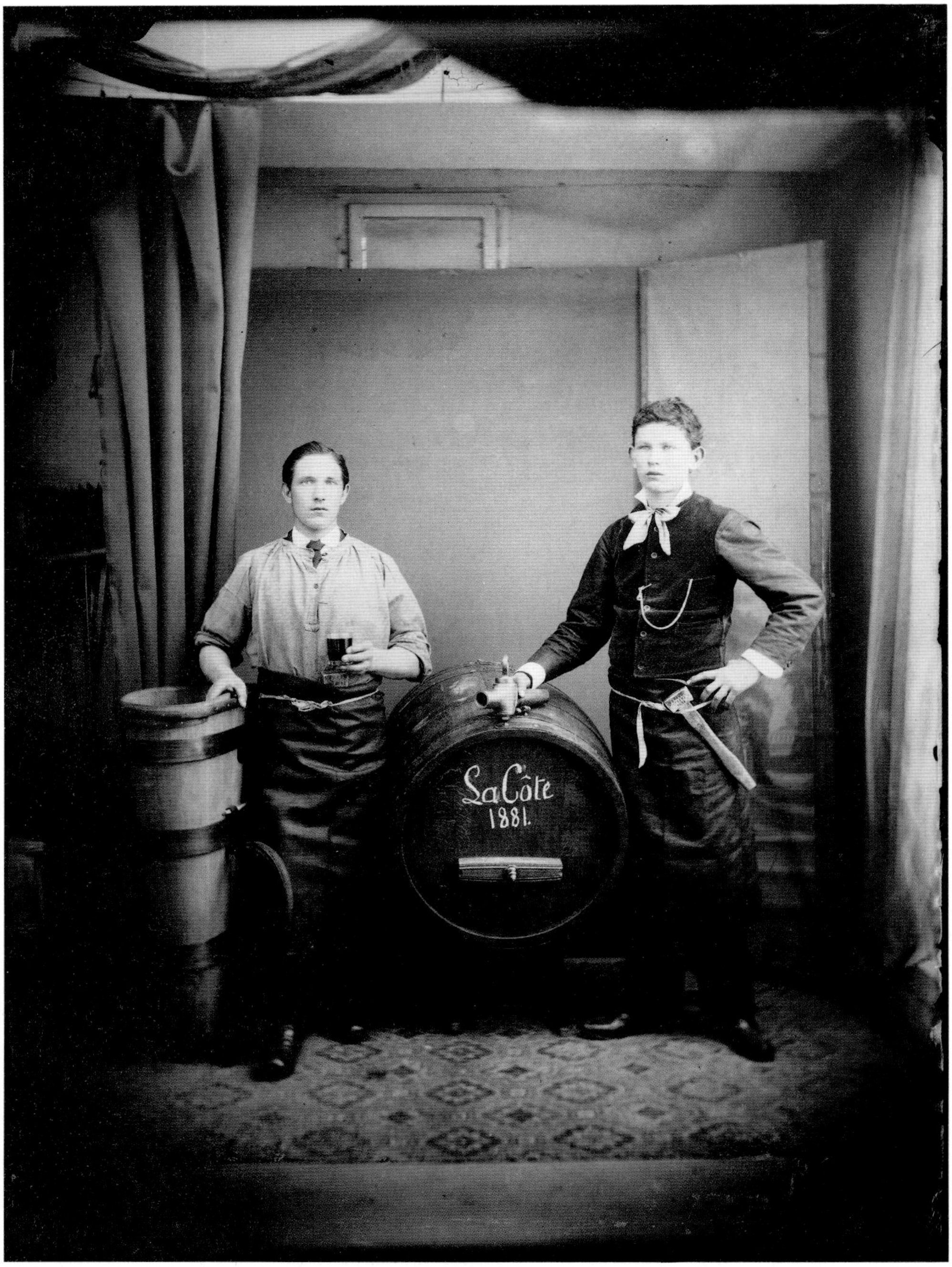

Morges. Vintners from la Côte, 1881.

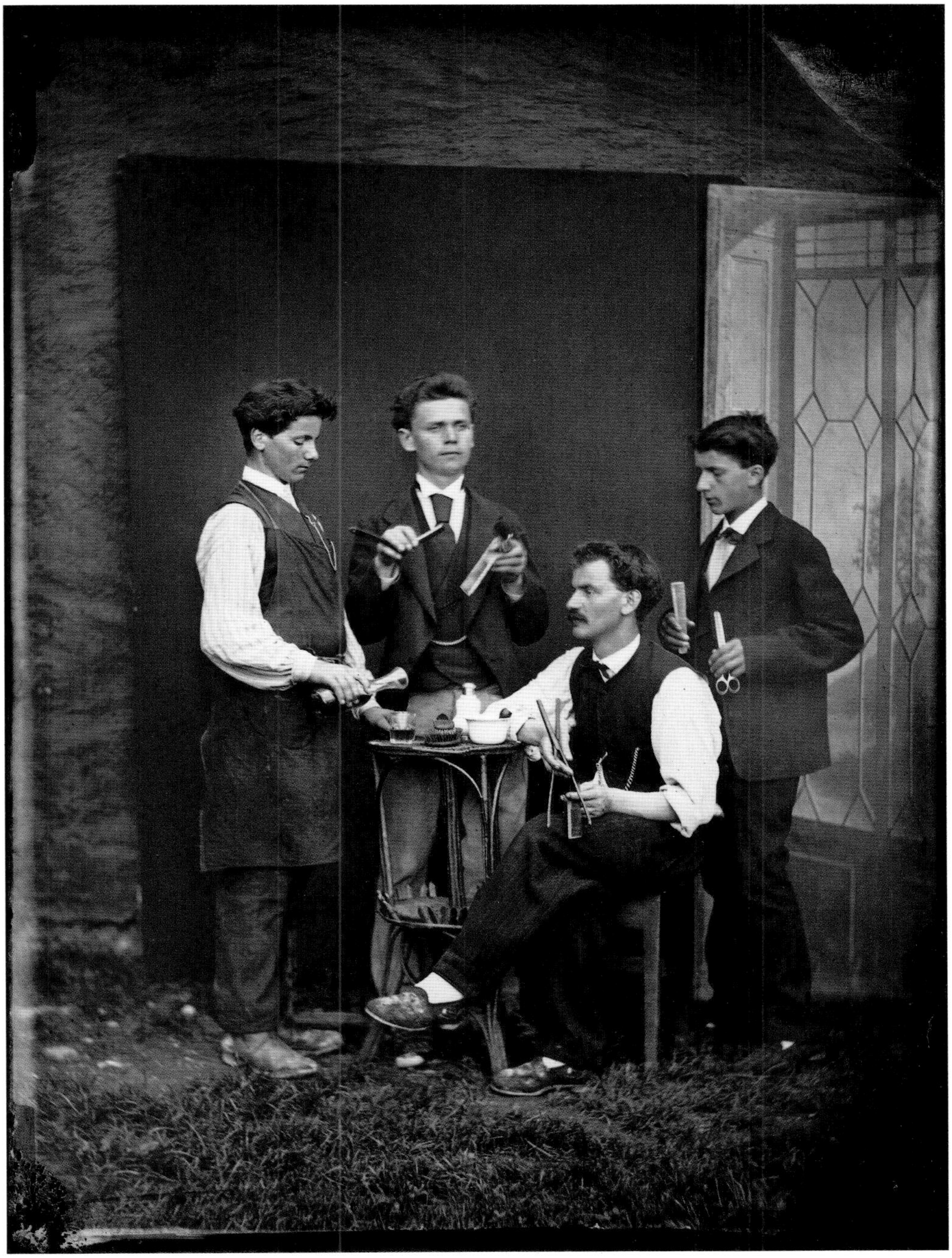

Barbers at the military barracks of Bière, 1882.

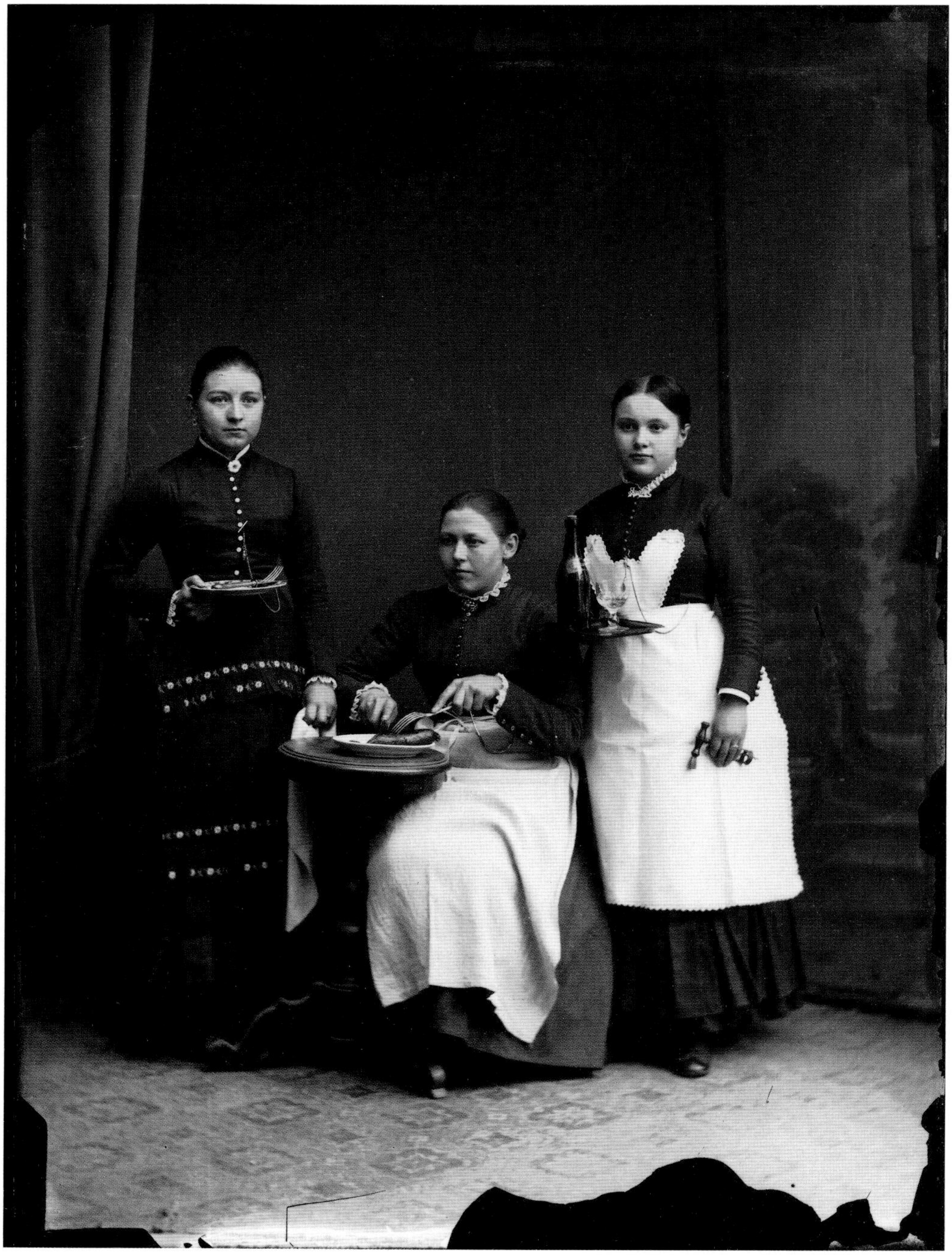

Morges. Hotel waitresses, 1879.

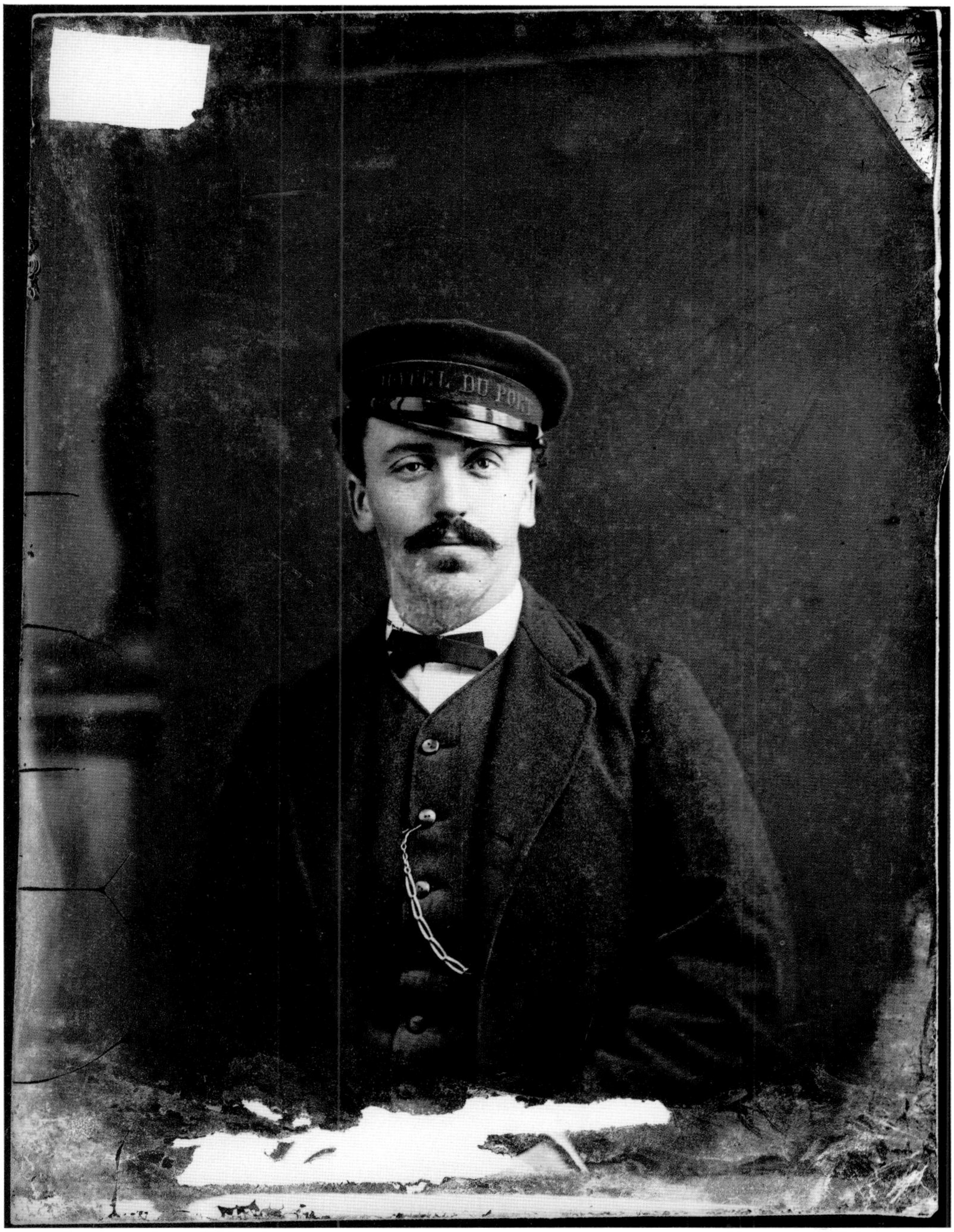

Morges. Studio portrait, 1872.

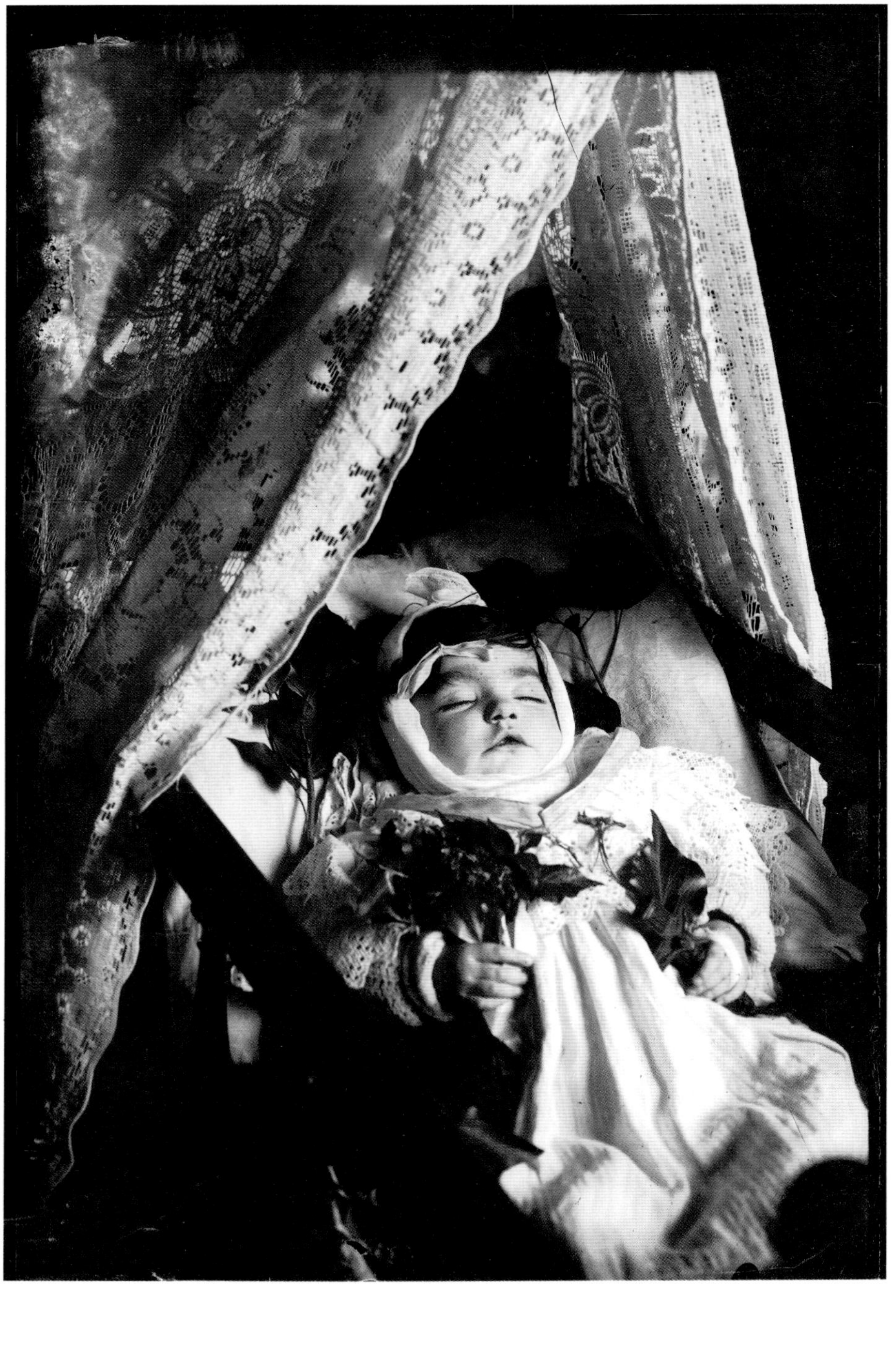

Morges. Photograph of a dead child, c. 1880.

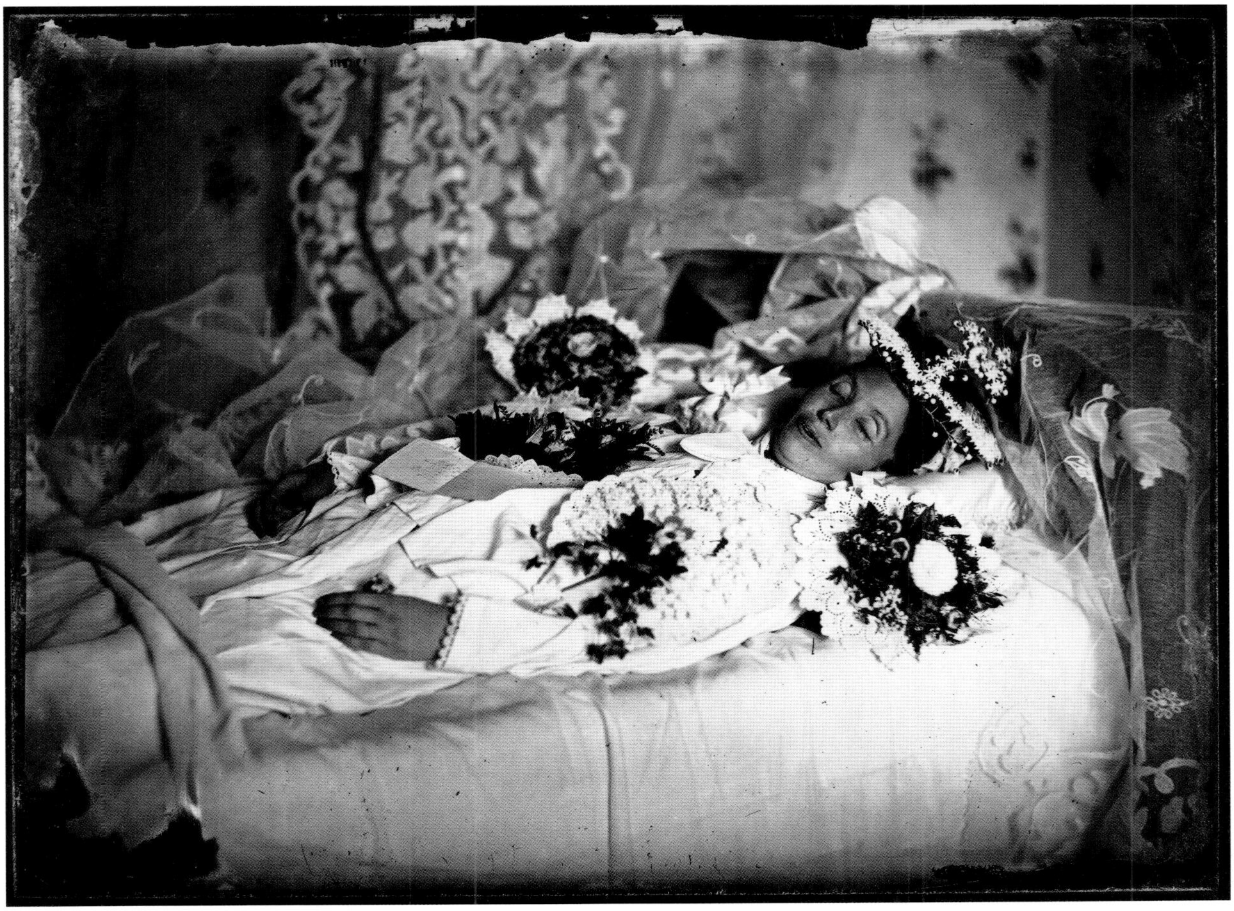

Morges. Photograph of a dead woman, c. 1880.

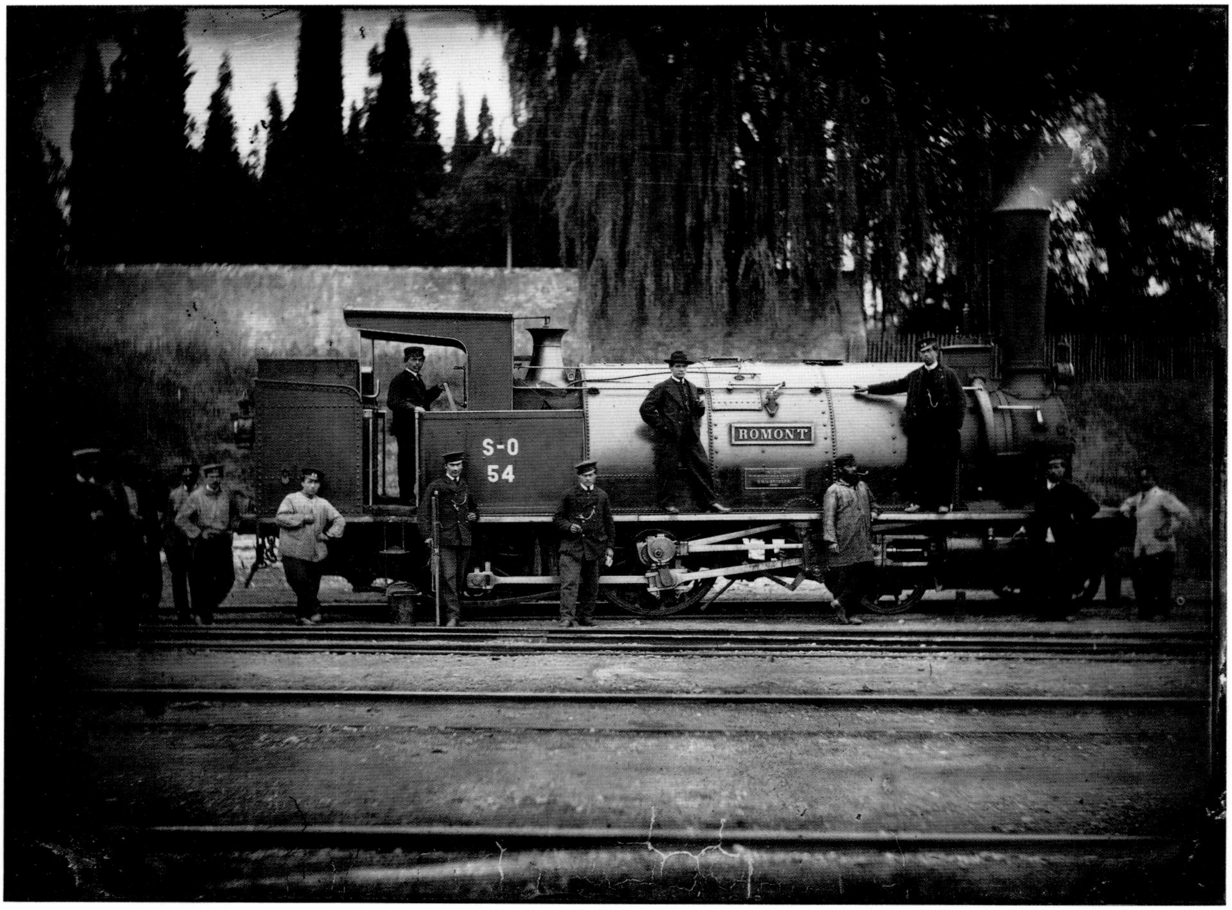

Morges. Locomotive, Compagnie Ouest-Suisse, 1872.

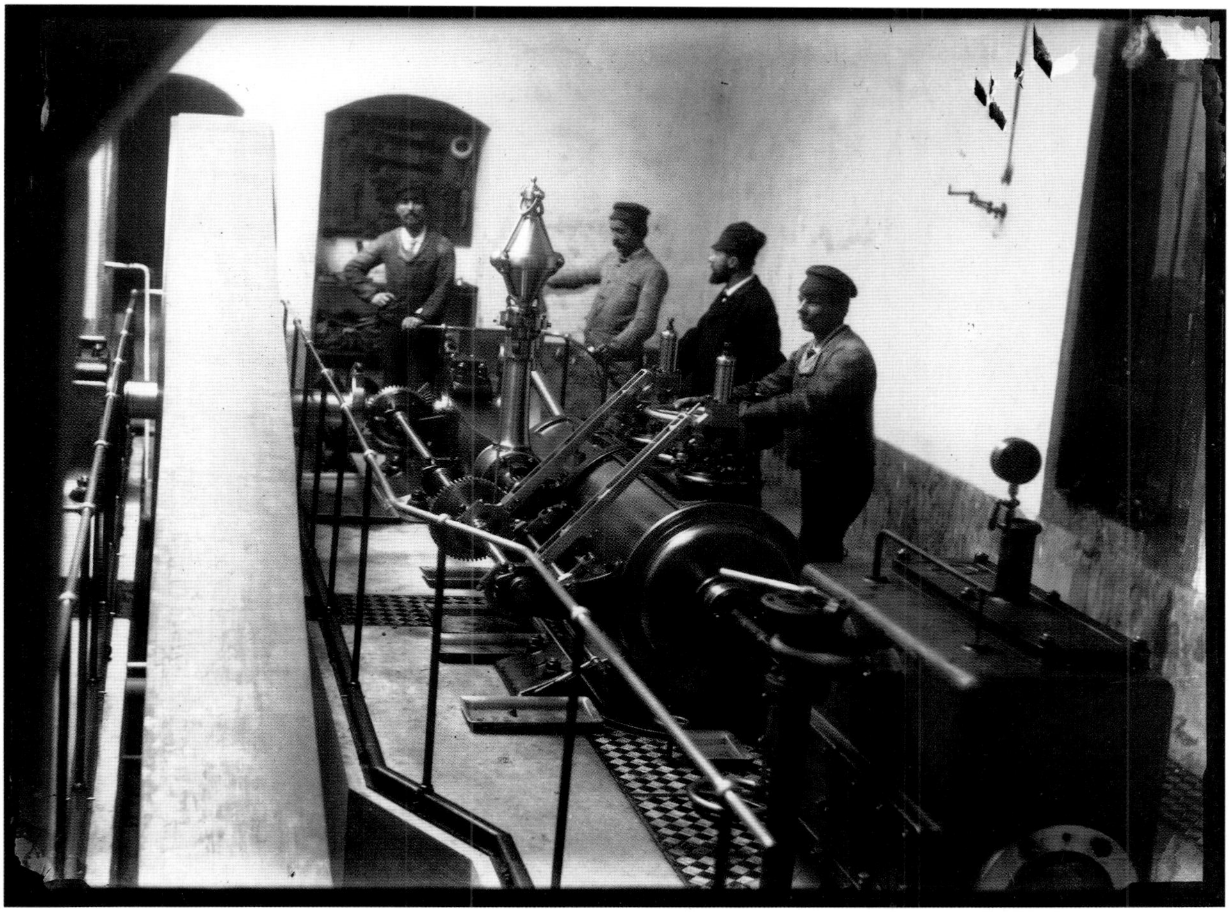

Electrical plant in Aubonne, 1874.

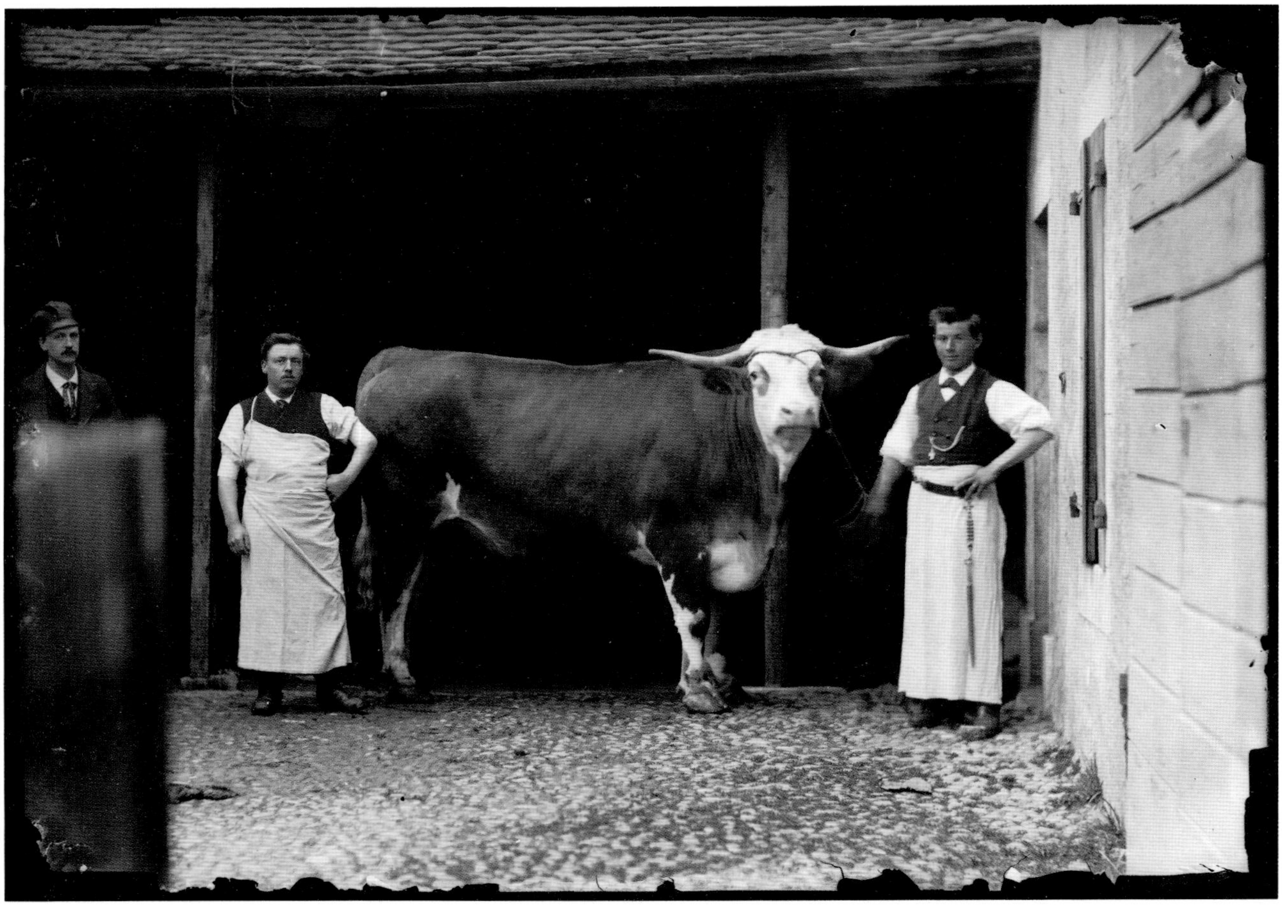

Morges. Butchers, 1876.

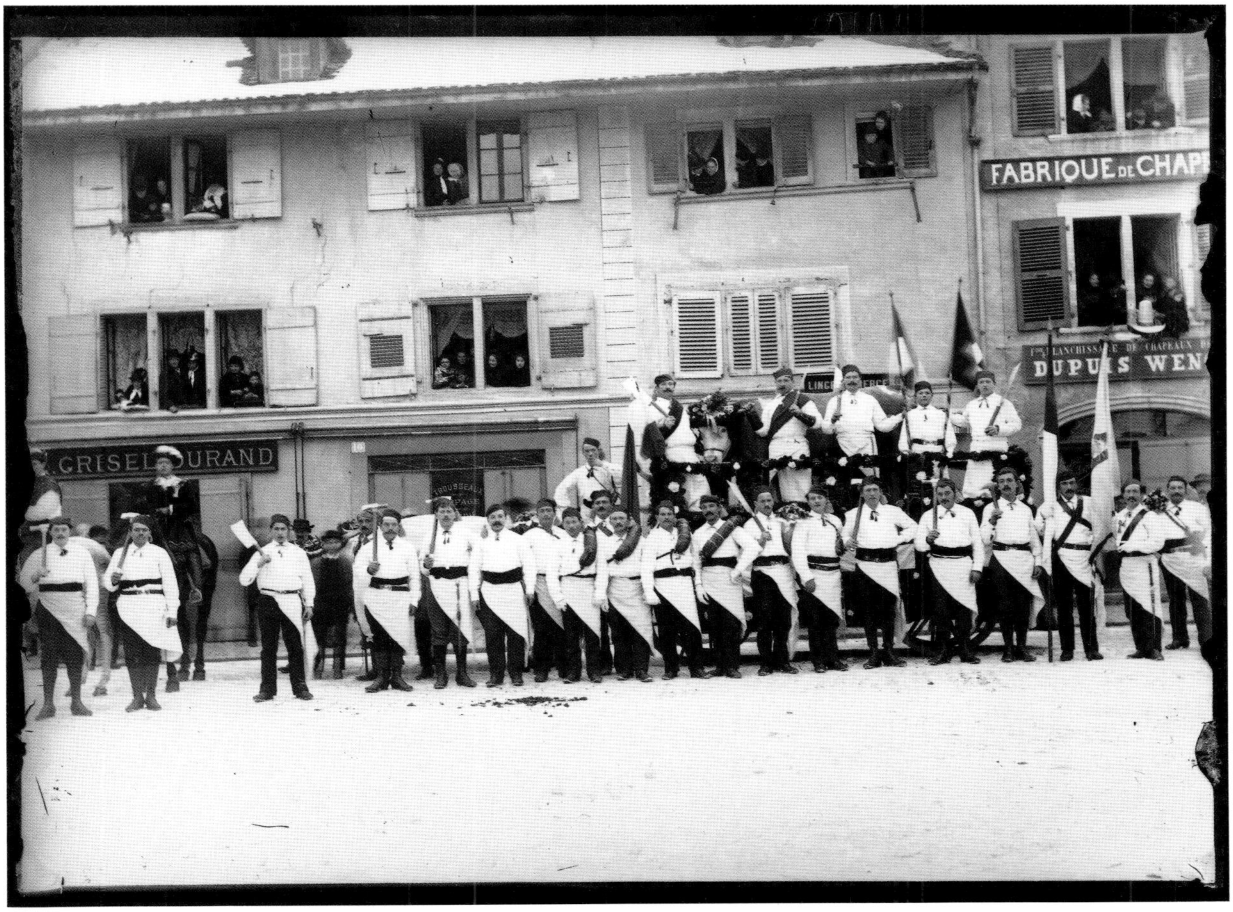

Morges. The butchers' festival, 1875.

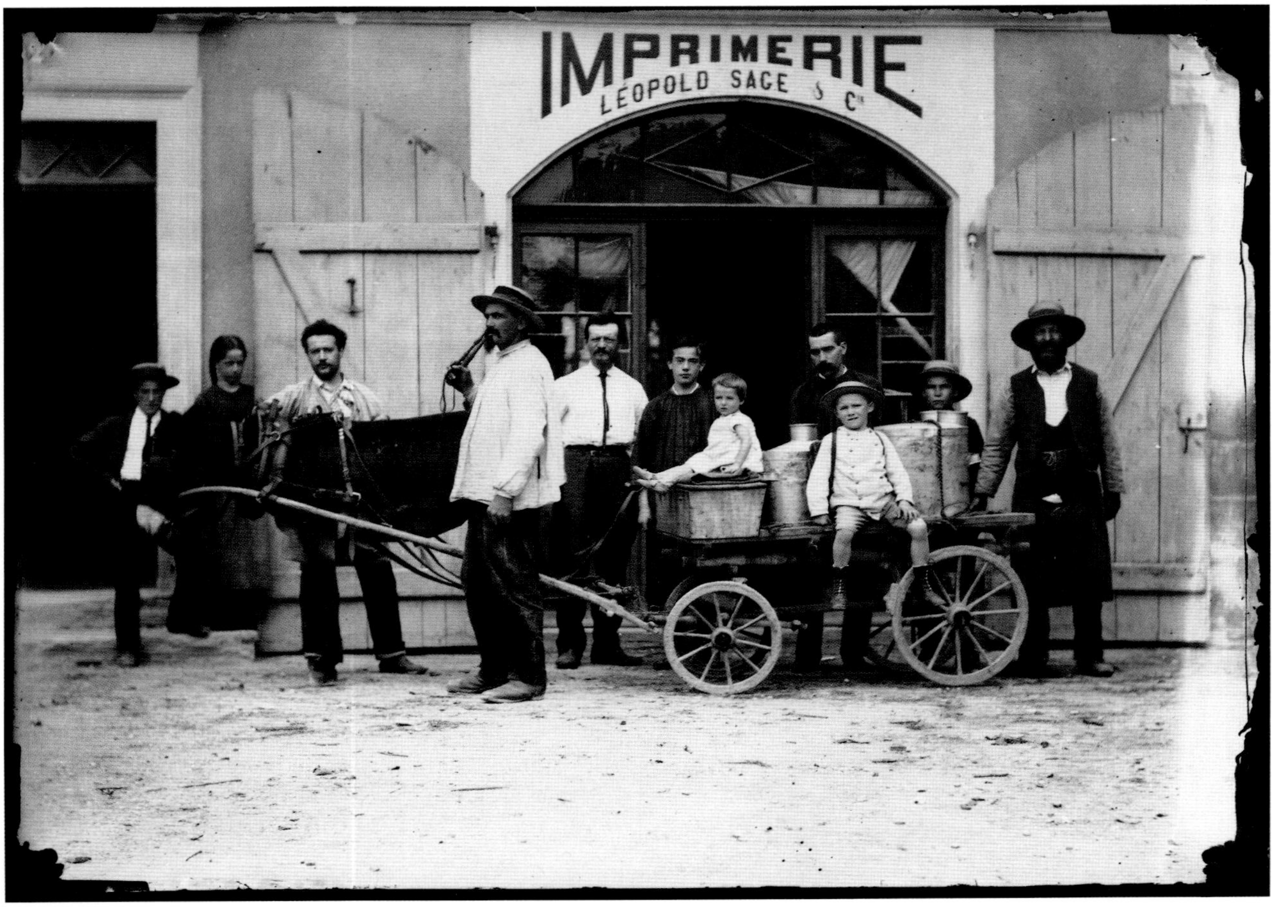

Morges. Sage Press, the editor of *«L'Ami de Morges»,* 1888.

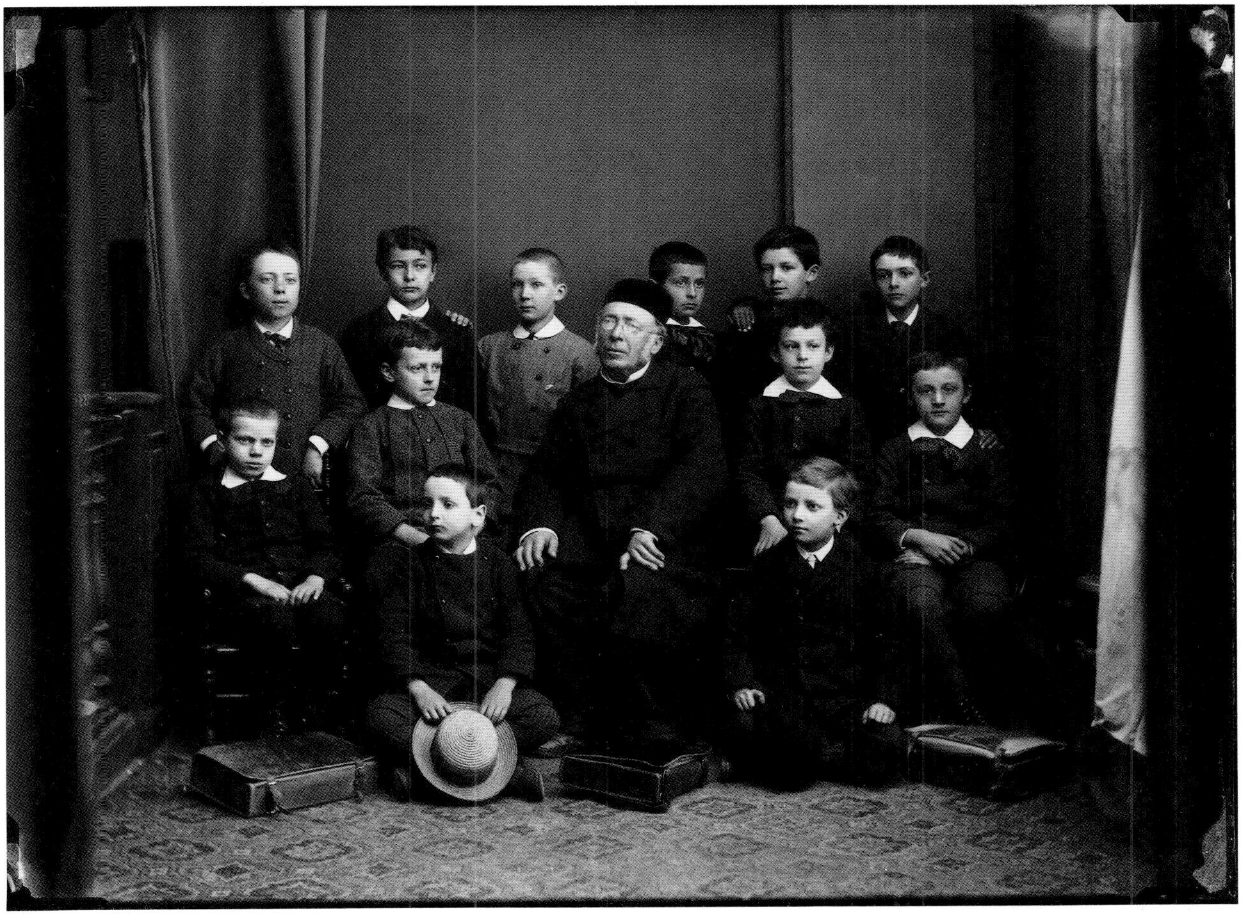

Students at the Collège Latin (Armand Deriaz, front row right), 1883.

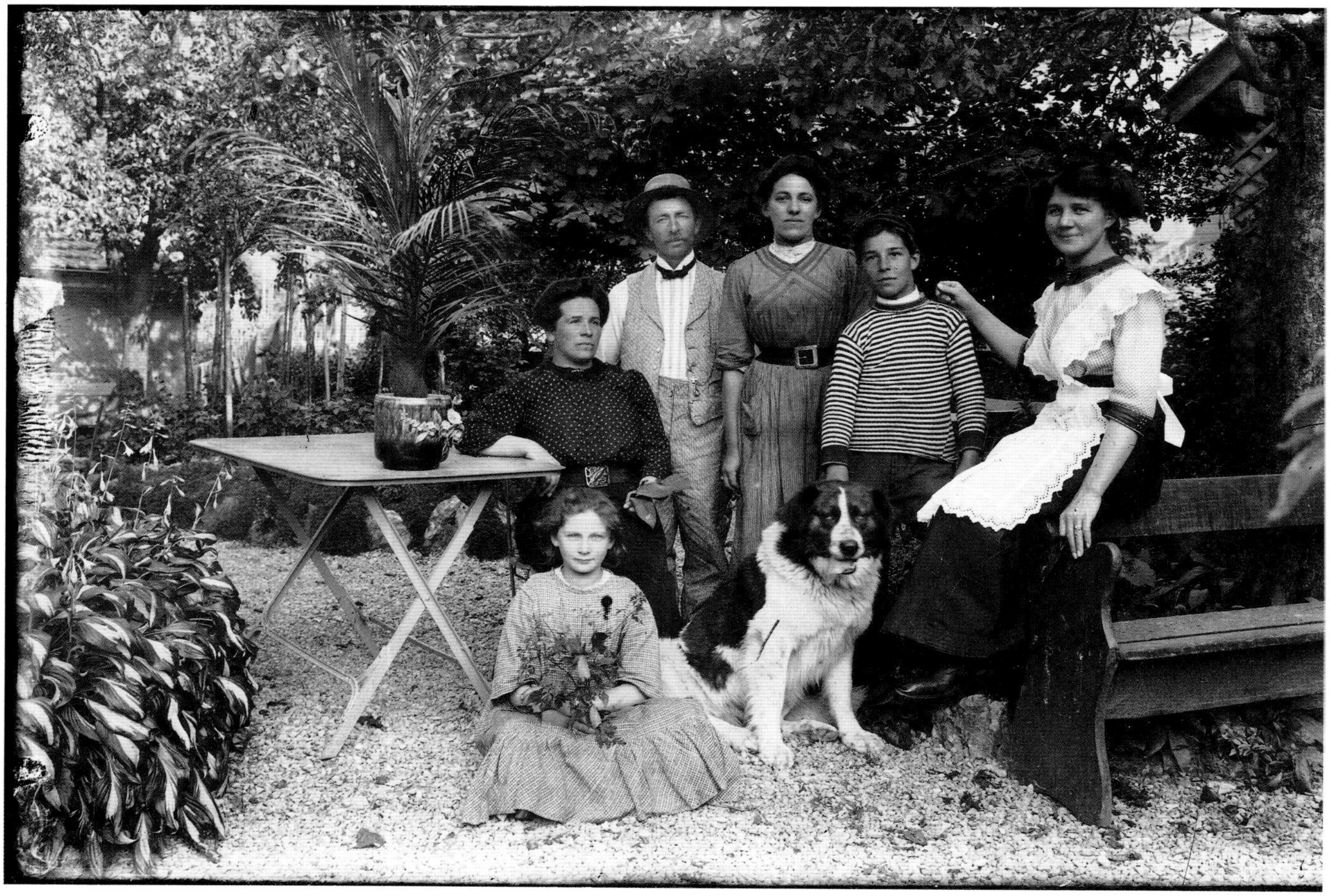

Morges. Family in a garden, 1882.

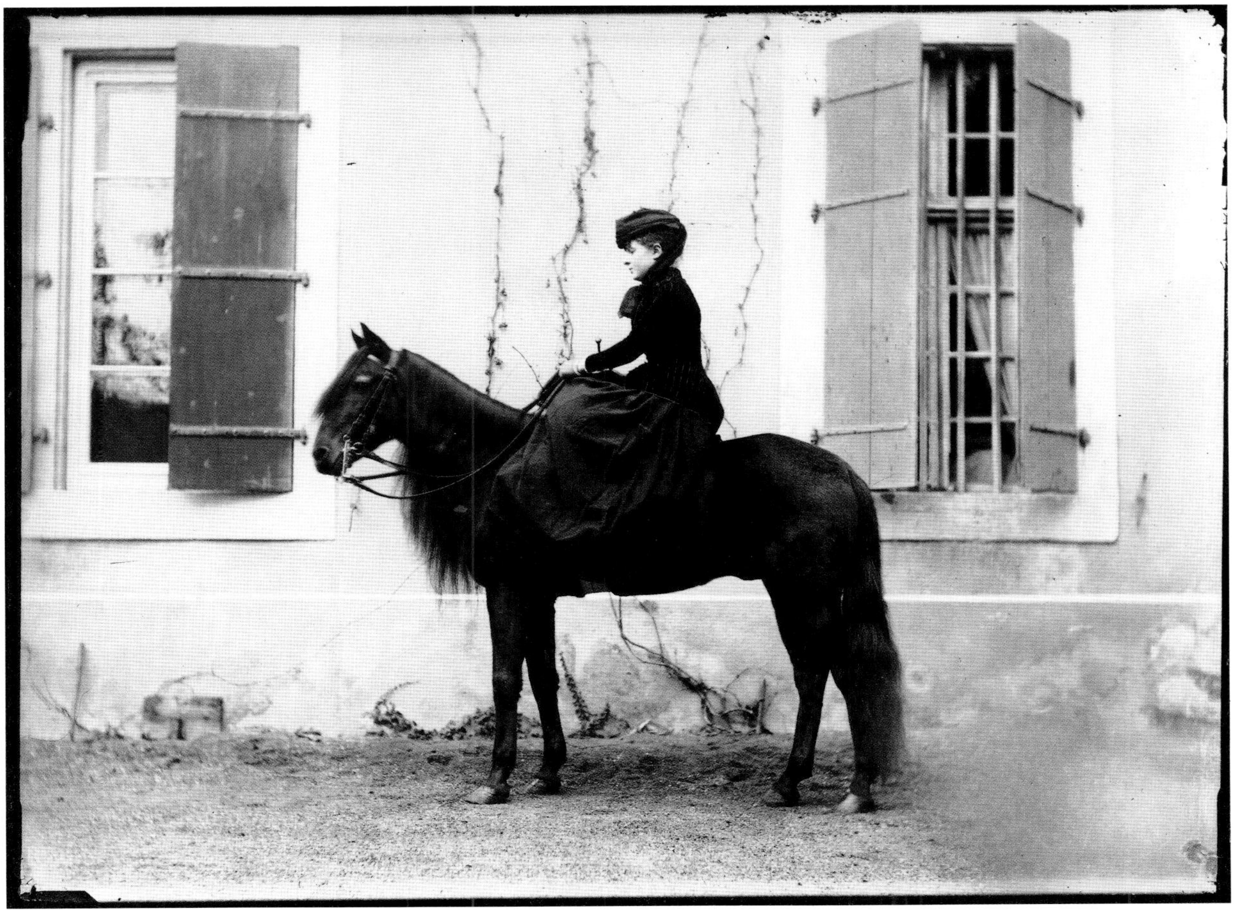

Morges. Horseback rider, 1872.

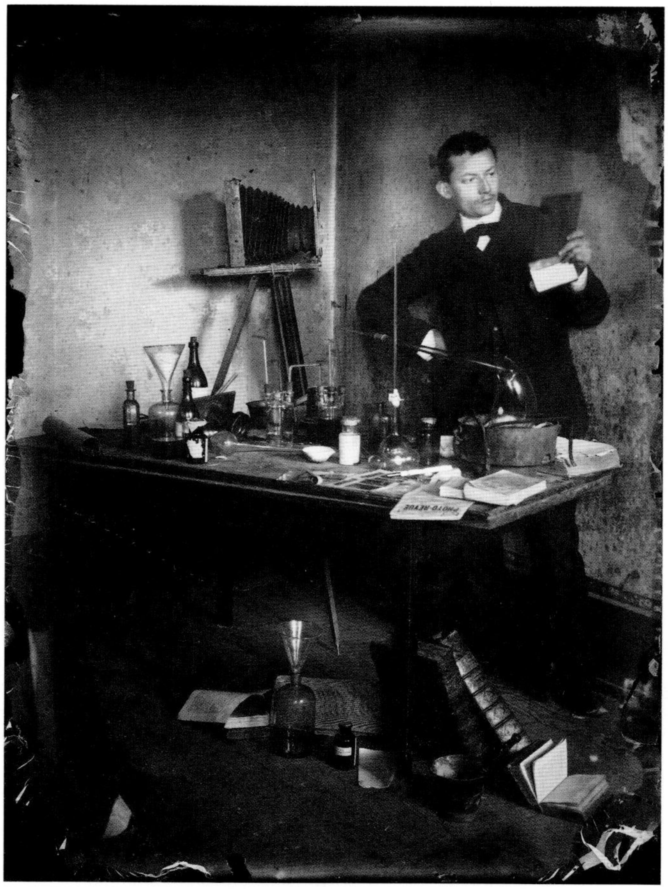

Armand Deriaz I

Born on August 18, 1873. Armand was only sixteen years old when his father Alphonse died and he suddenly inherited the family business. With the development of the calotype, he was able to publish post cards and alpine panoramas.

Having settled in Baulmes, at the foot of the Jura mountains, he photographed the surrounding region and the local people. His work offers a remarkable account of the changes that took place in the region during the first quarter of the century.

He died on May 19, 1932.

Baulmes. Self-portrait, 1896.

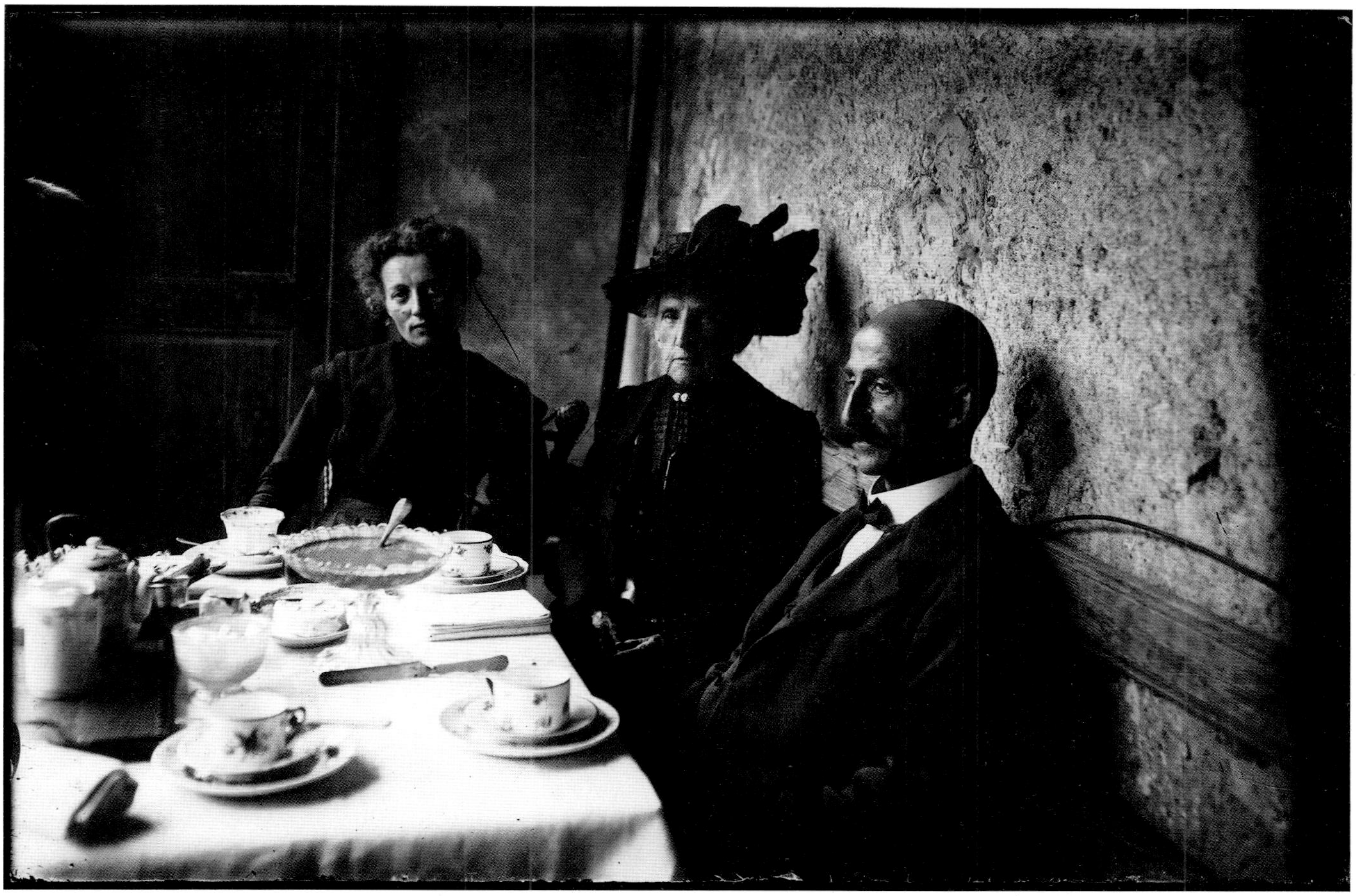

Baulmes. A Sunday afternoon, 1914.

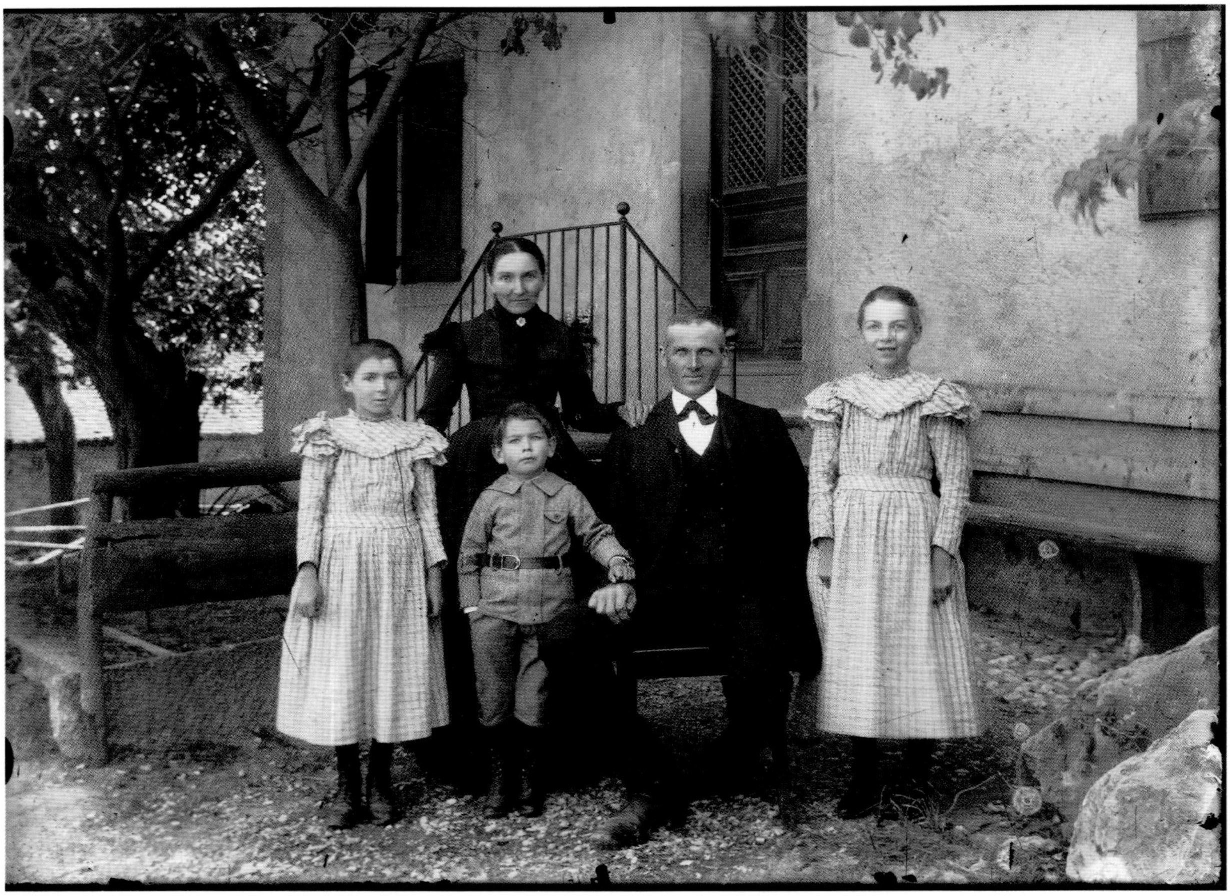

Baulmes. César Cachemaille and his wife Jenny, their daughters Olga and Hélène and son Clément, 1905.

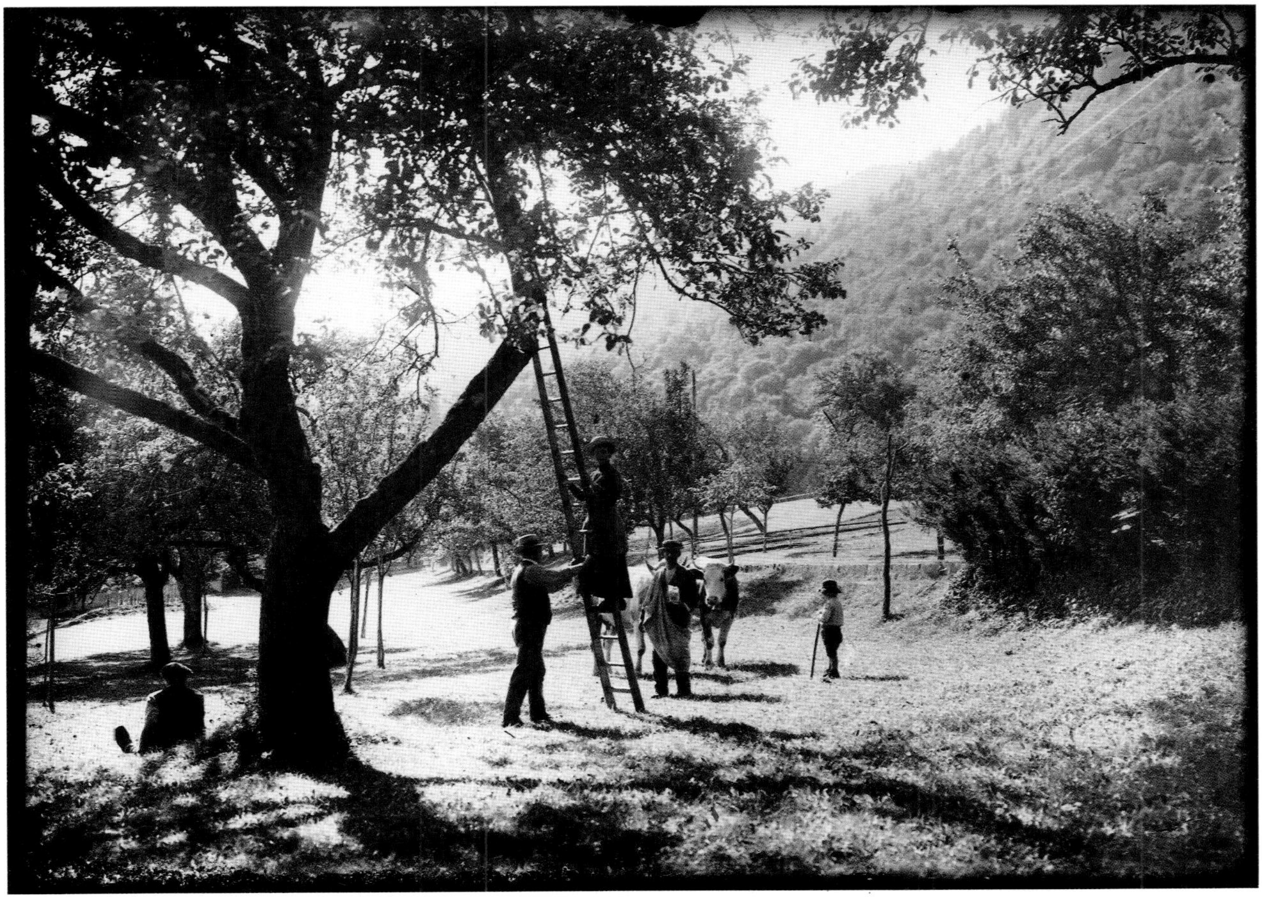

Baulmes. The chapel orchard, with Elise Deriaz on the ladder, 1915.

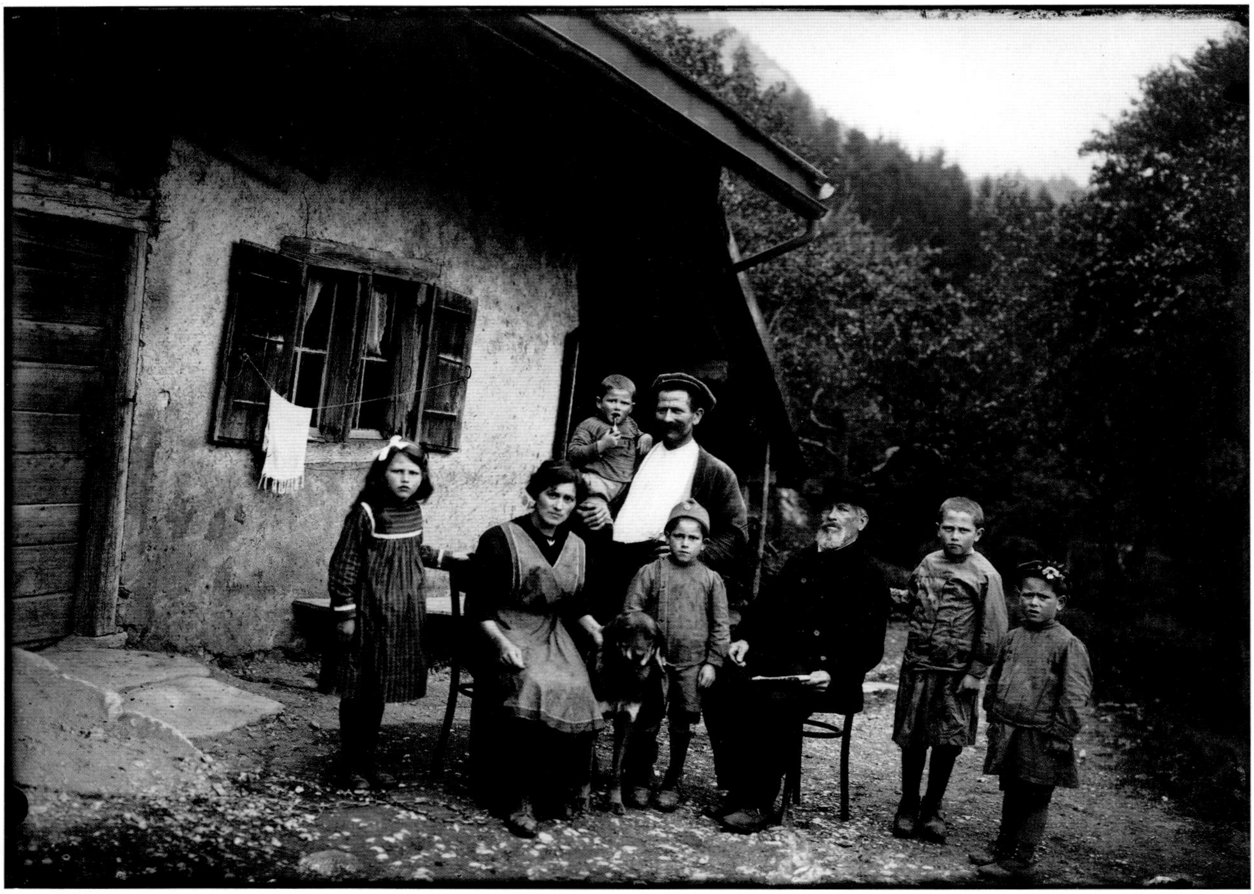

Baulmes. Albert "Lonzi" Deriaz and his family, Praz-Mincin, 1909.

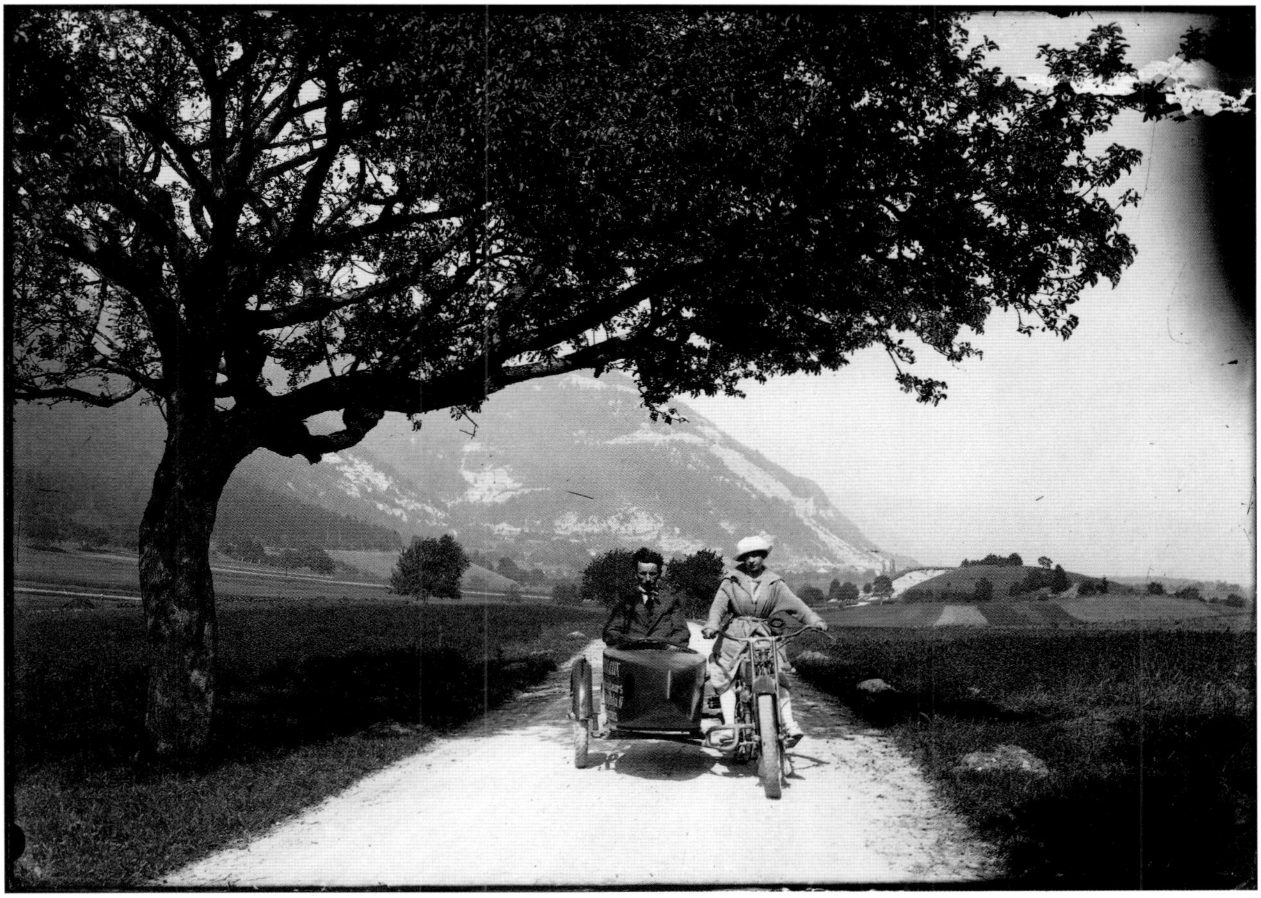

Baulmes. Sidecar on the road to Vallorbe, 1923.

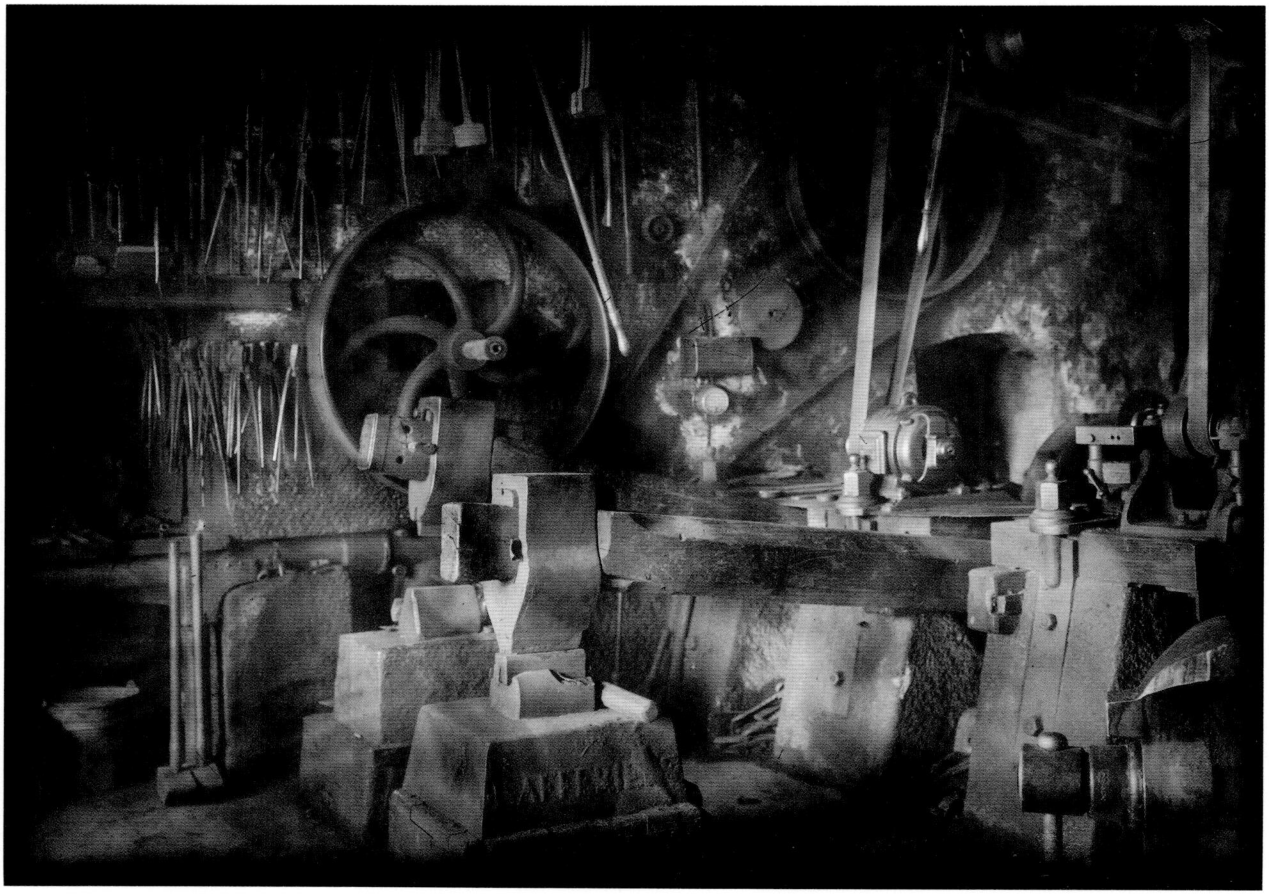

Baulmes. The ironworks, 1899.

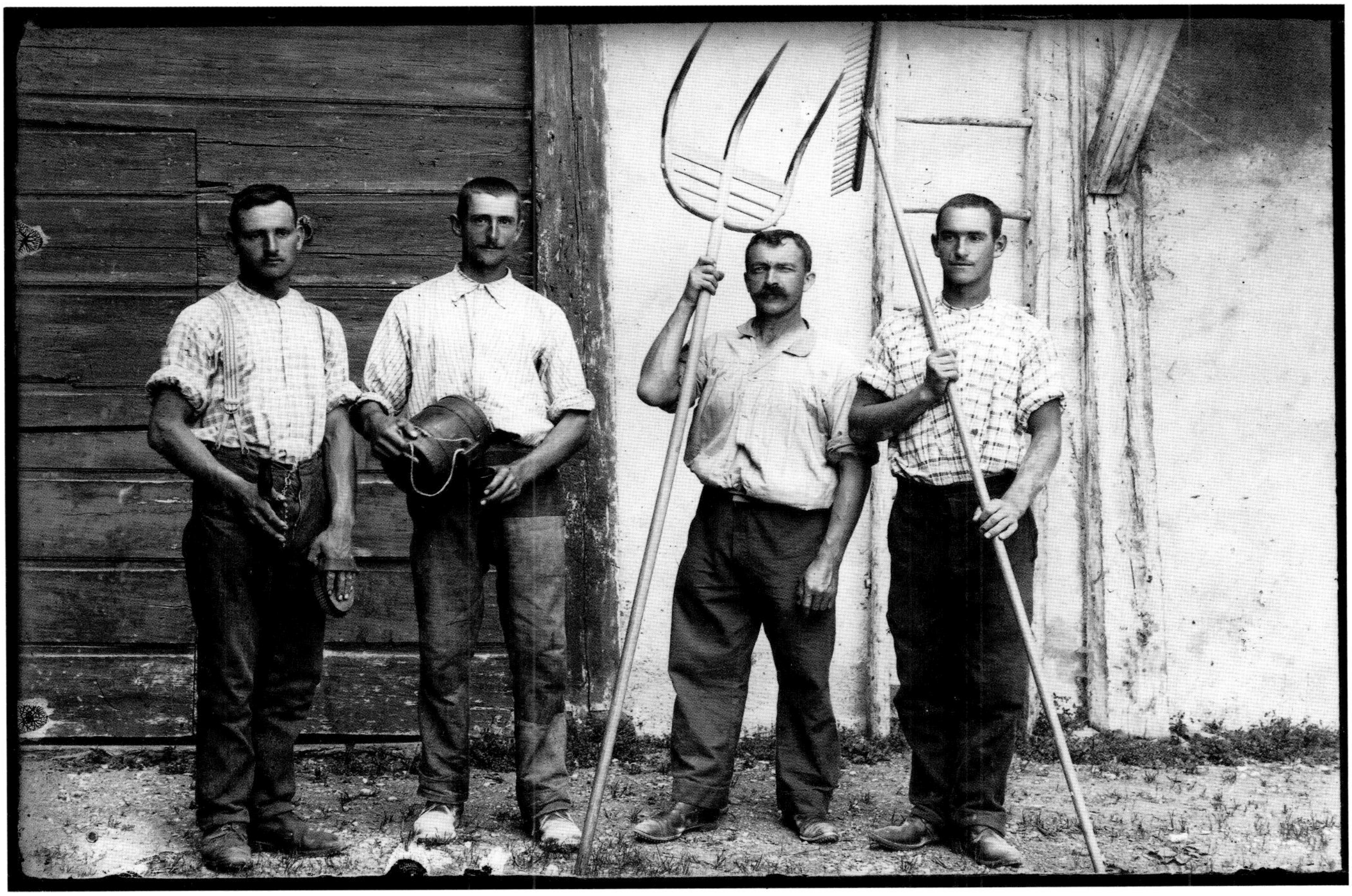

Baulmes. Farm workers, 1903.

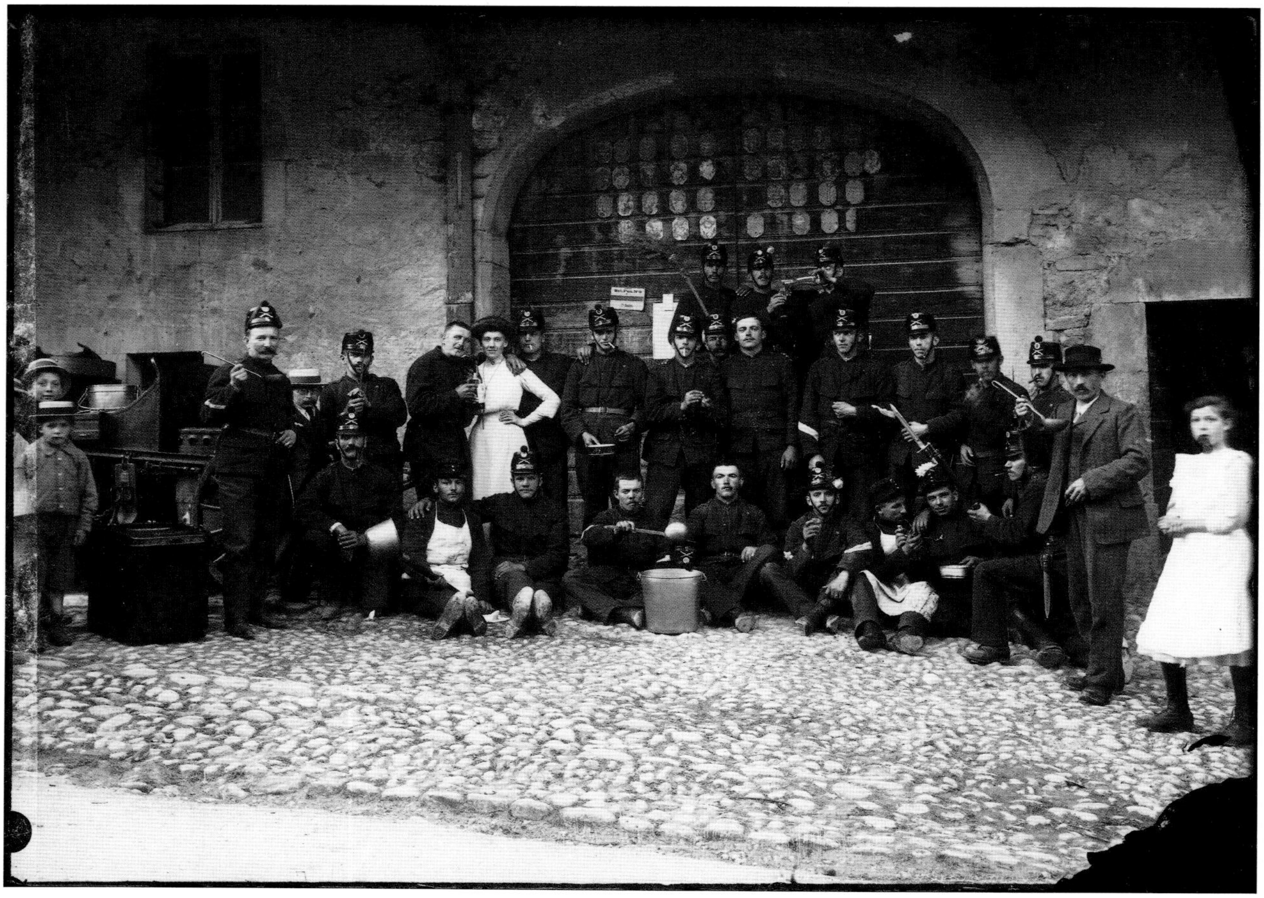

Baulmes. Riflemen in the Fifth Battalion, 1912.

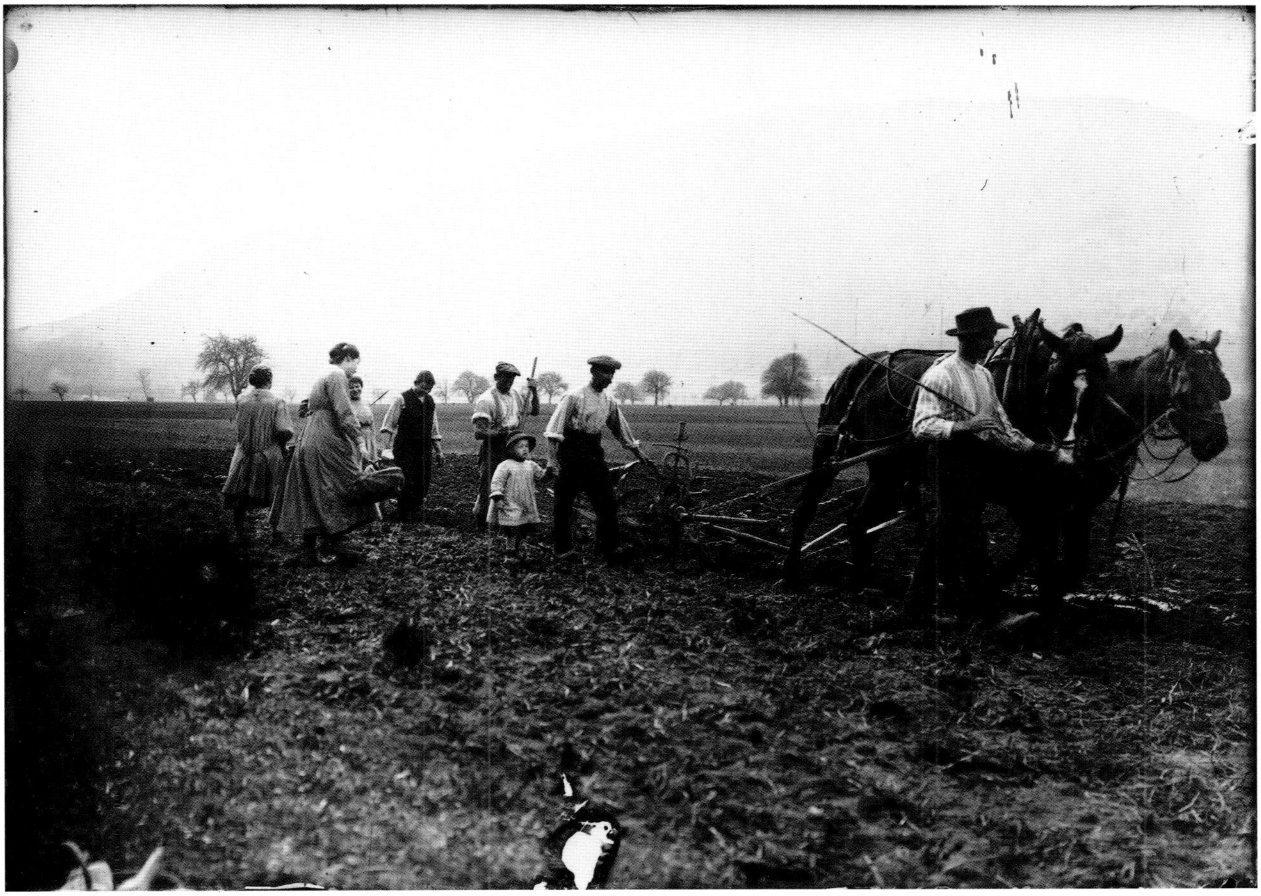

Baulmes. Farmhands, Freddy and Julien Cachemaille with their nephew Alphonse Deriaz, 1918.

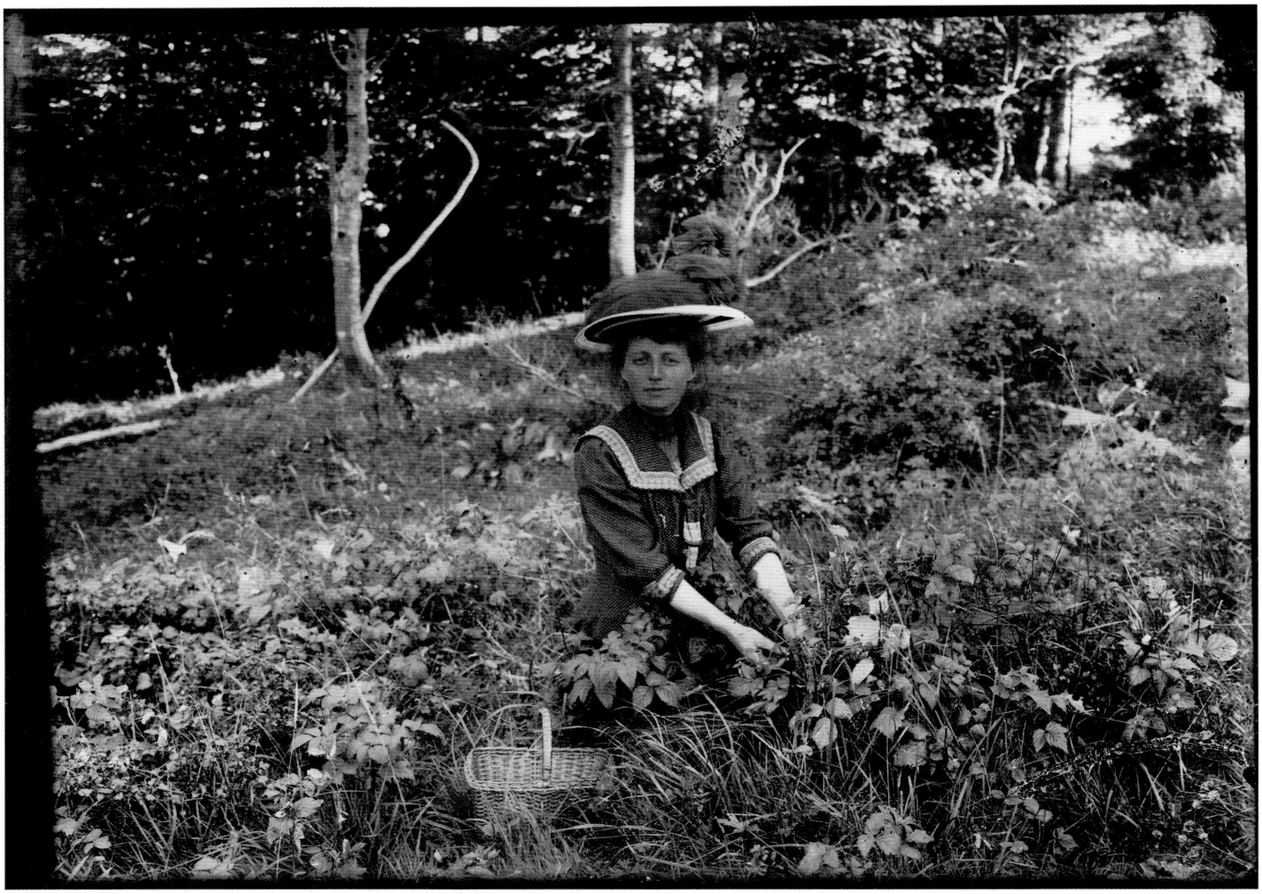

Baulmes. Elise Cachemaille, Armand's future wife, 1909.

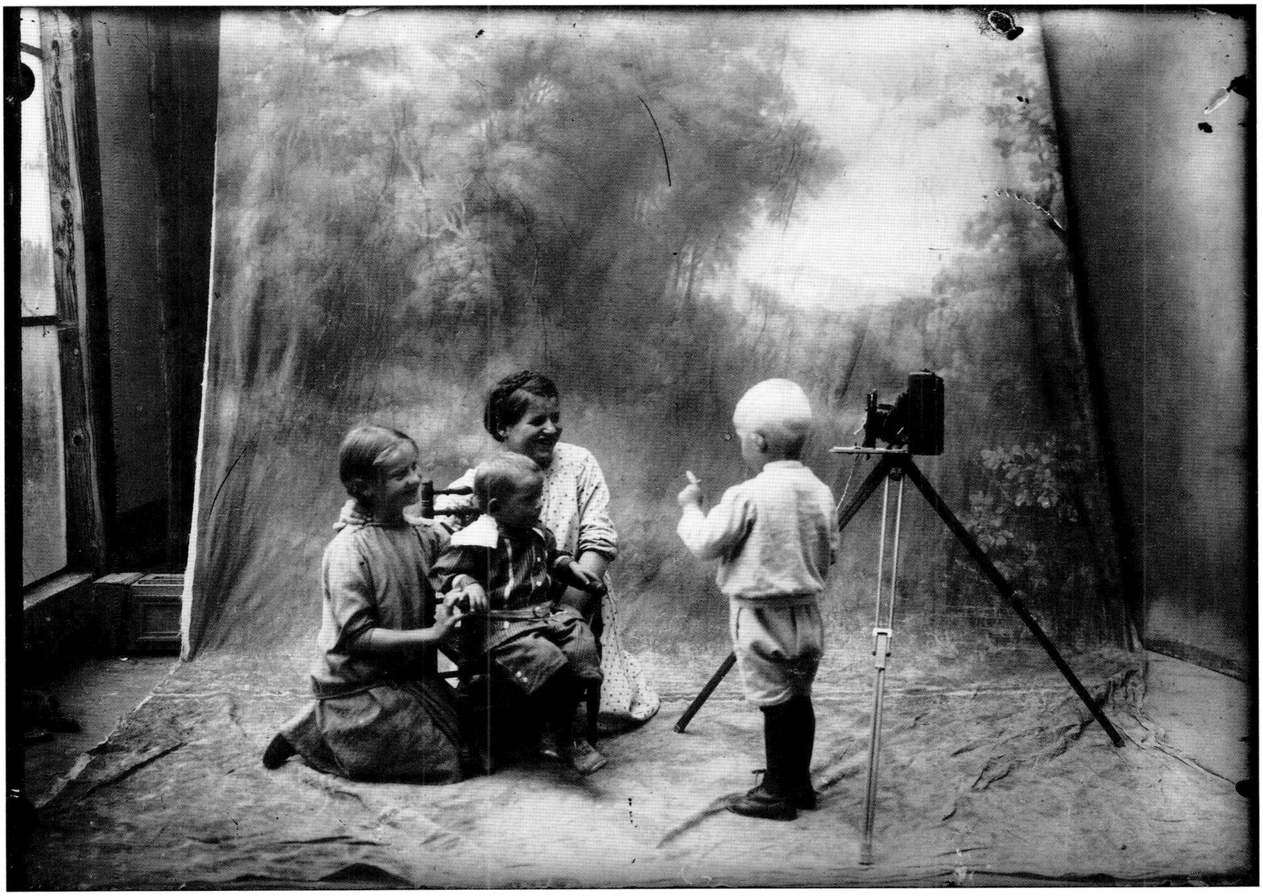

Baulmes. The photographer's son, 1920.

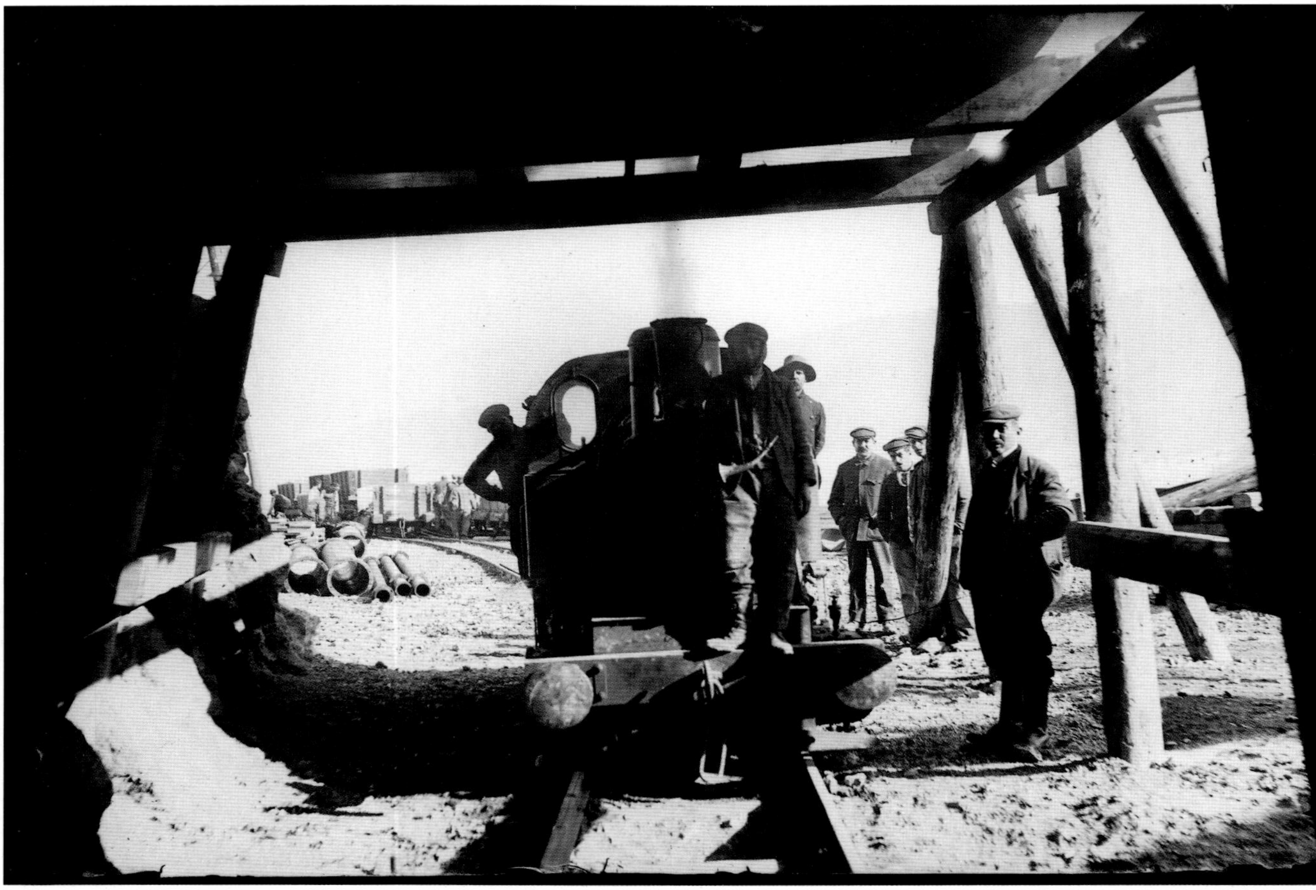

Construction of the Mont-d'Or tunnel between Vallorbe, Switzerland and Frasnes, France, c. 1911.

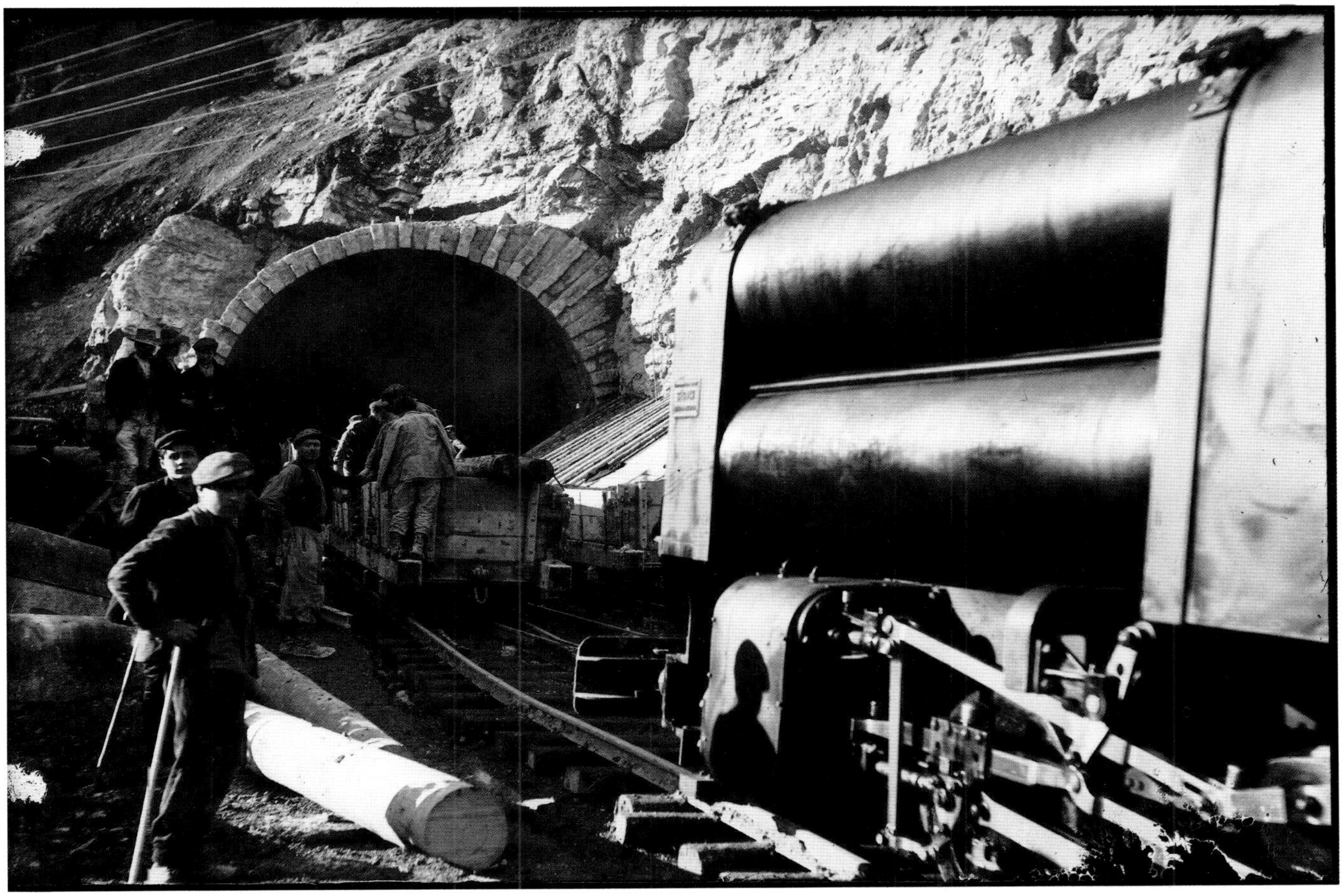

Construction of the Mont-d'Or tunnel between Vallorbe, Switzerland and Frasnes, France, c. 1911.

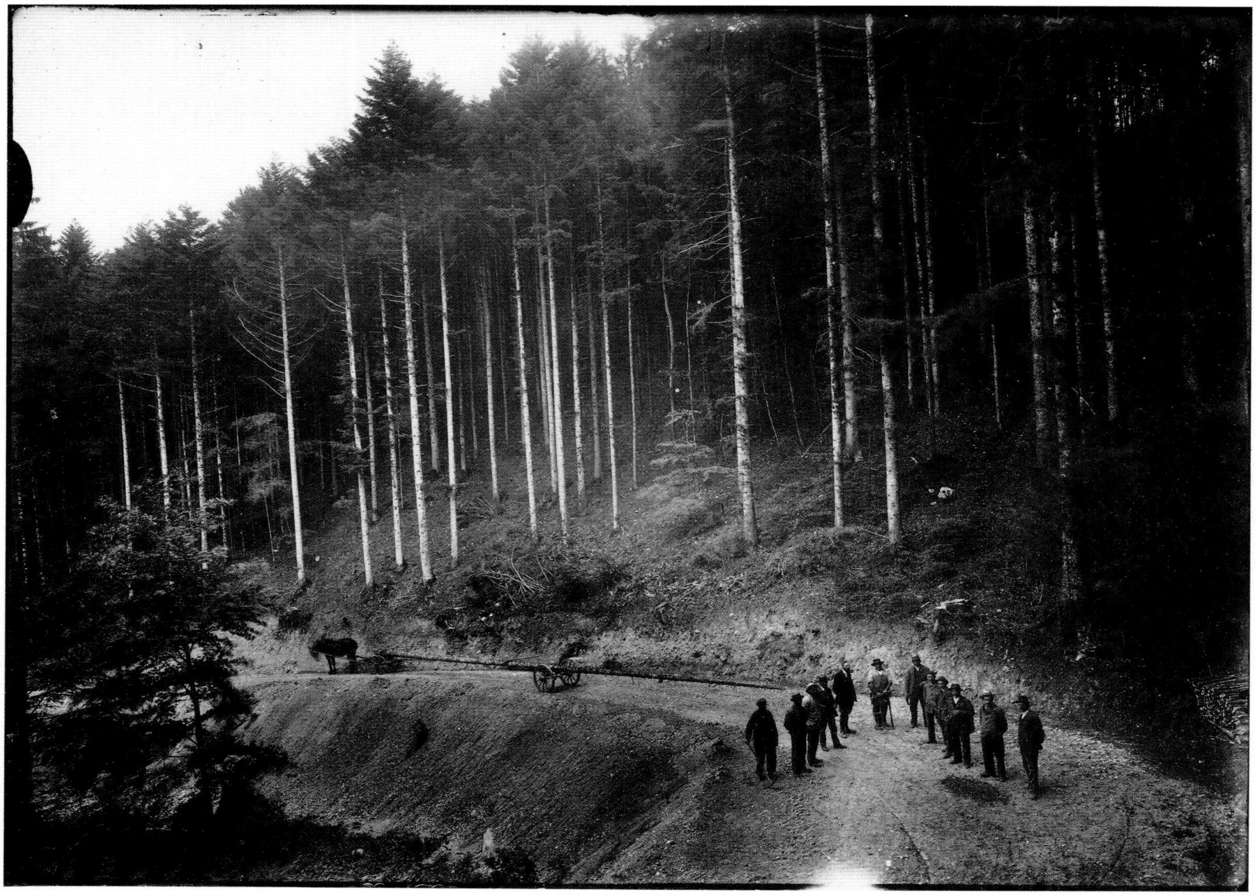

Baulmes. Transporting a white fir from the Bataillard forest, 1910.

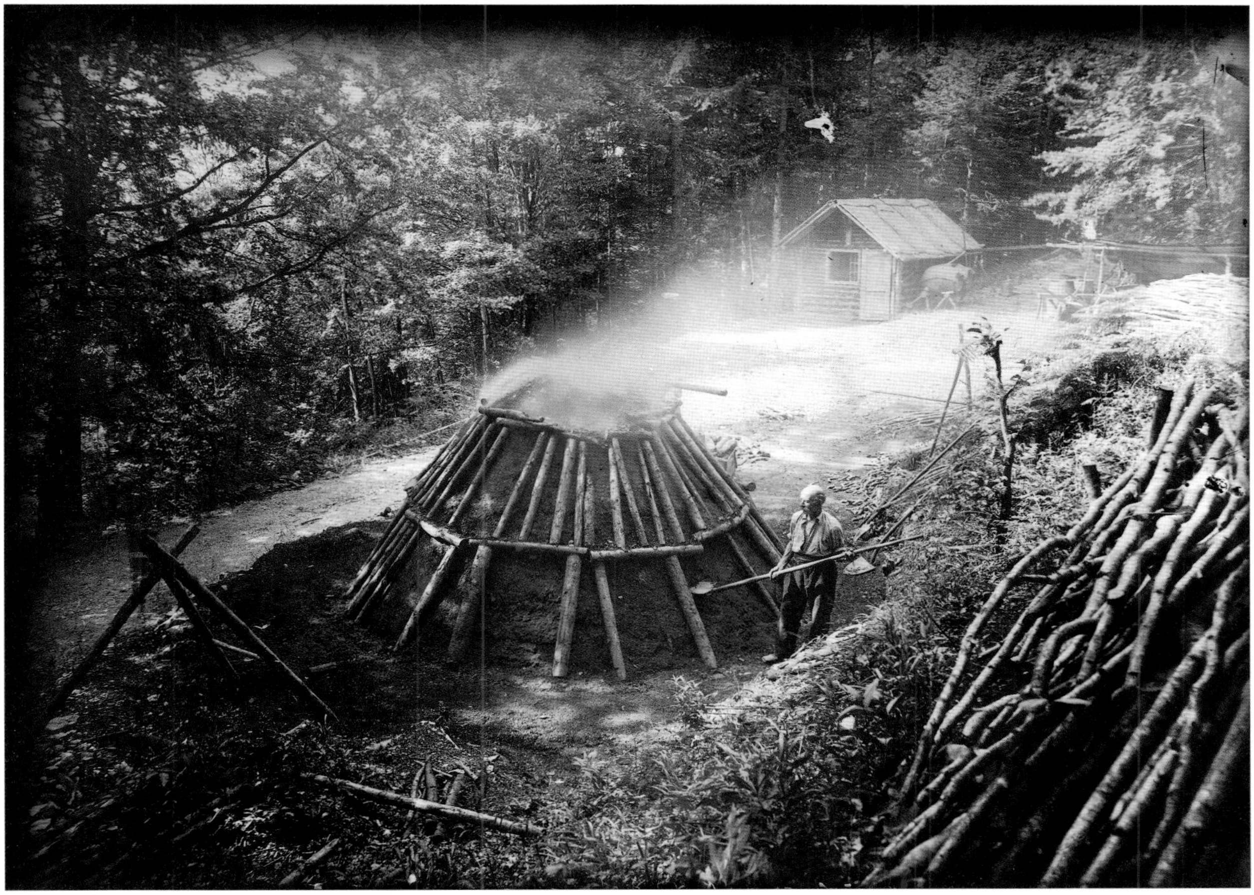

Baulmes. Charcoal production, 1905.

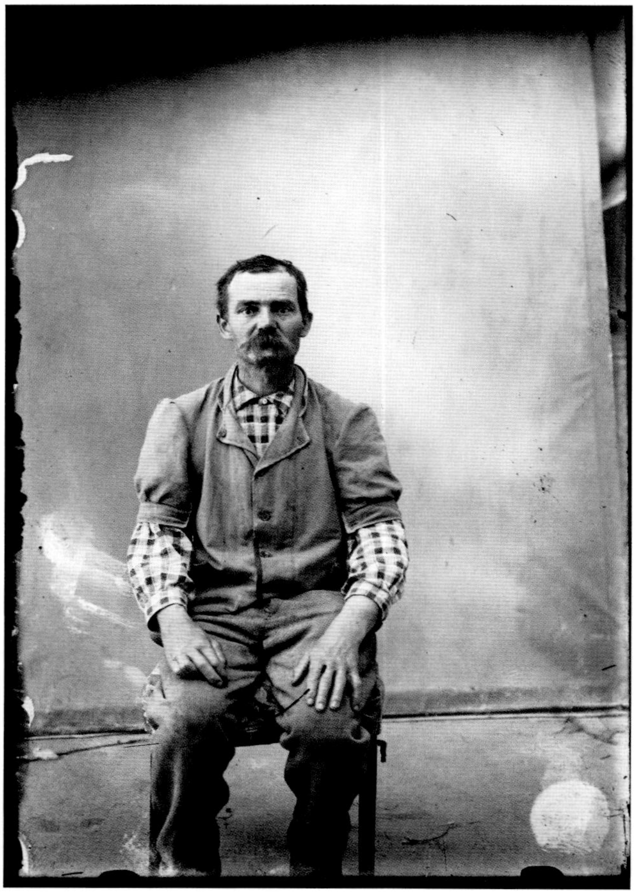

Baulmes. Tenant farmer of le Suchet mountain, 1908.

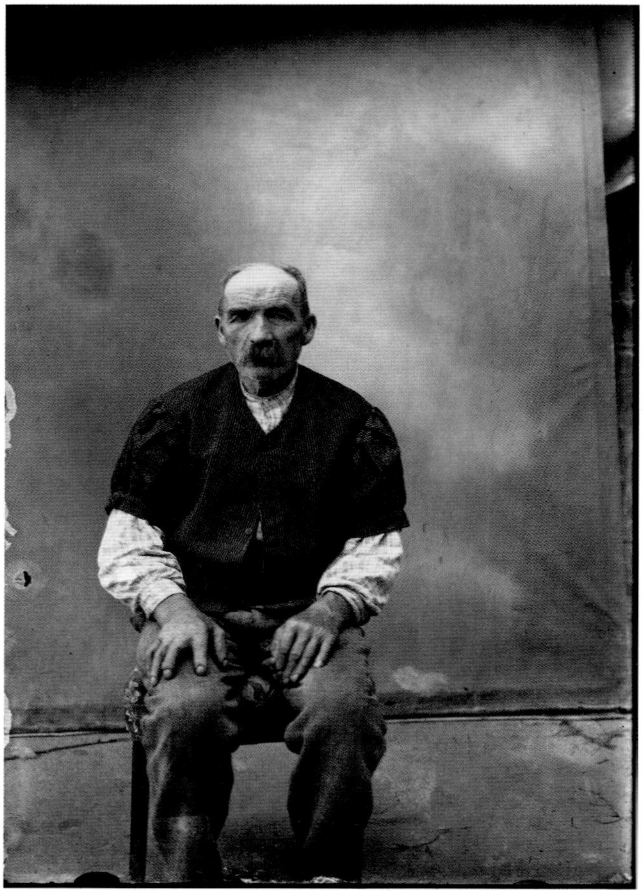

Baulmes. Emile (Pélac) Deriaz, Limasse shepherd, 1910.

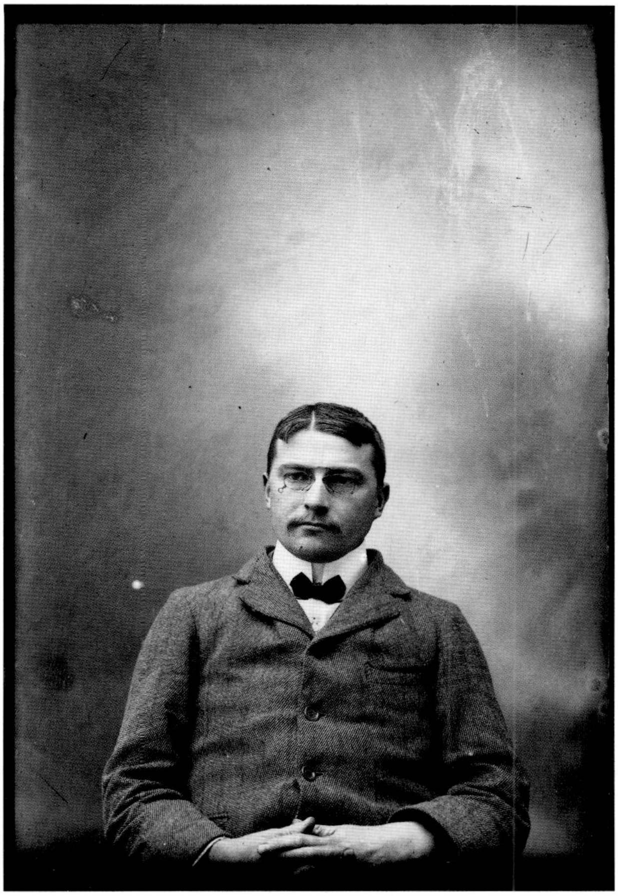

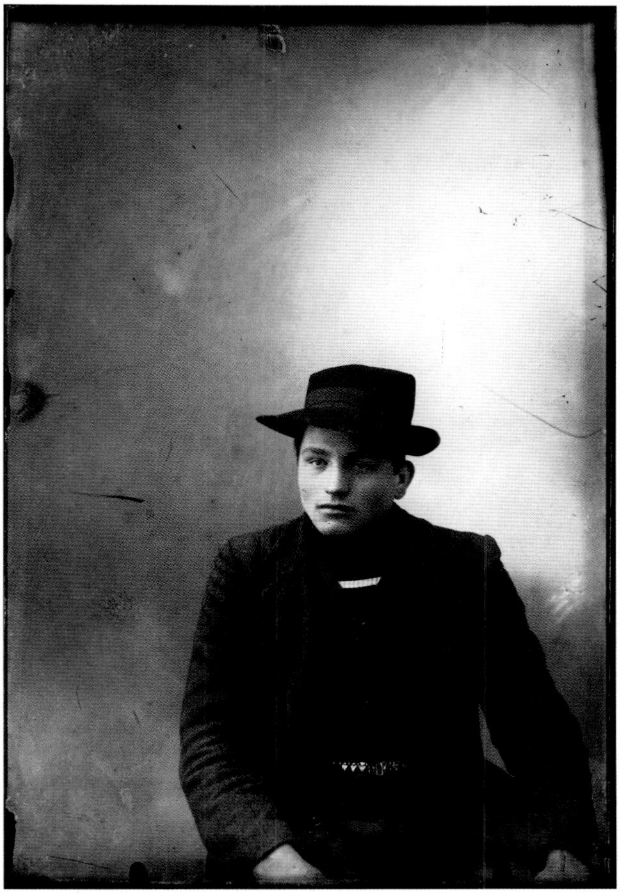

Baulmes. Dr. William Roullier, 1914.

Baulmes. Laborer from Trentin, 1900.

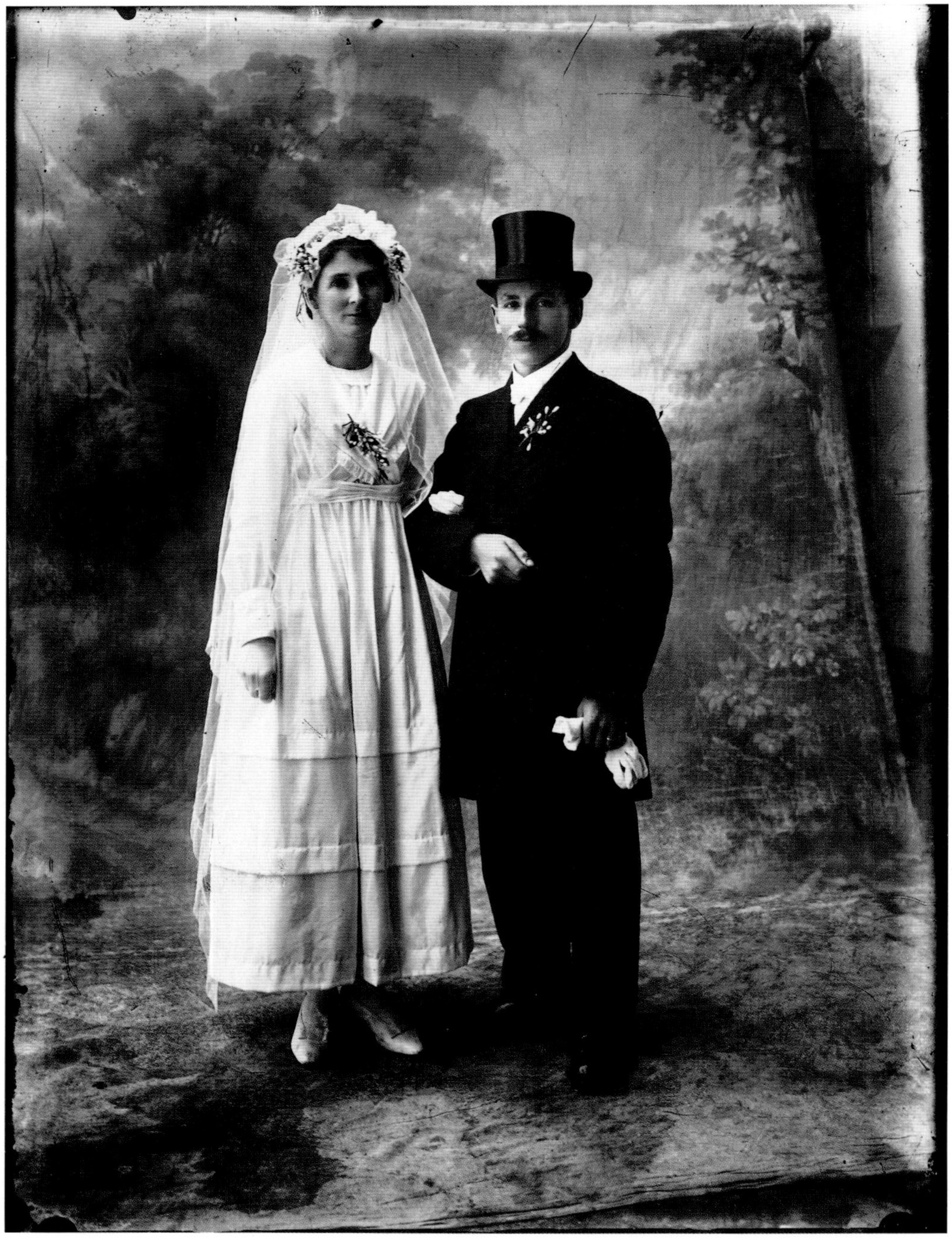

Baulmes. Hélène and Louis-François Pillevuit, December 27, 1919.

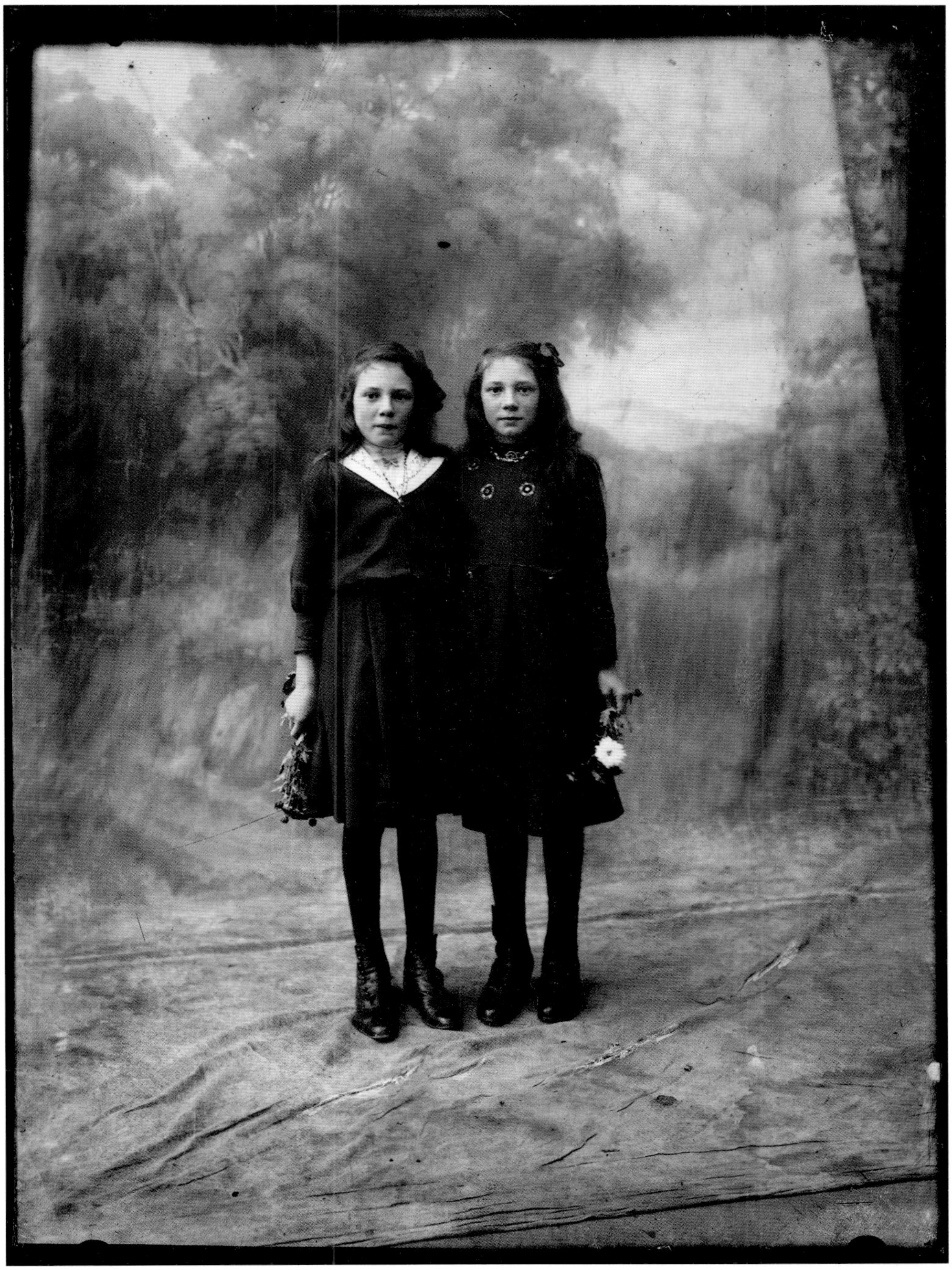

Baulmes. The Gonthier twins, 1919.

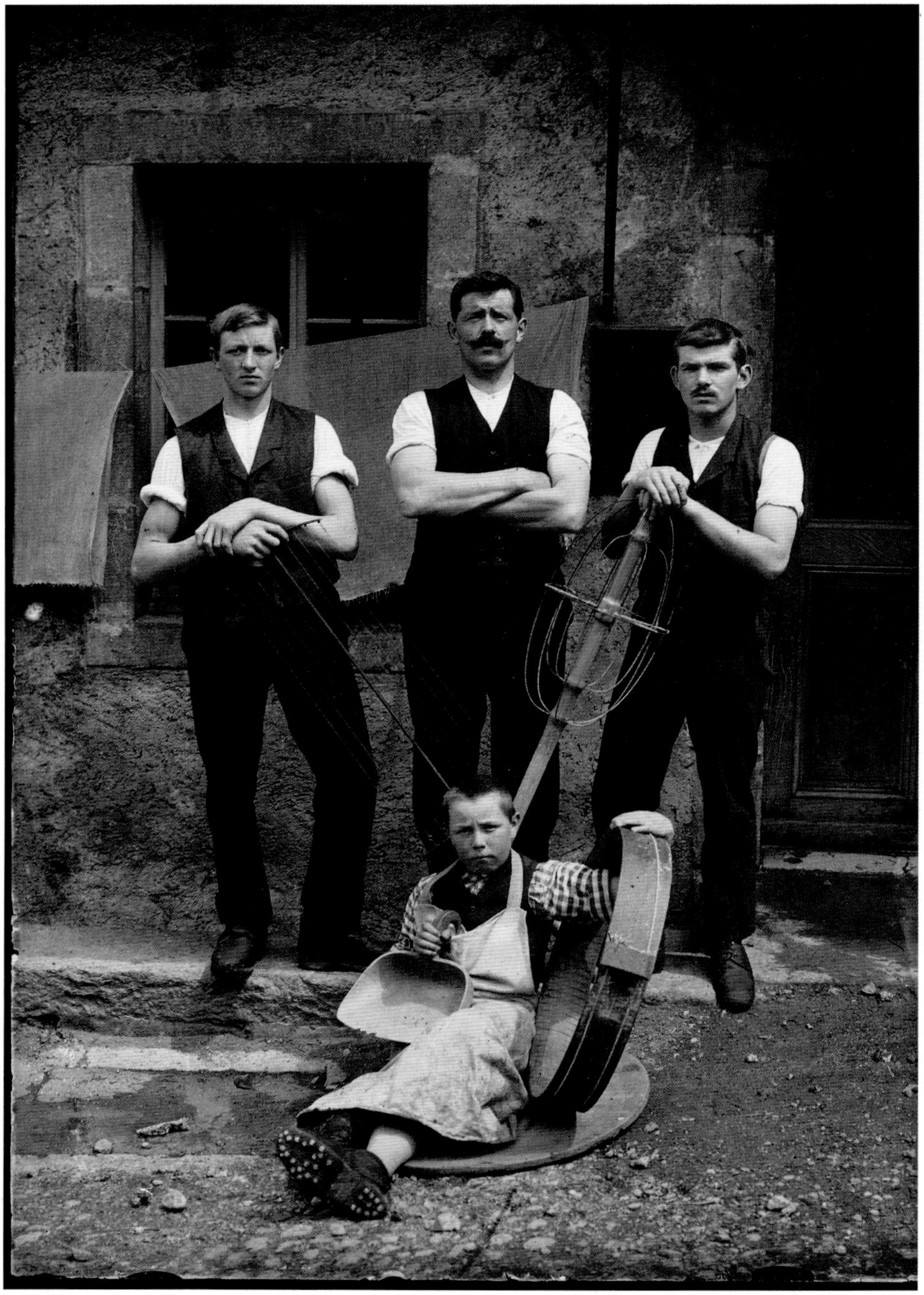

Cheese makers at a Baulmes dairy, 1910.

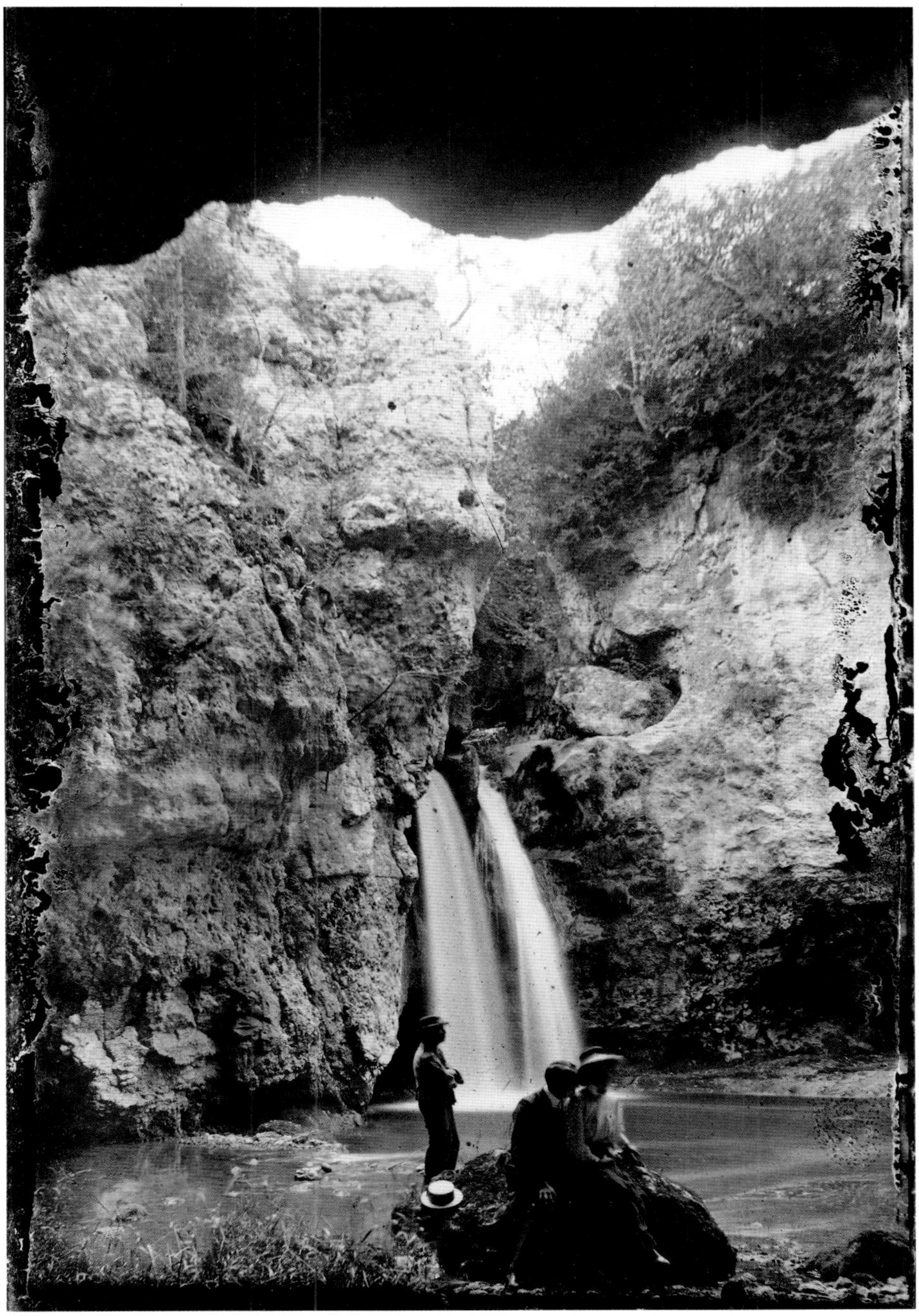

The Nozon waterfall, near Croy, Switzerland, 1907.

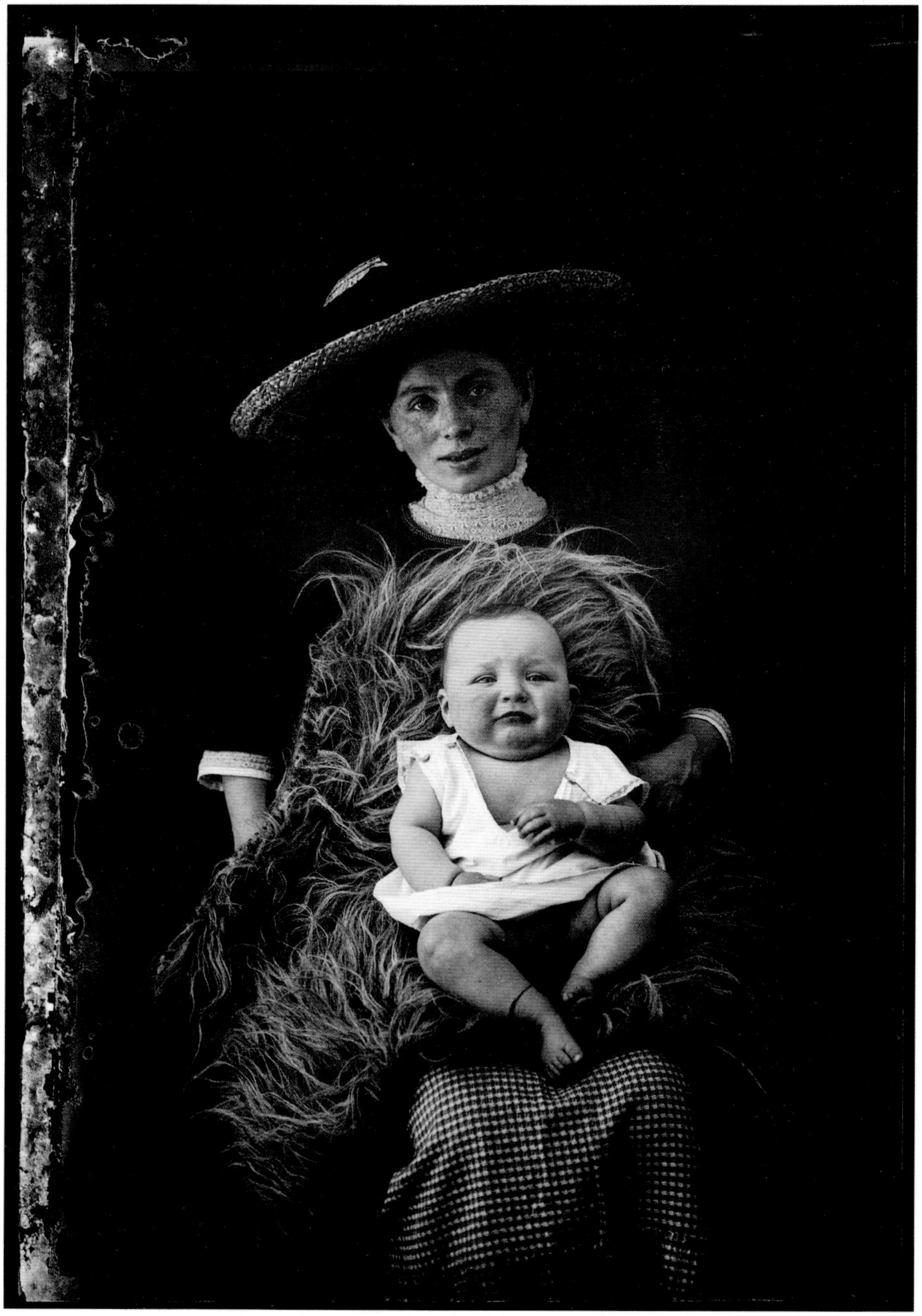

Baulmes. Mother and son, 1909.

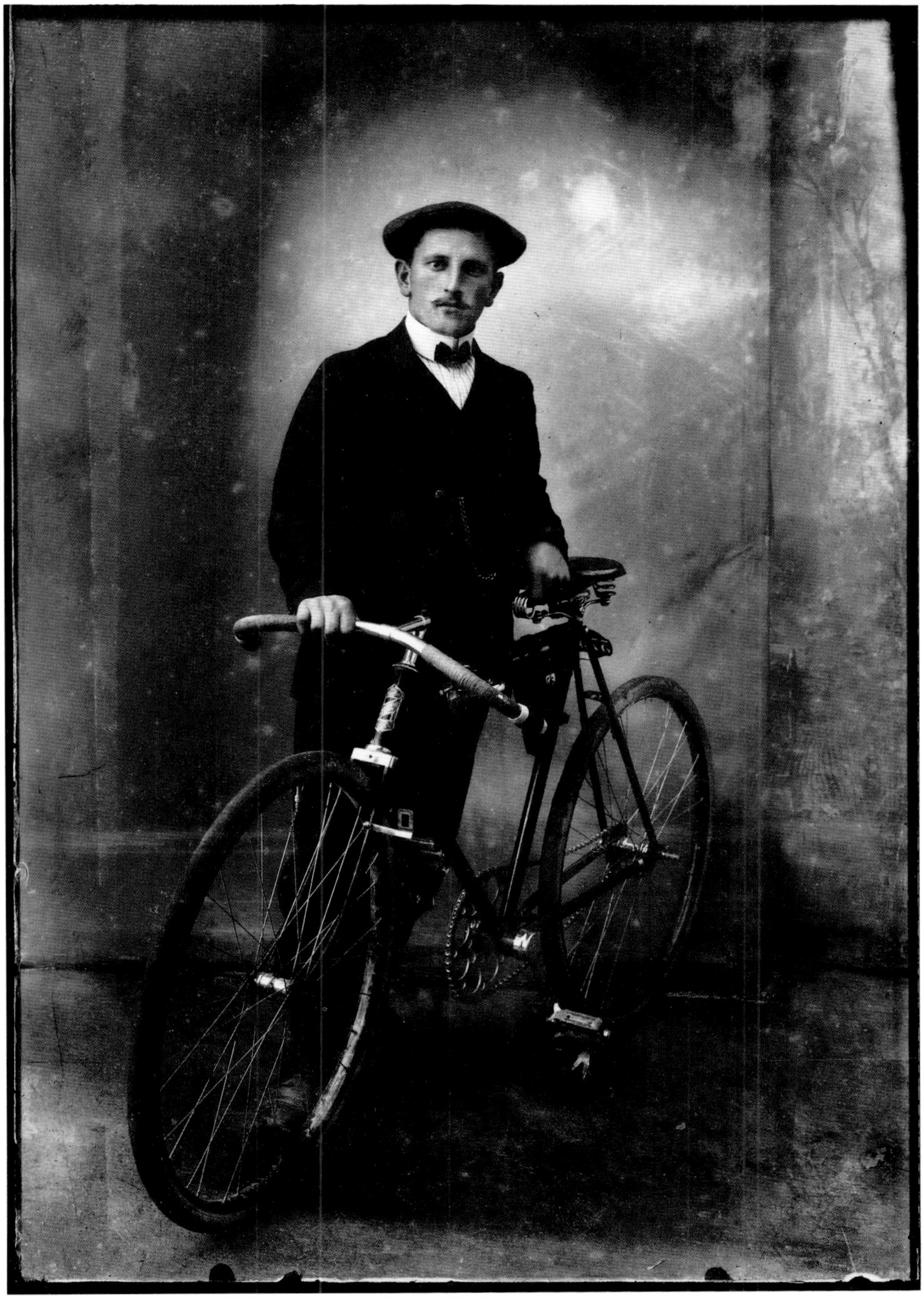

Baulmes. Cyclist, 1912.

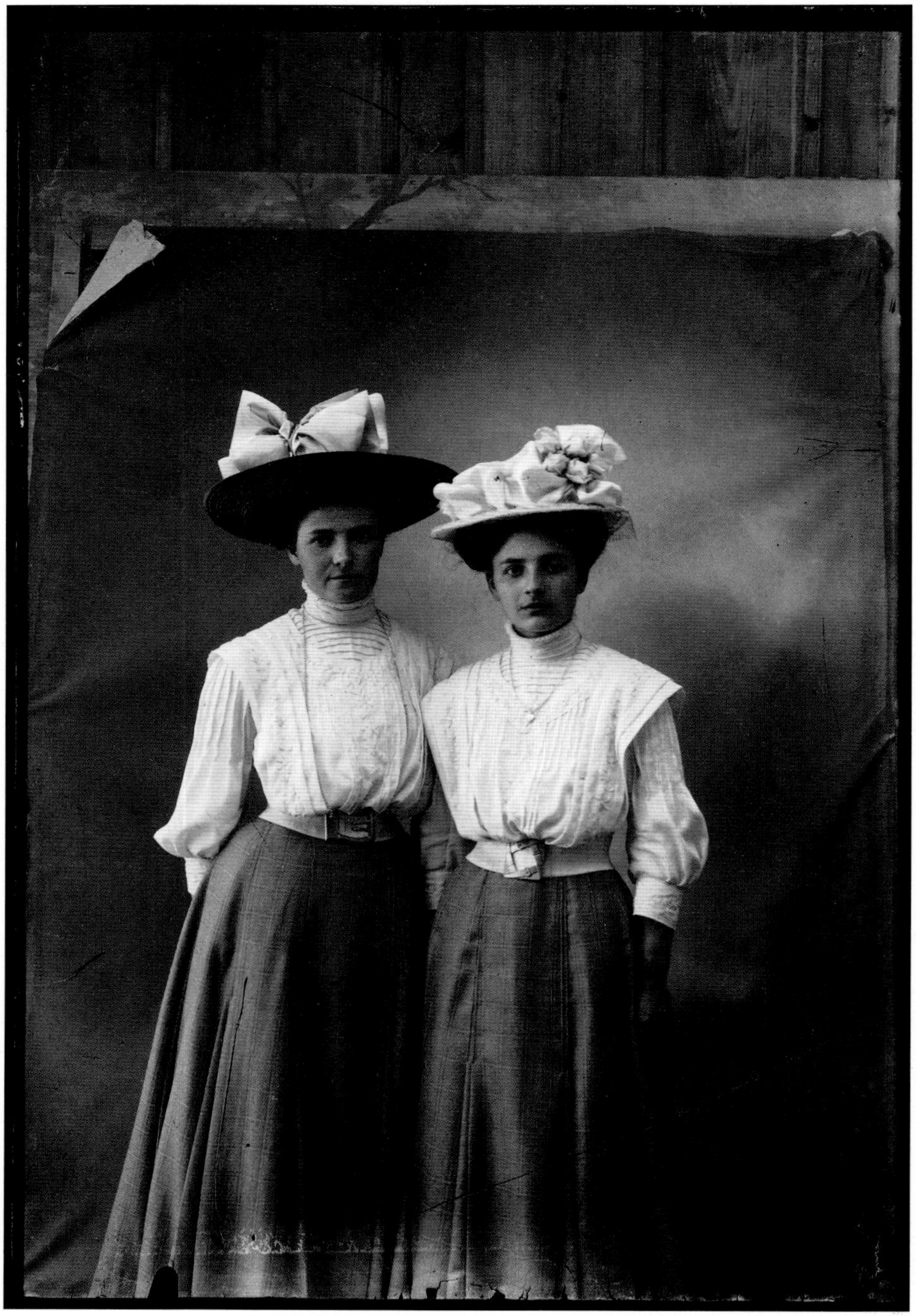

Baulmes. Ida and Marthe Deriaz, 1912.

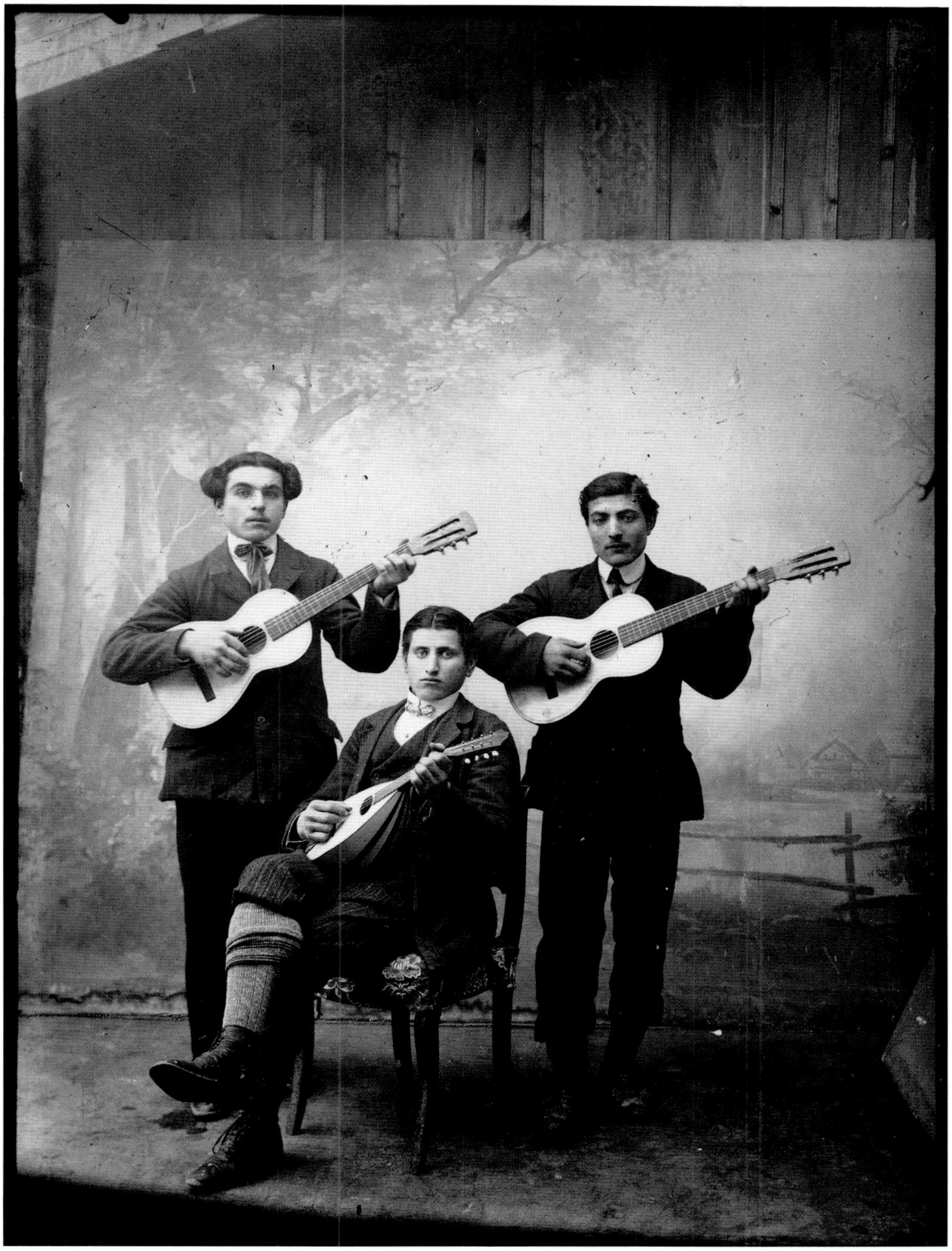

Baulmes. Musicians, three workers from the Bollini Construction Company, 1899.

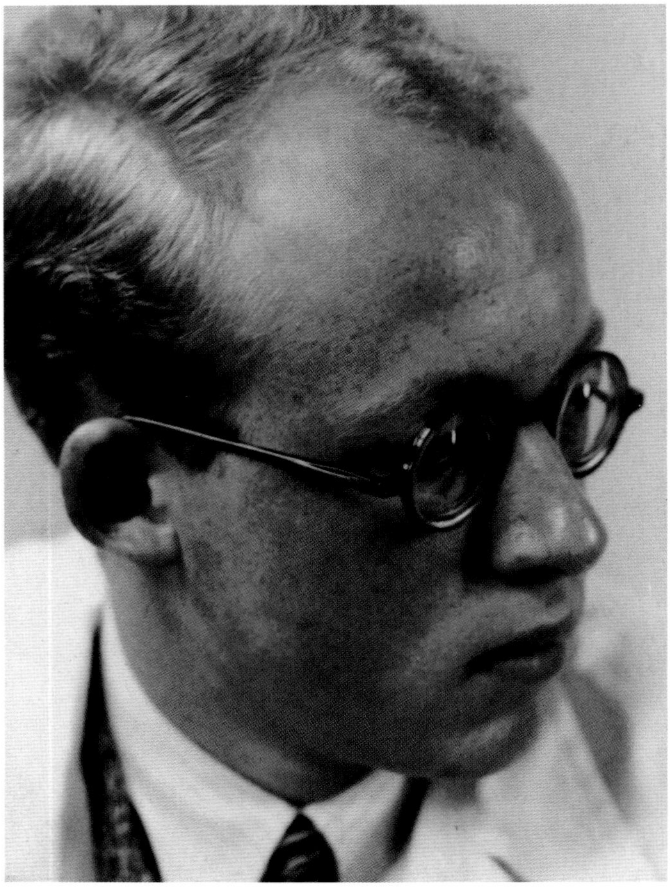

Alphonse Deriaz II

Born on February 16, 1915, and named after his grandfather, founder of the dynasty.

When his father Armand Deriaz died in 1932, he took over the photography studio and the post card publishing. He was among the first to use airplanes in order to take mountain photographs from a completely new angle, not to mention aerial views of the cities and towns of the canton of Vaud.

His work employs impeccable technique, developed in Vienna and Berlin, in combination with a natural visual sensibility.

Vienna. Self-portrait, 1934.

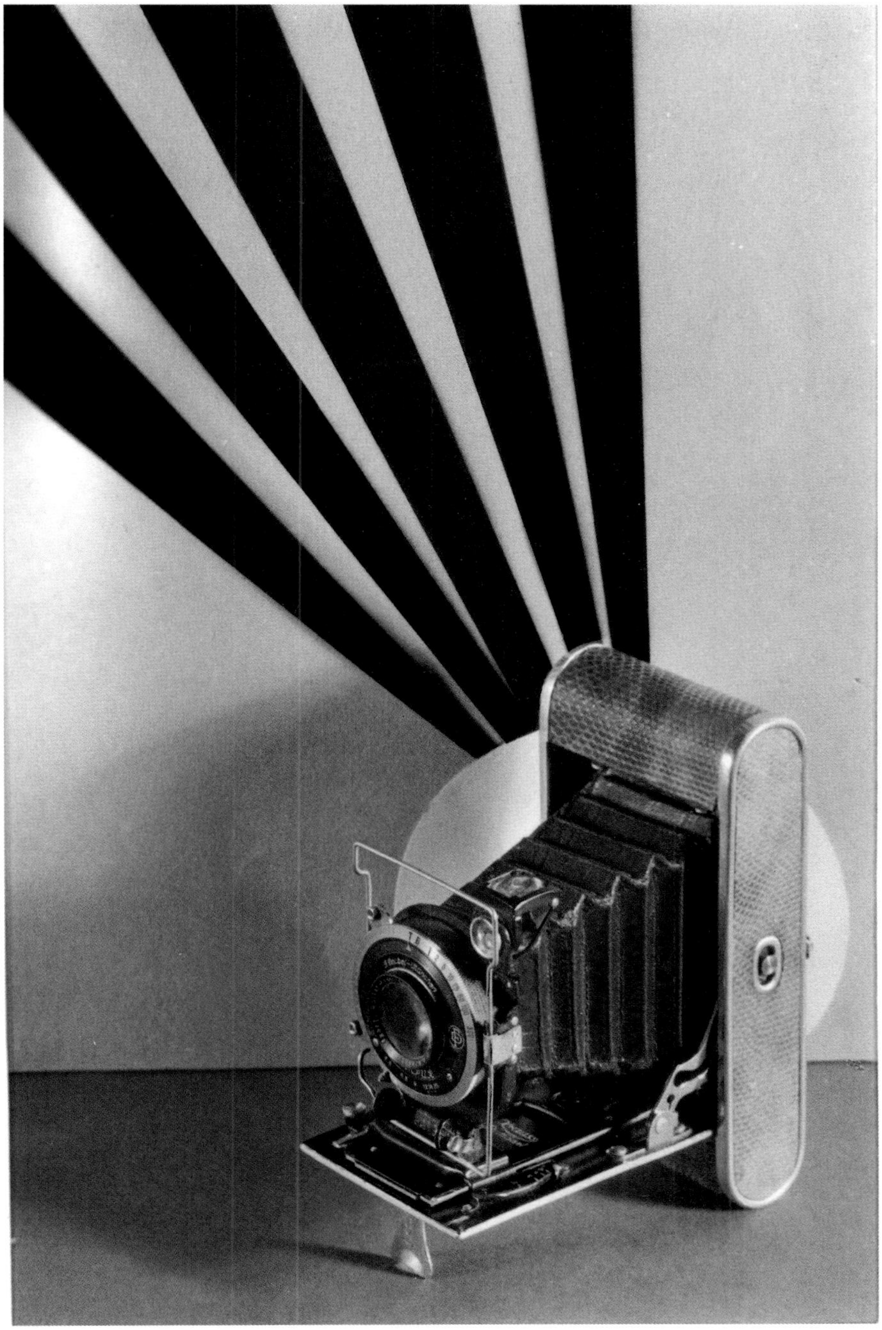

Vienna. Advertisement, project for the School of Photography, 1934.

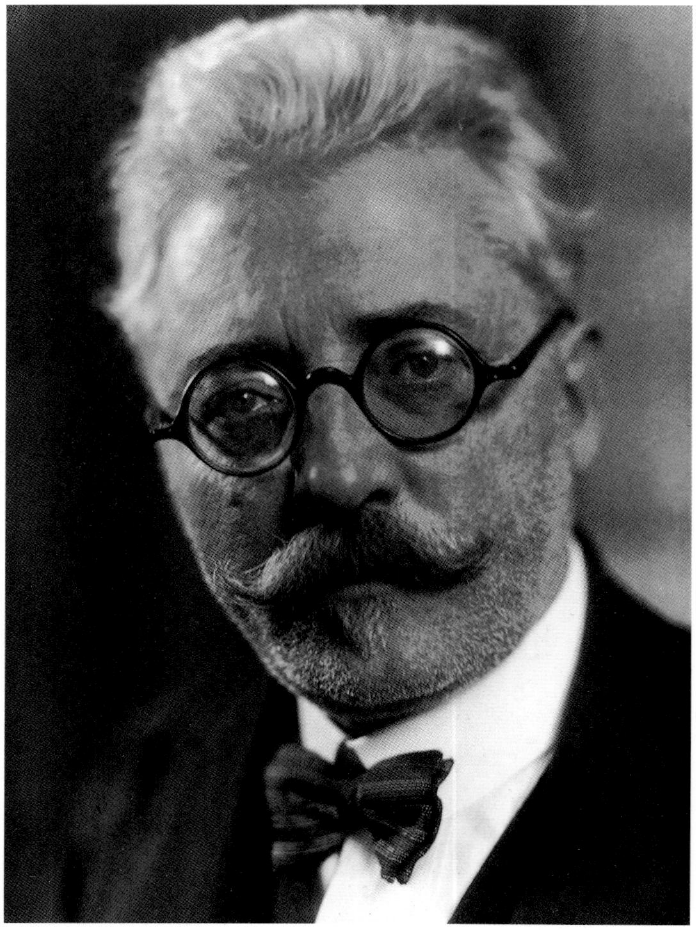

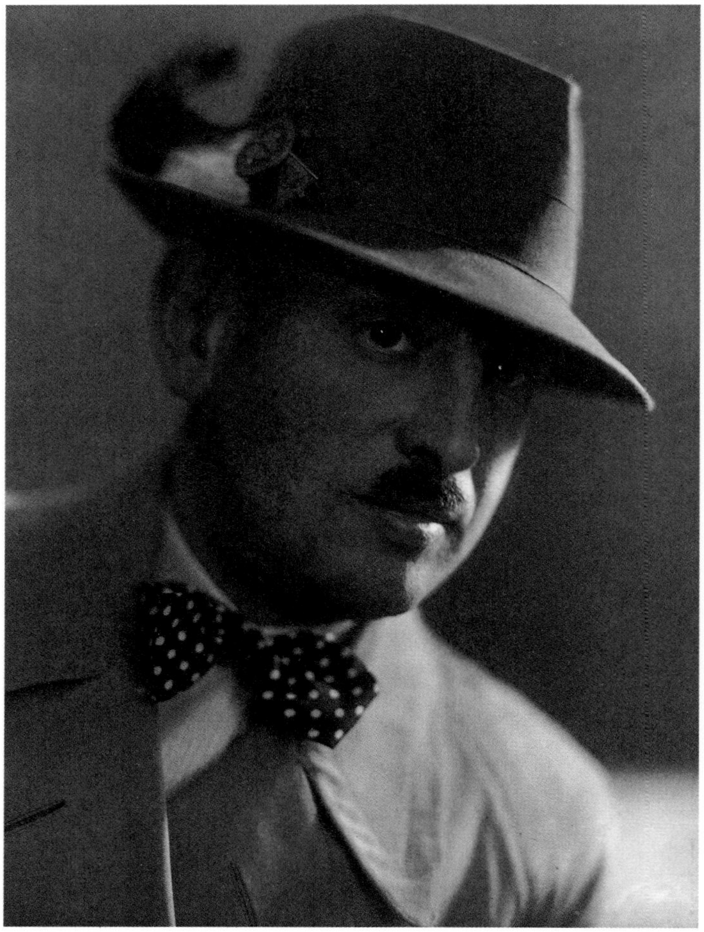

Vienna. Portrait, 1934.

Vienna. Portrait, 1934.

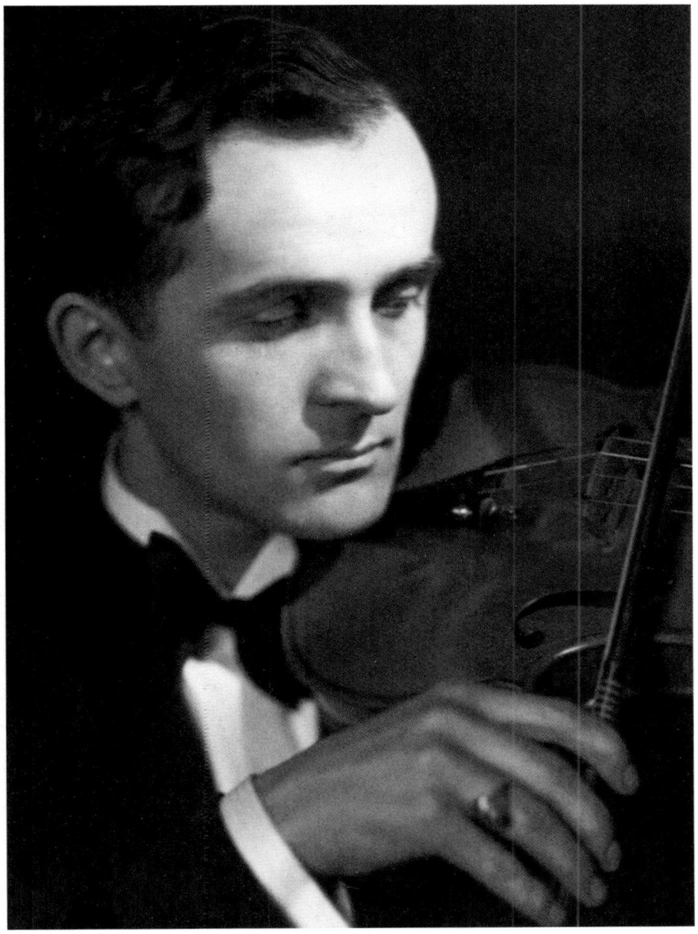

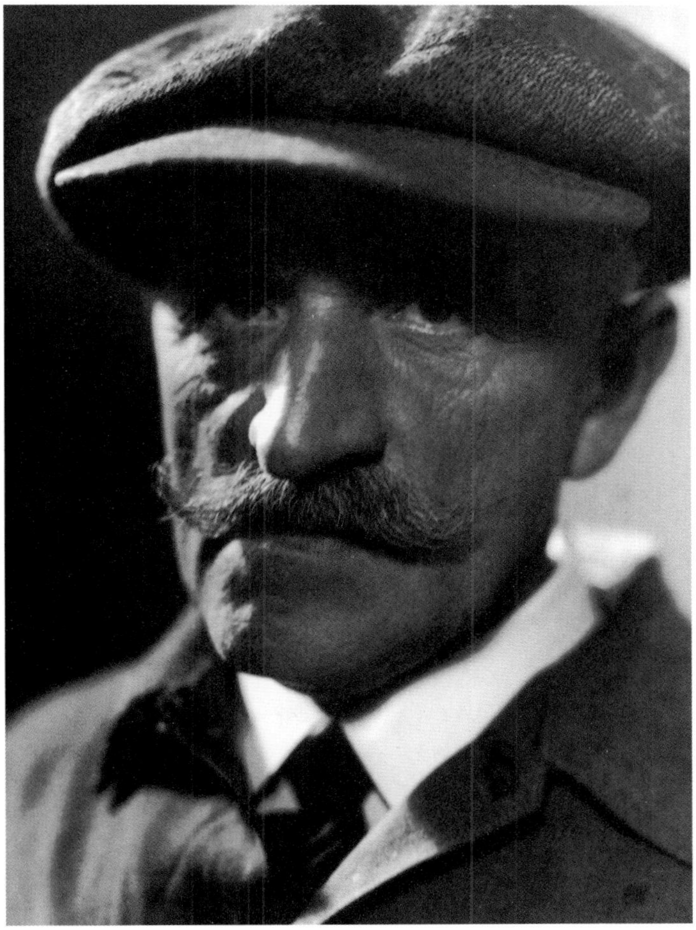

Vienna. Portrait, 1934.

Vienna. Portrait, 1934.

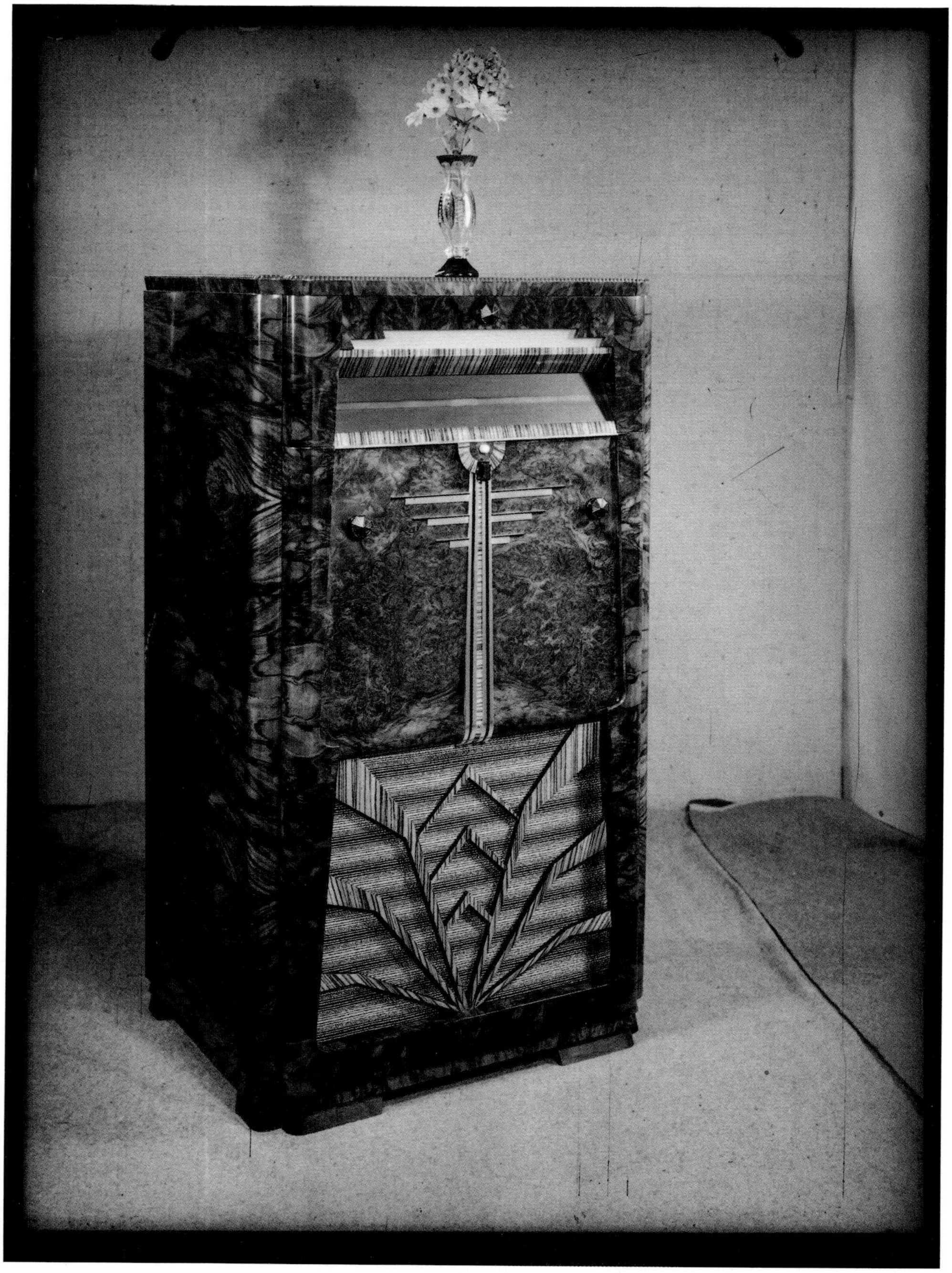

Baulmes. Radio-gramophone, 1938.

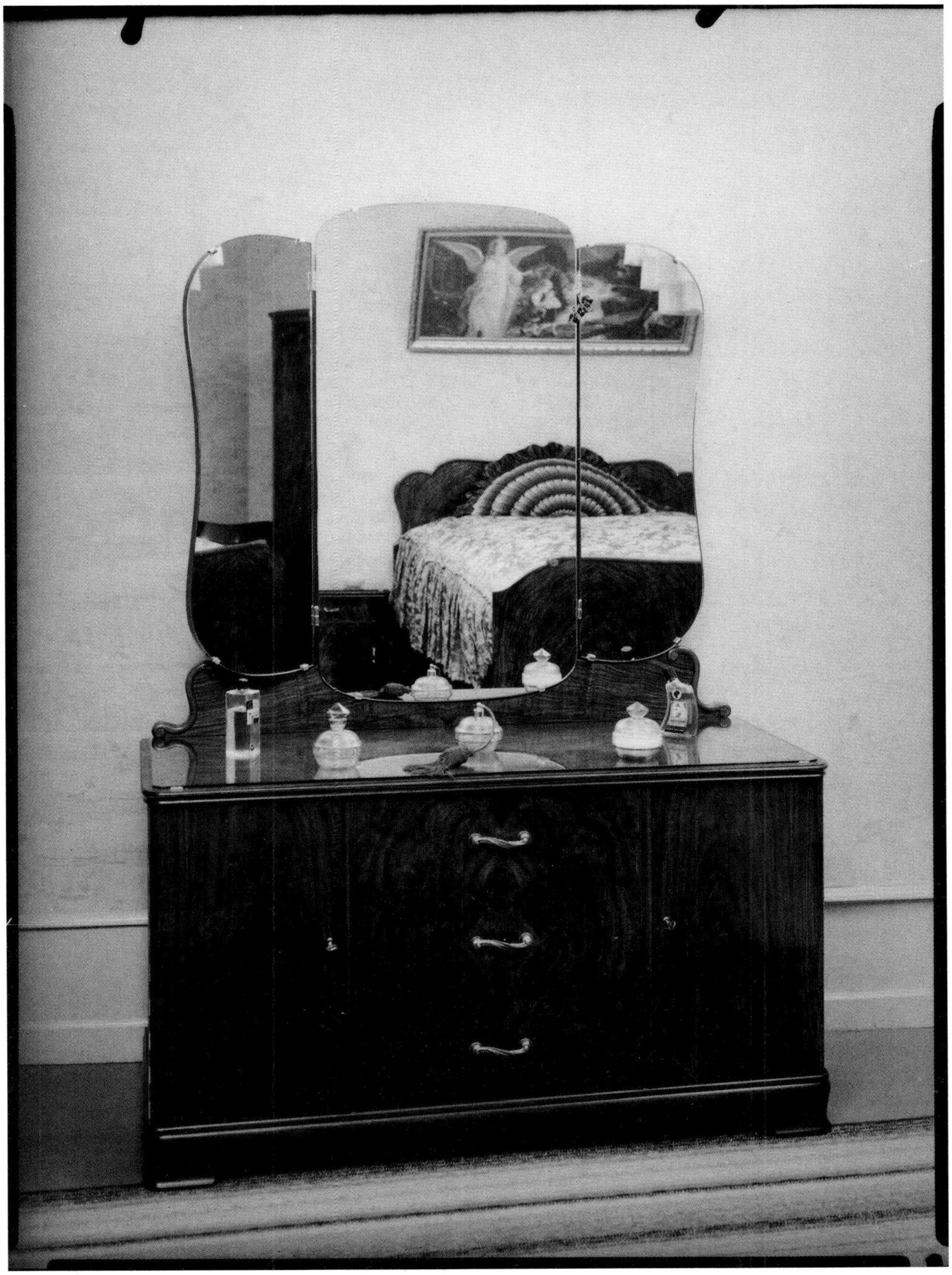

Baulmes. Dressing table and the matrimonial bed, 1938.

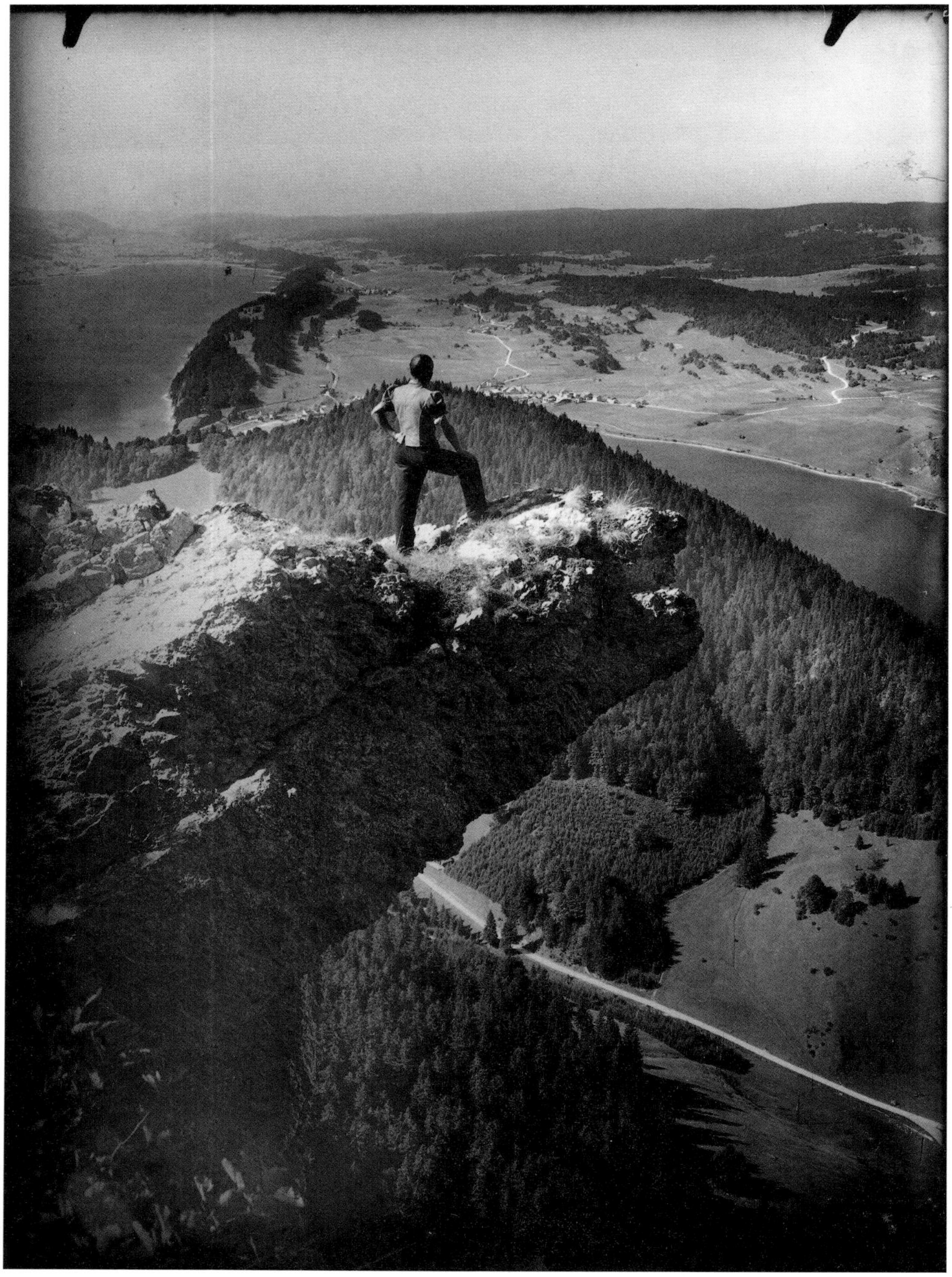

At the top of la Dent-de-Vaullion, Switzerland, 1937.

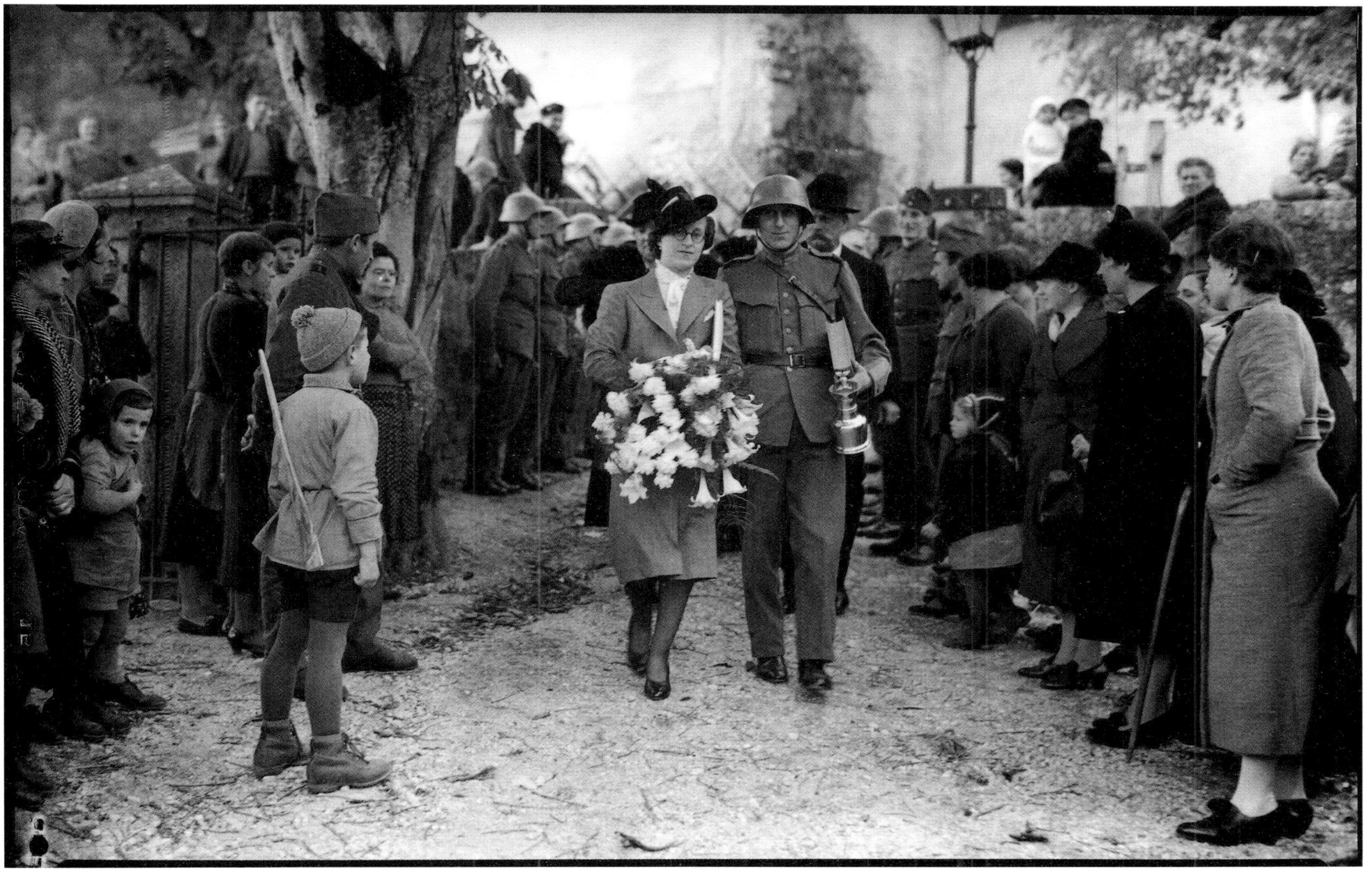

Baulmes. Military wedding, 1940.

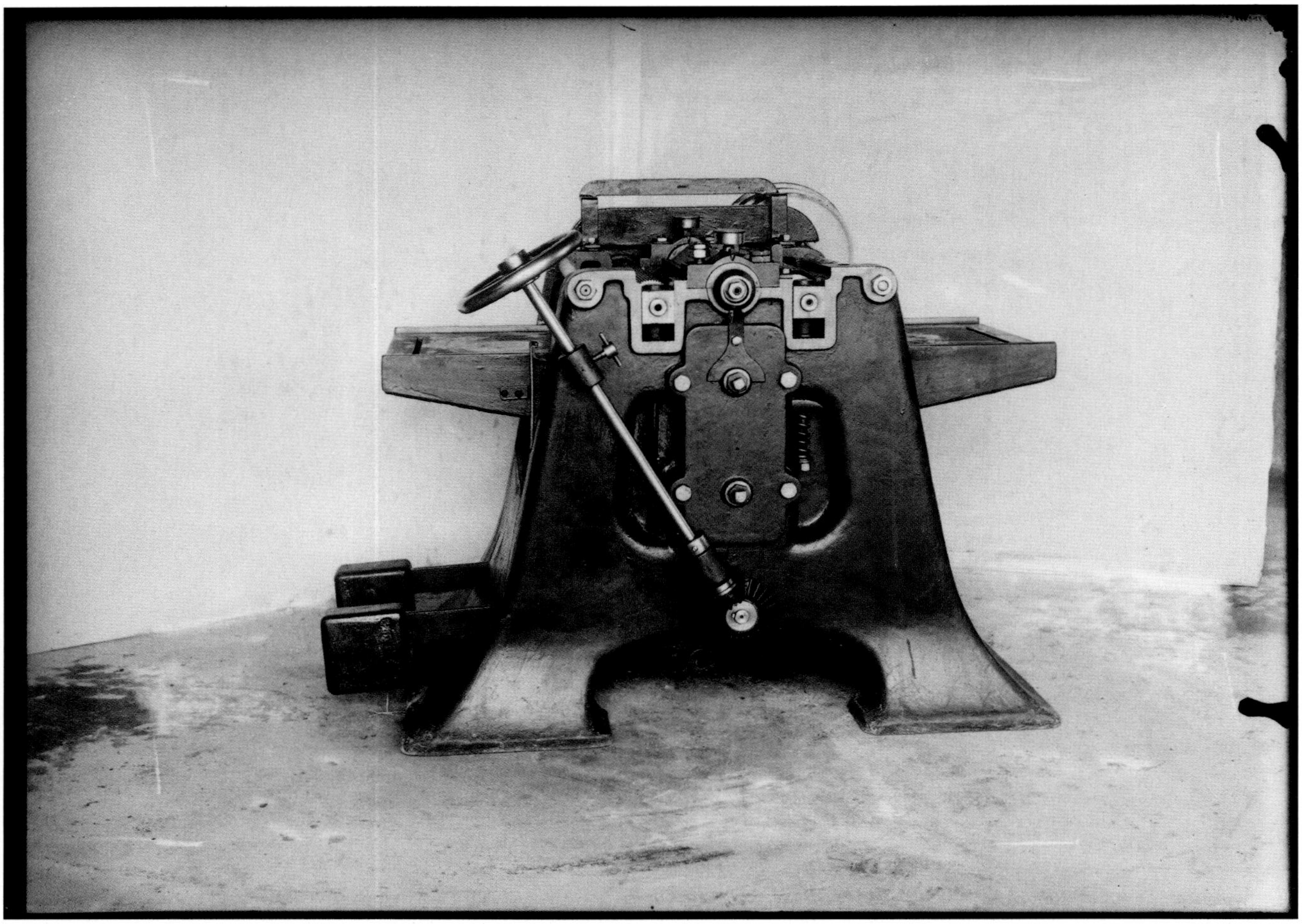

Baulmes. Electric plane, 1933.

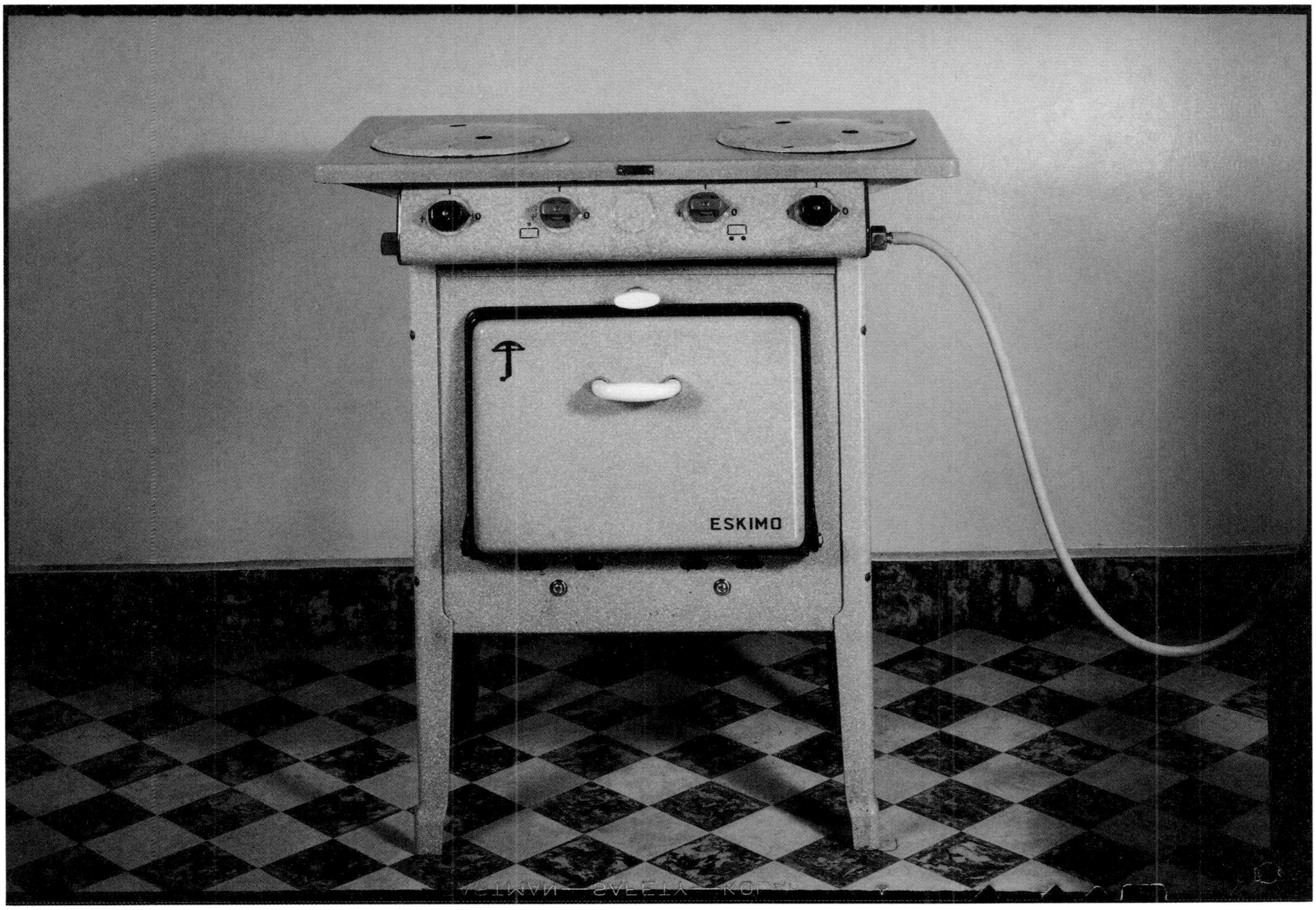

Baulmes. Gas stove, 1938.

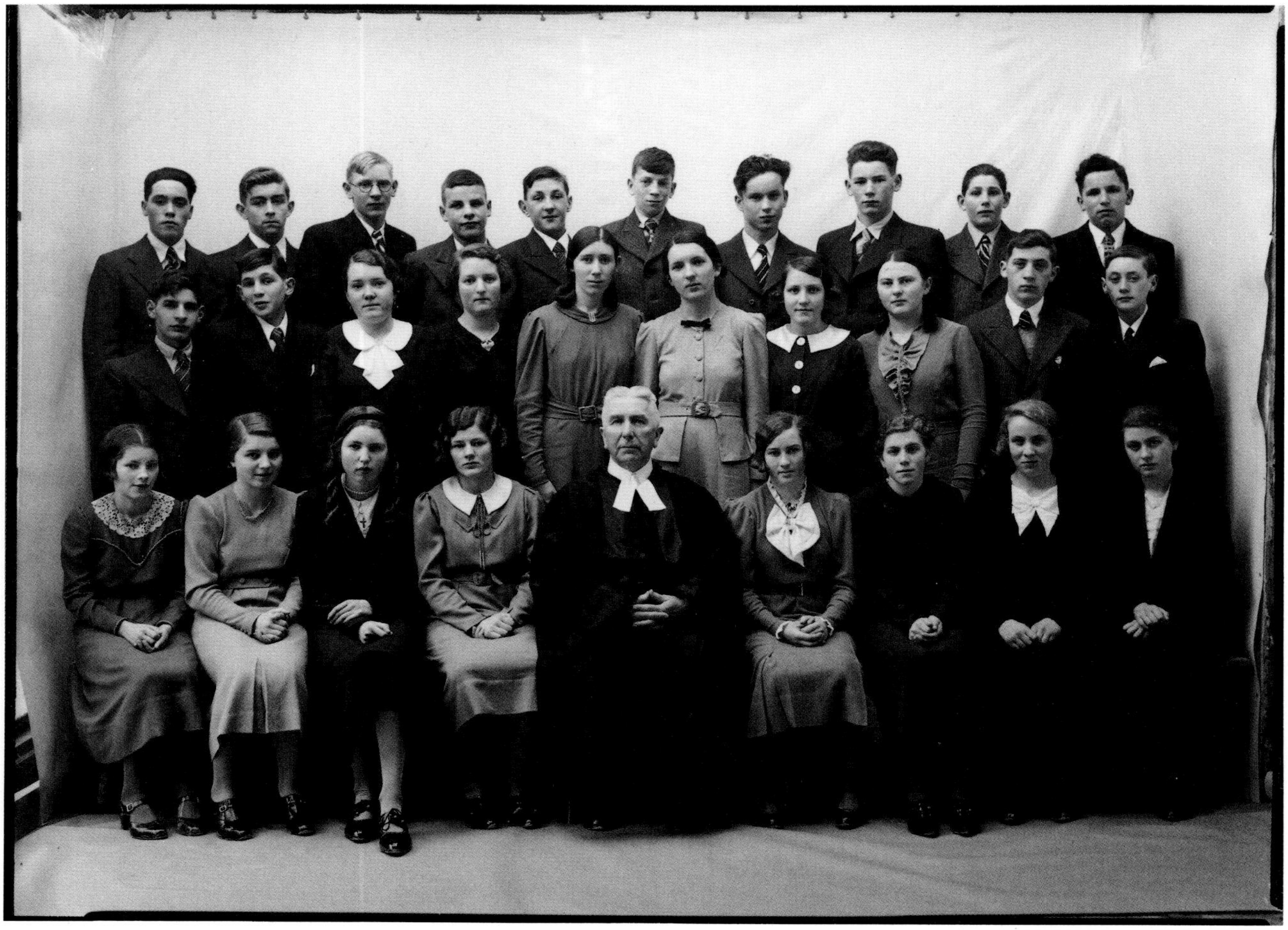

Baulmes. Confirmation class, 1938.

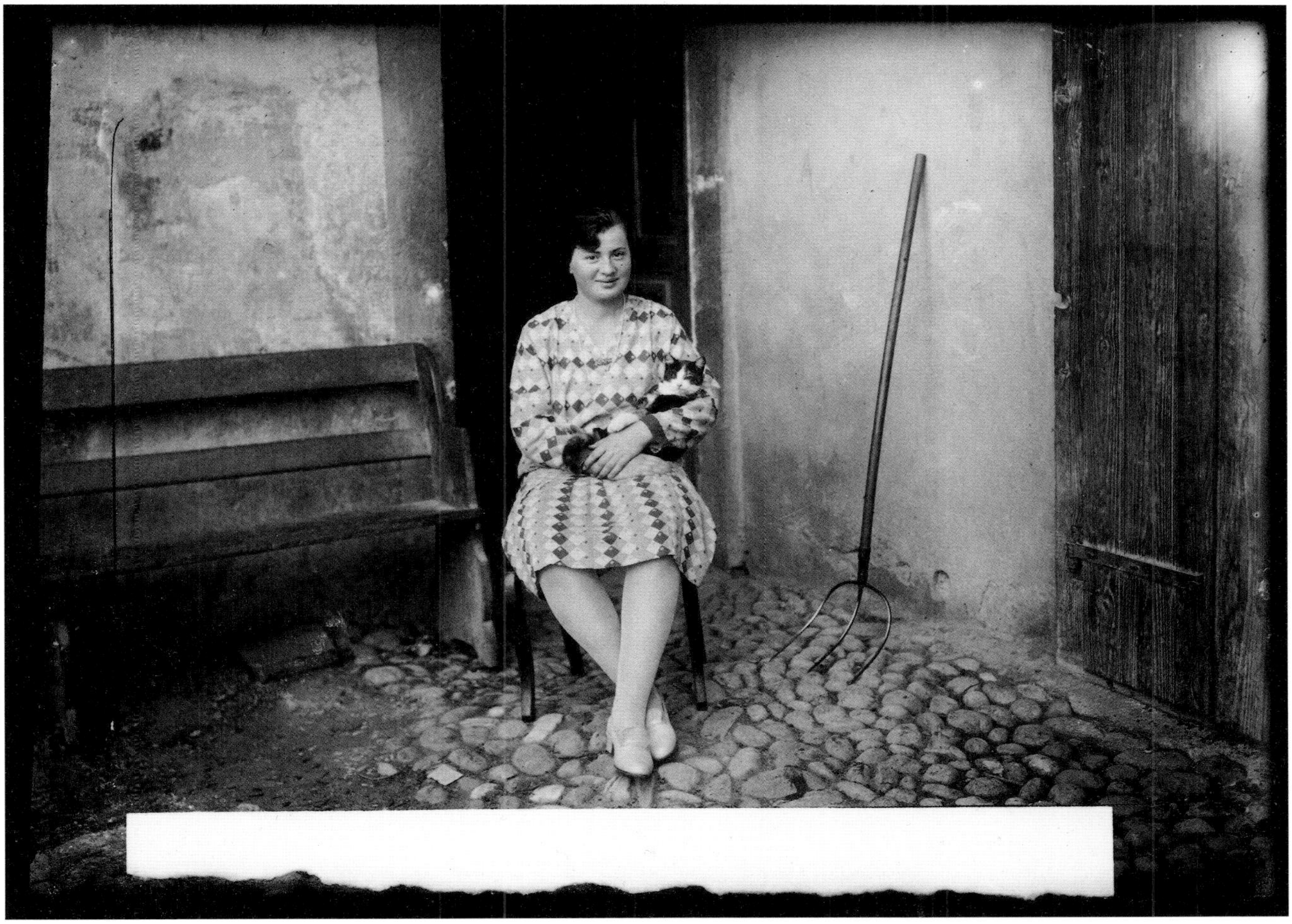

Baulmes. Hélène Collet, 1933.

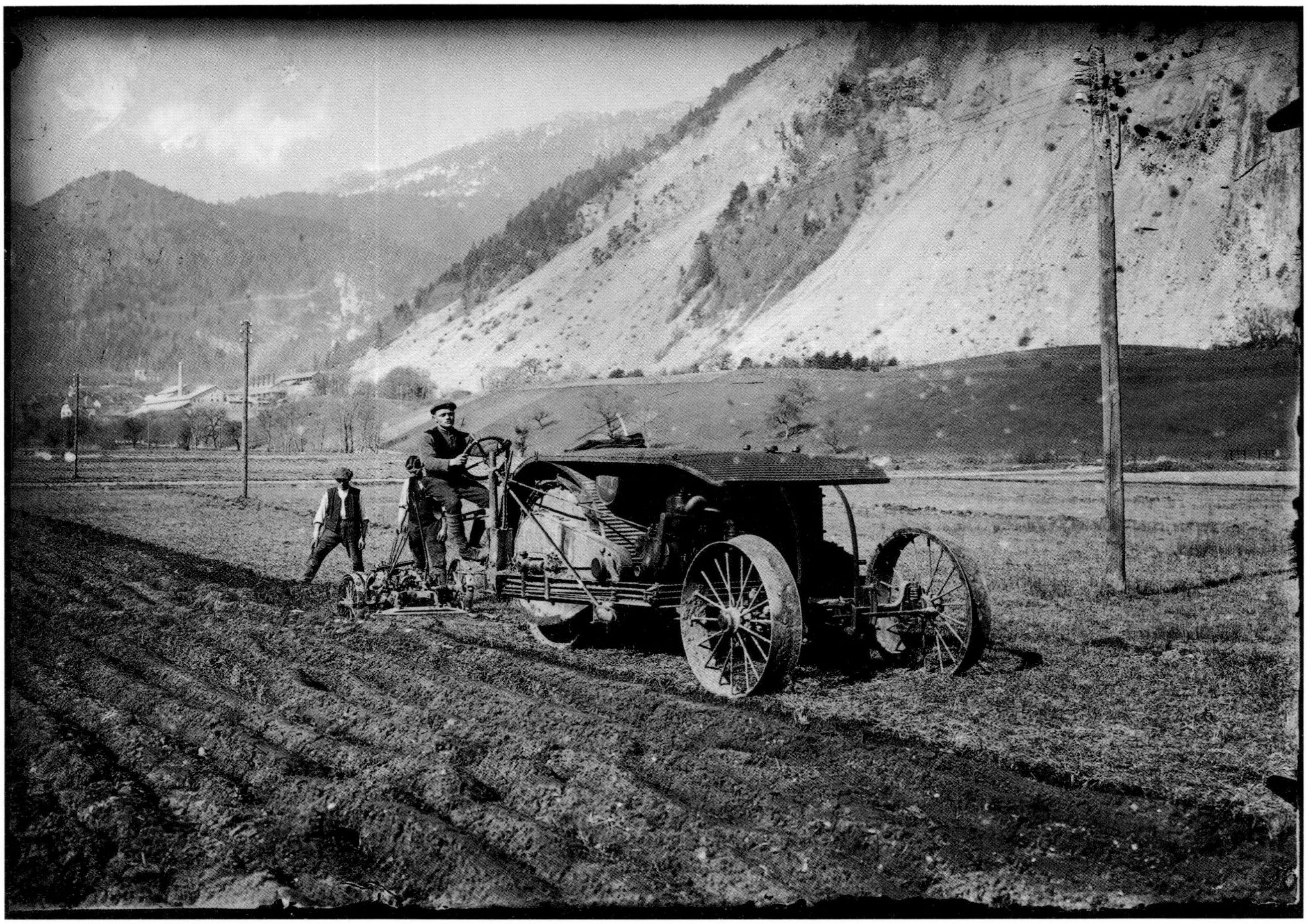

Baulmes. First tractor, 1934.

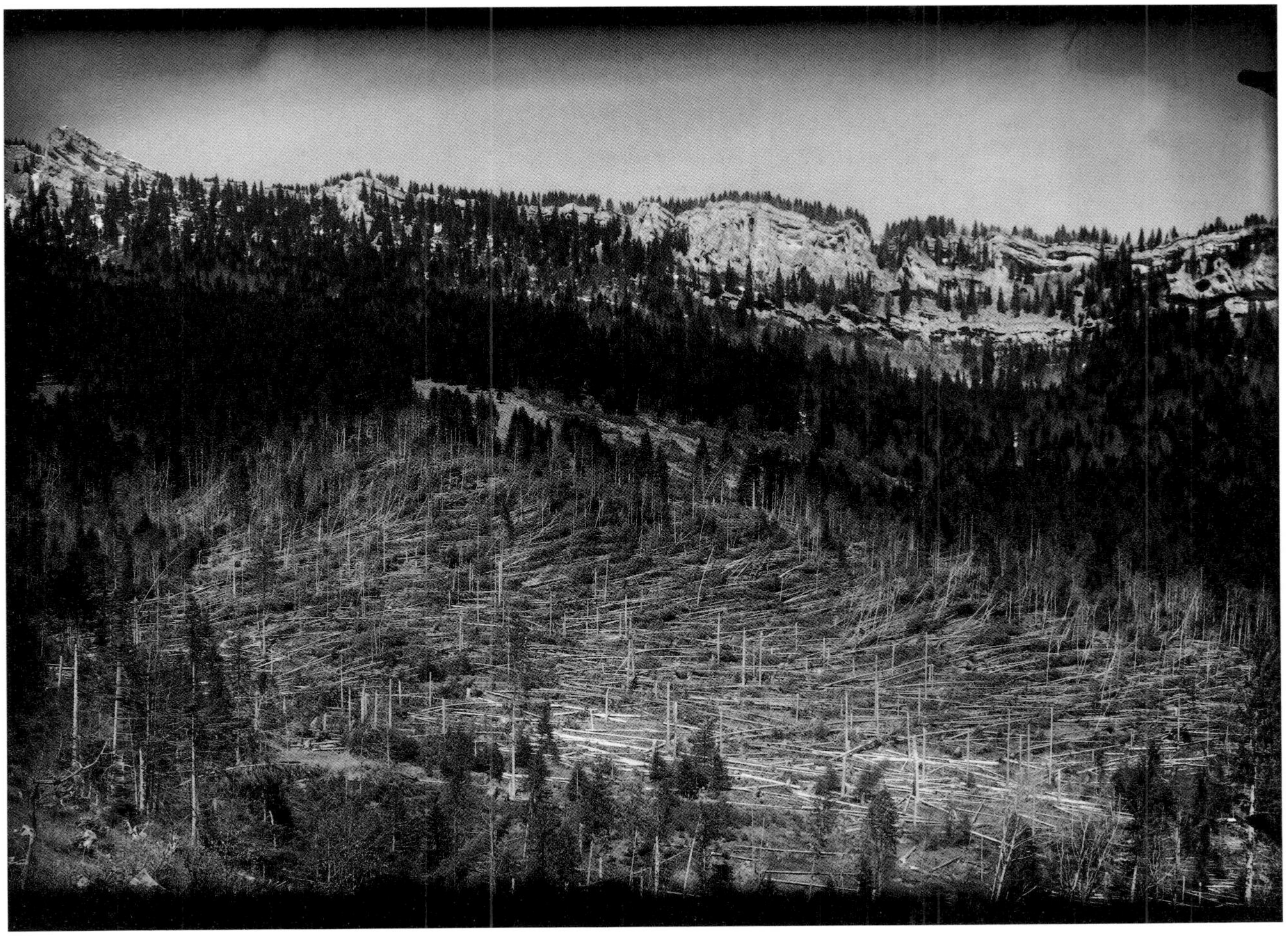

Hurricane over Baulmes, 1935.

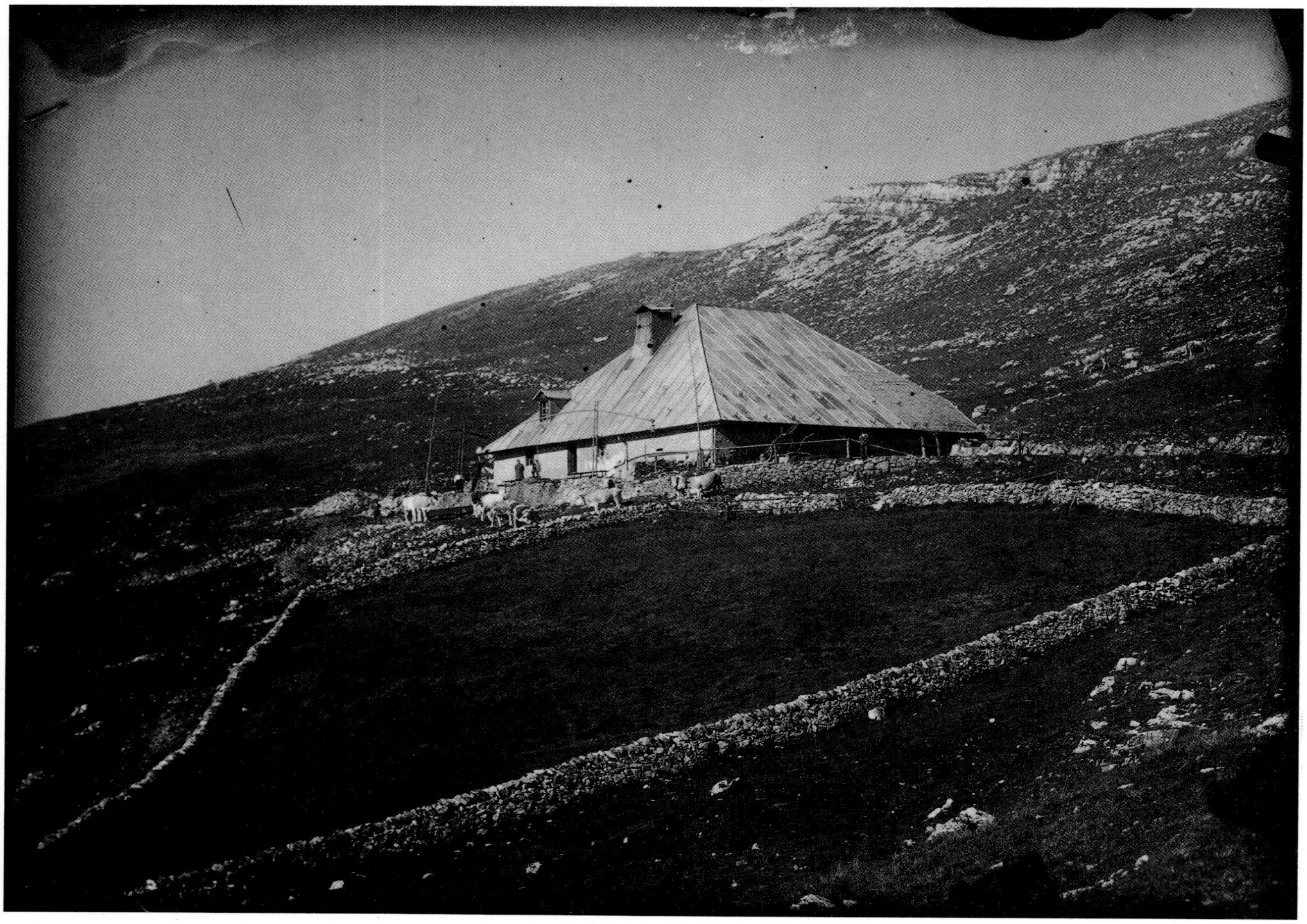

At the top of le Suchet, Switzerland, 1932.

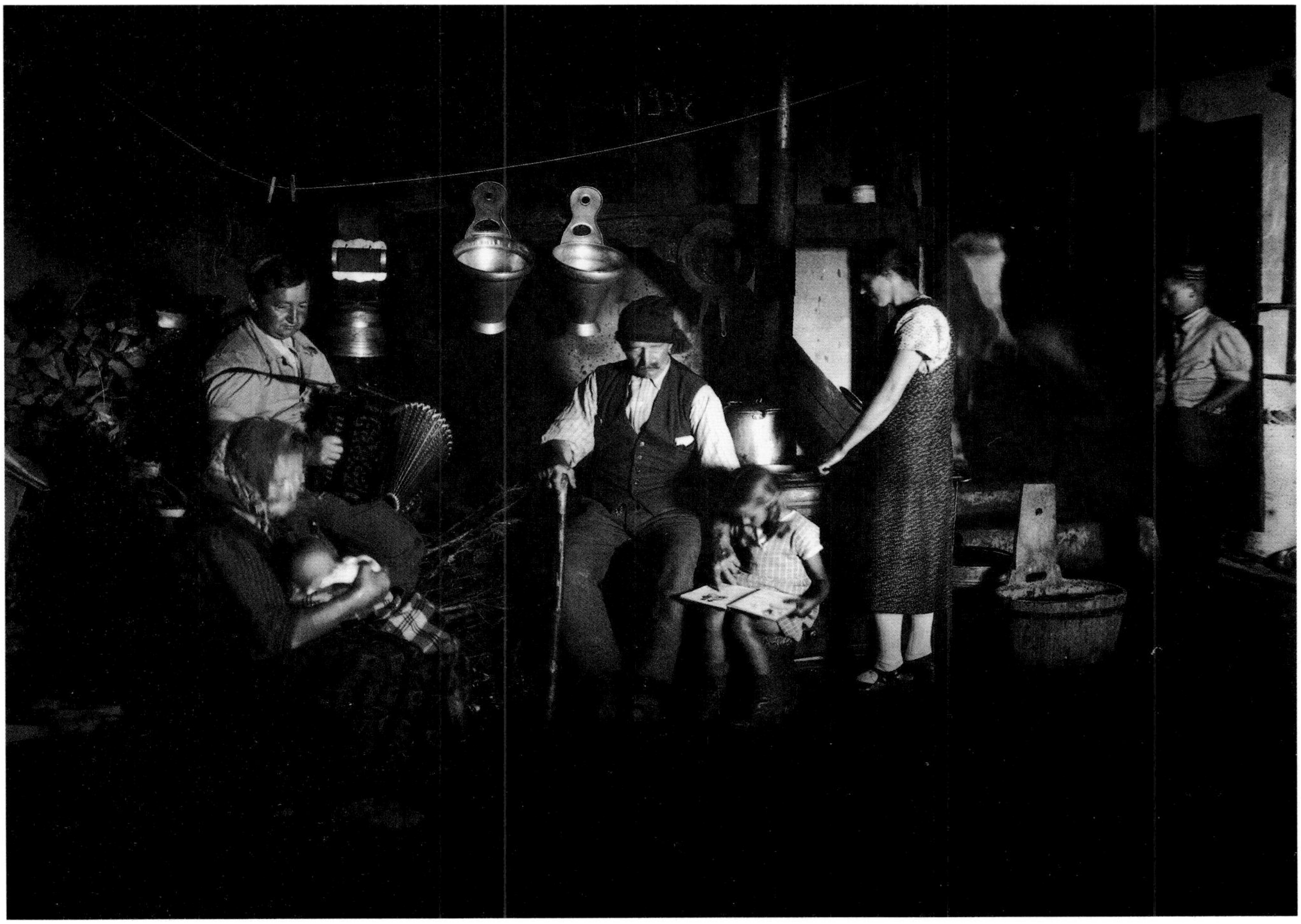

Le Suchet. Mountain pasture, 1932.

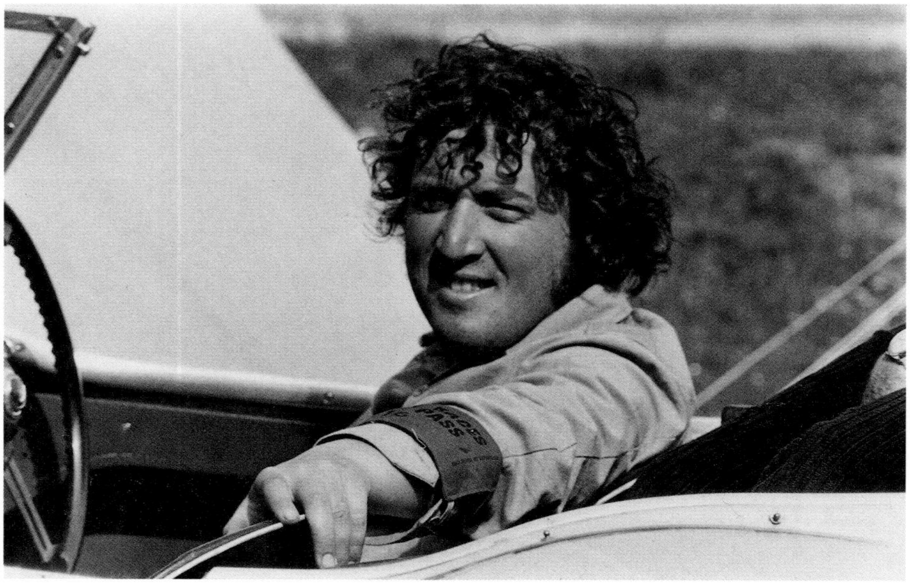

The Isle of Man, United Kingdom. Photograph by Françoise Deriaz, his wife, 1971.

Armand Deriaz II

Born on August 1, 1942. Following the familiy tradition, he was named after his grandfather.

Trained at the School of Photography of Vevey, he was drawn to photojournalism early on, and has reported from Senegal to the Caucasus, from Jordan to Northern Ireland, as well as on his own Switzerland, where he concentrates on traditional festivals and political demonstrations. Author and filmmaker, he also collaborates in the family business, now over a hundred years old, alongside his father Alphonse Deriaz who was his first mentor as a photographer. In addition, he is currently the director of *News Productions,* which publishes post cards and posters for the Swiss photography museum, le Musée de l'Elysée in Lausanne, and distributes them throughout the world.

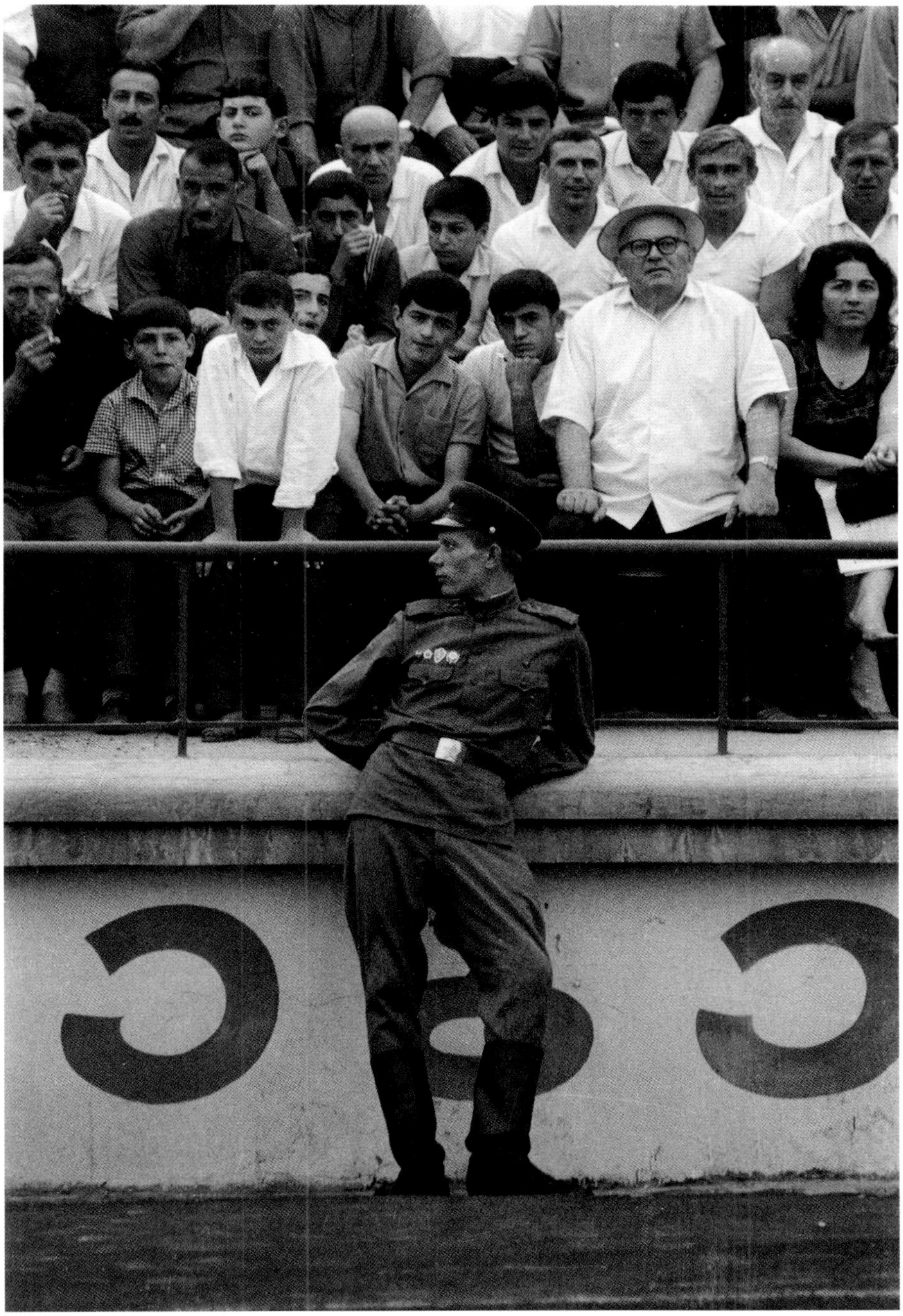

Tbilissi stadium, USSR. Soviet soldier during a Greece–USSR soccer match, 1967.

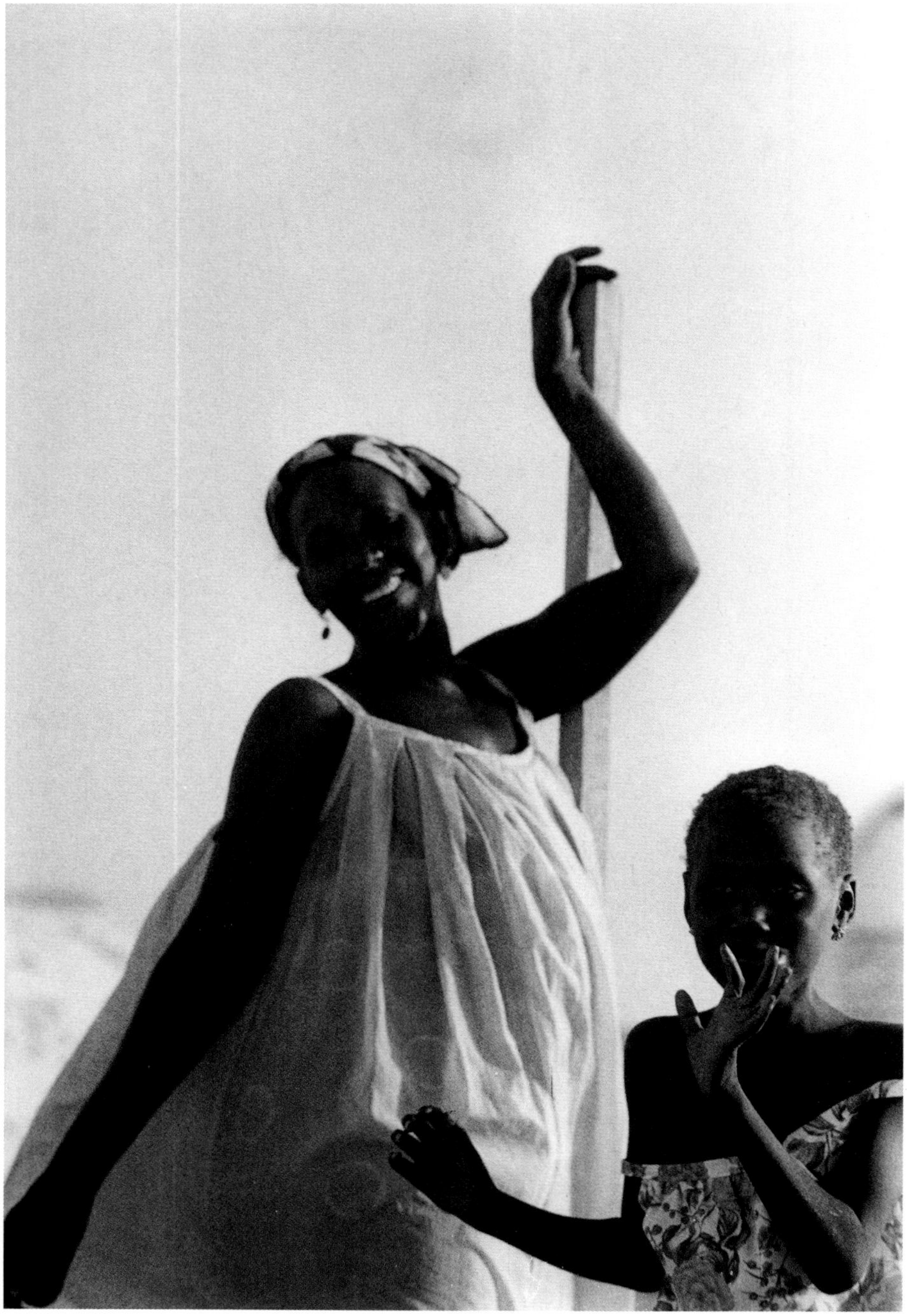

Peul women in Podor, Senegal river valley, 1965.

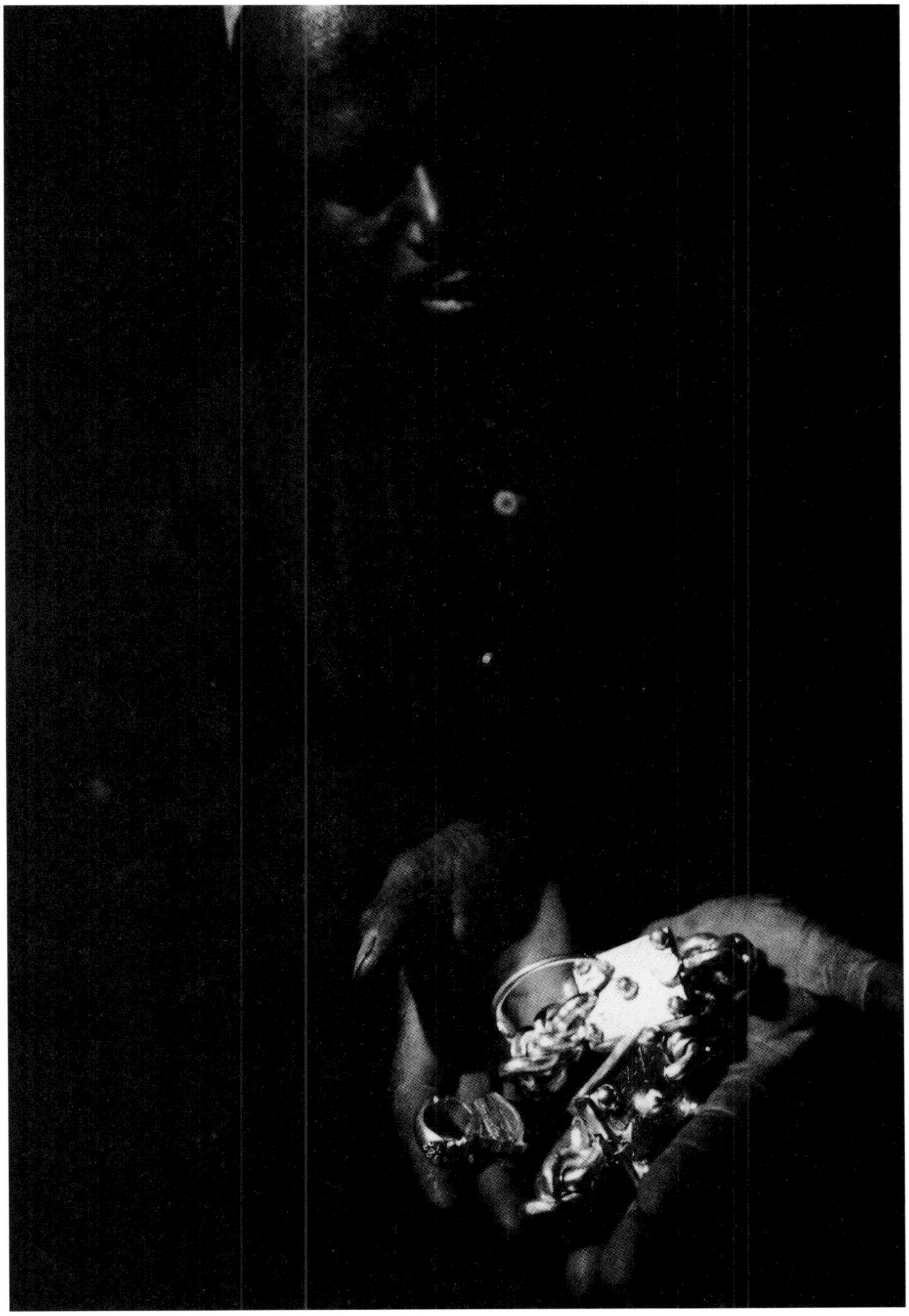

Paris, France. Jeweler and tailor selling gifts to workers returning home to Senegal, their "fortunes" made, 1969.

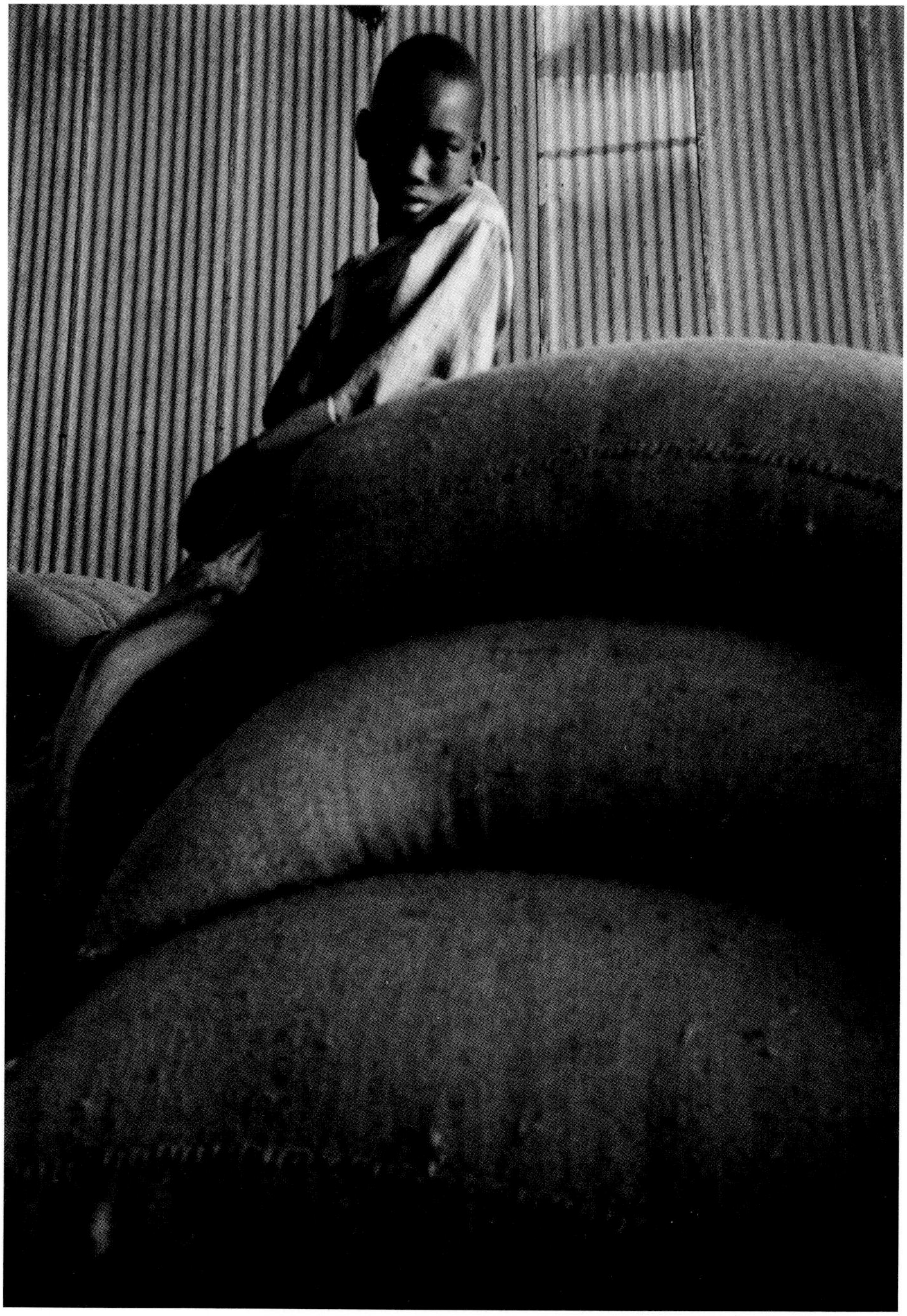

Peanut harvest in Bathurst, Gambia, 1965.

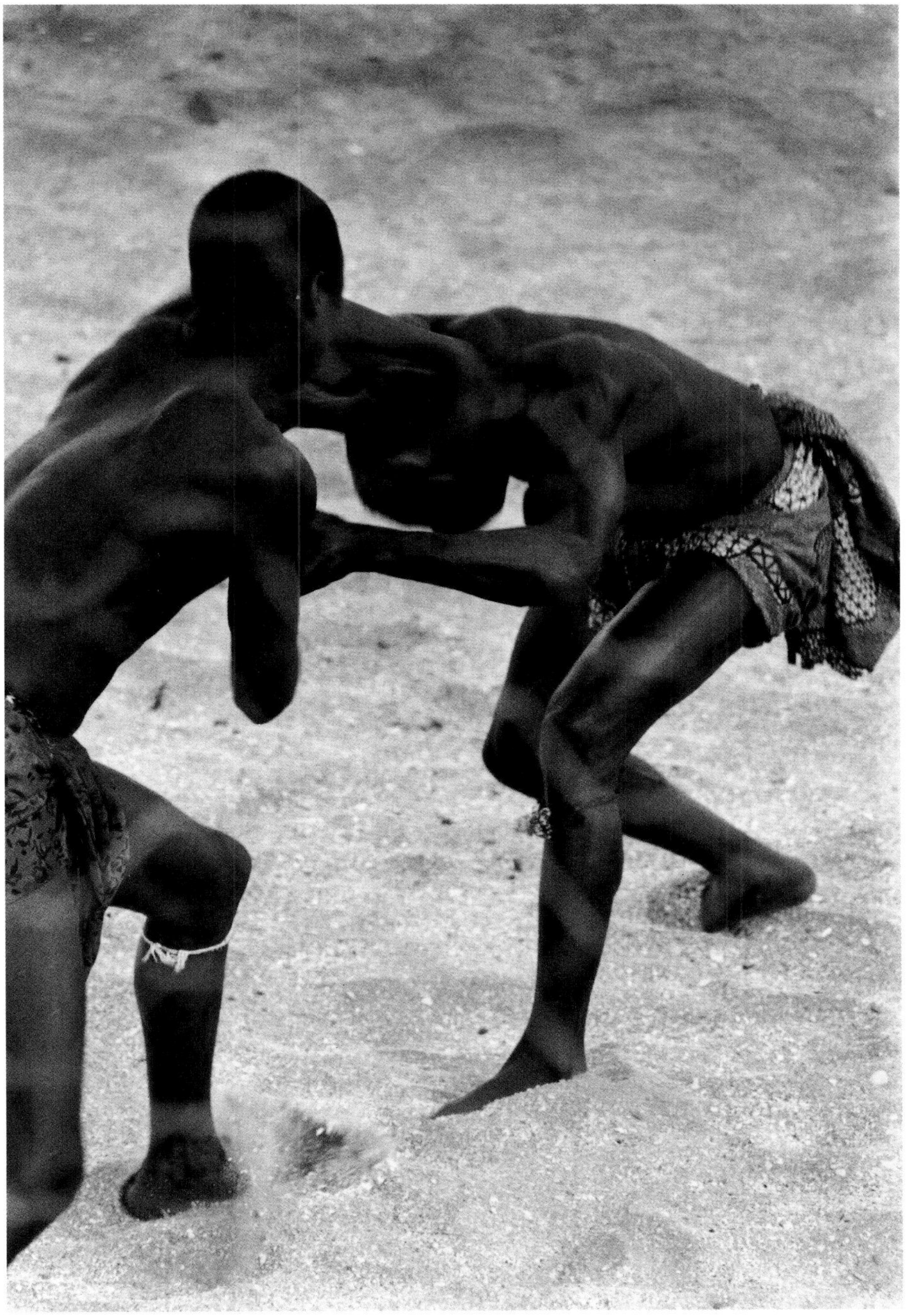

Rufisque. "La lutte sénégalaise", a Senegalese ritual, 1965.

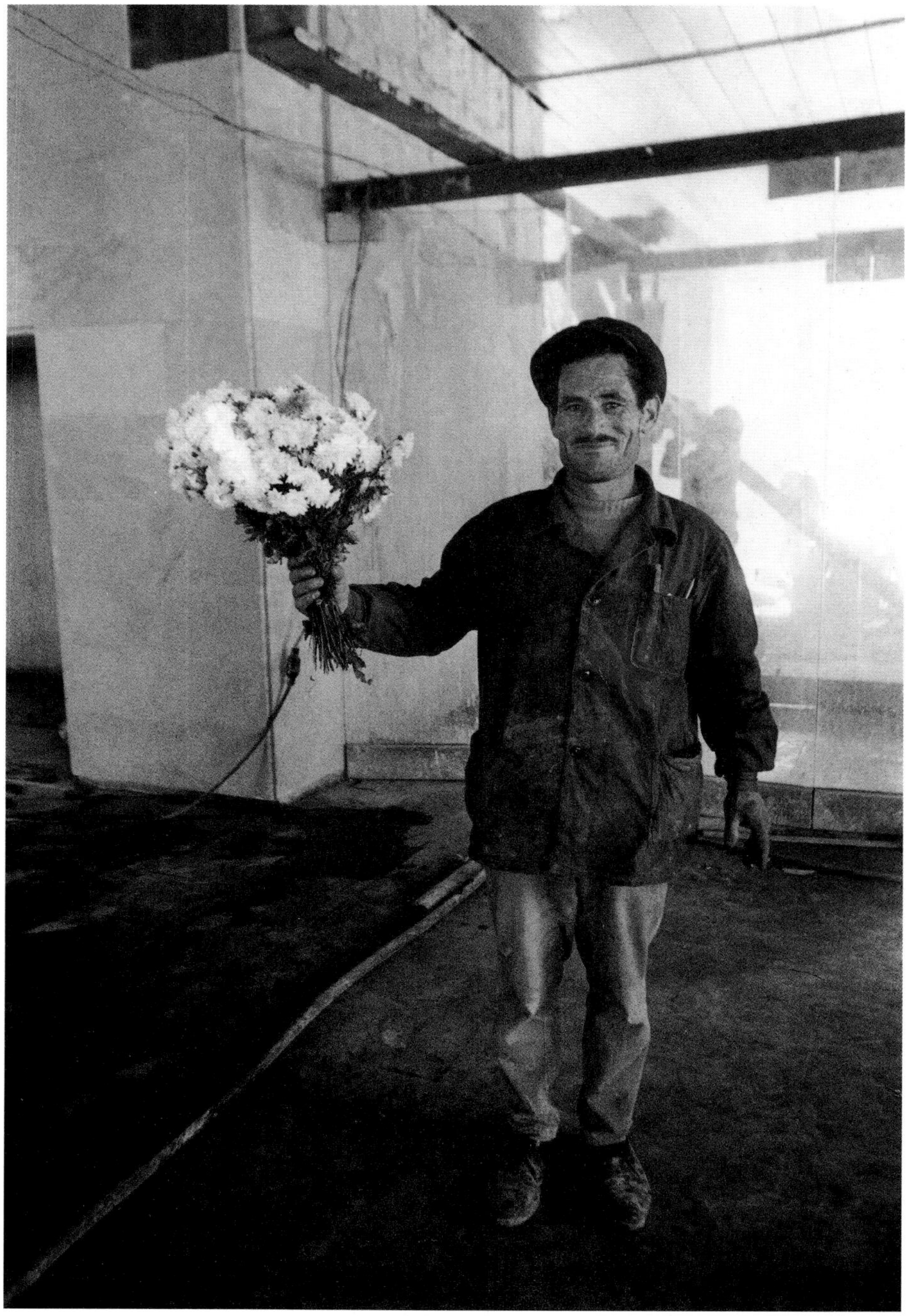

Tbilissi, USSR. An Azerbaidjani worker greets visitors, 1967.

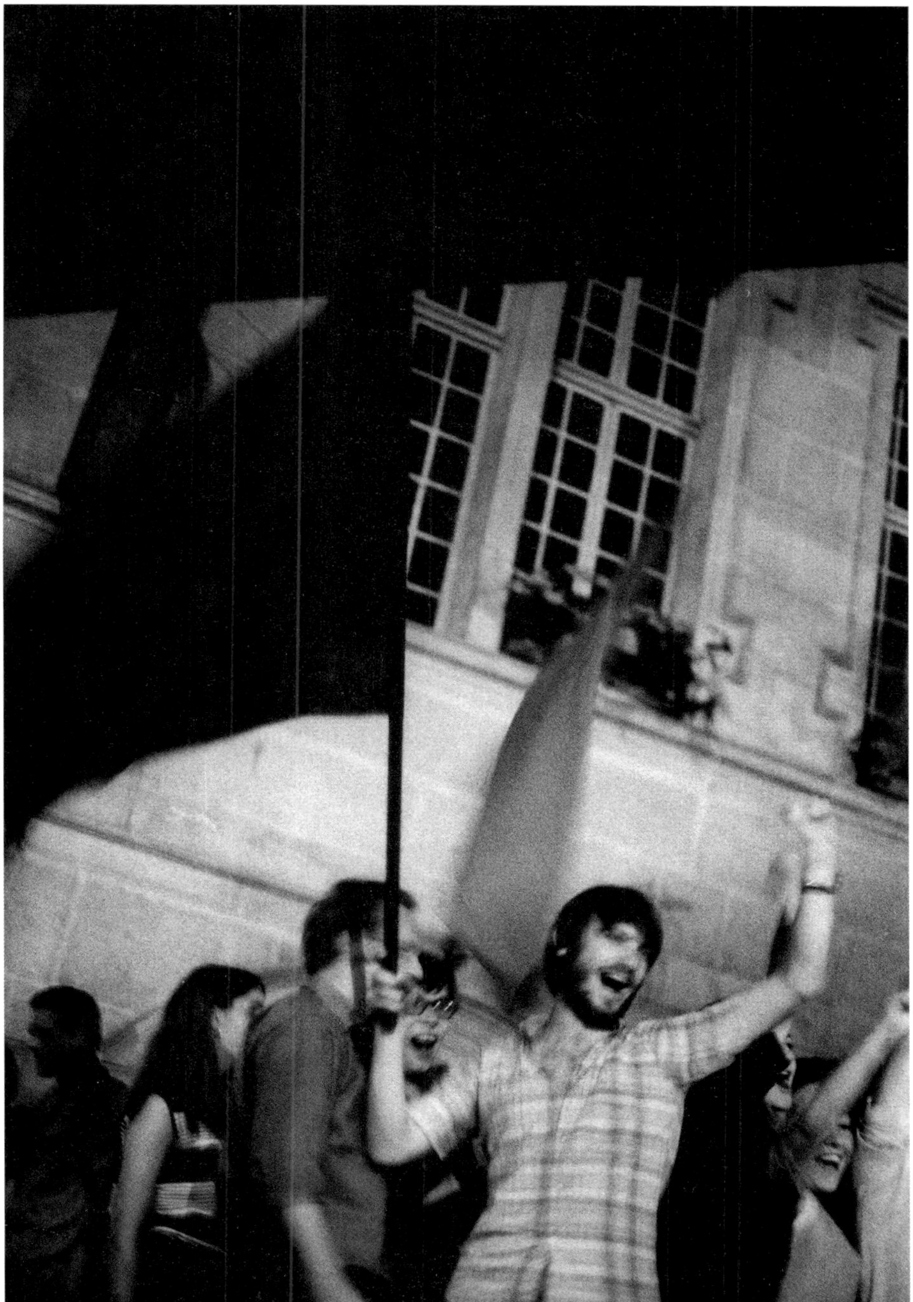

Lausanne, Switzerland. Students in front of the Hôtel de Ville, 1968.

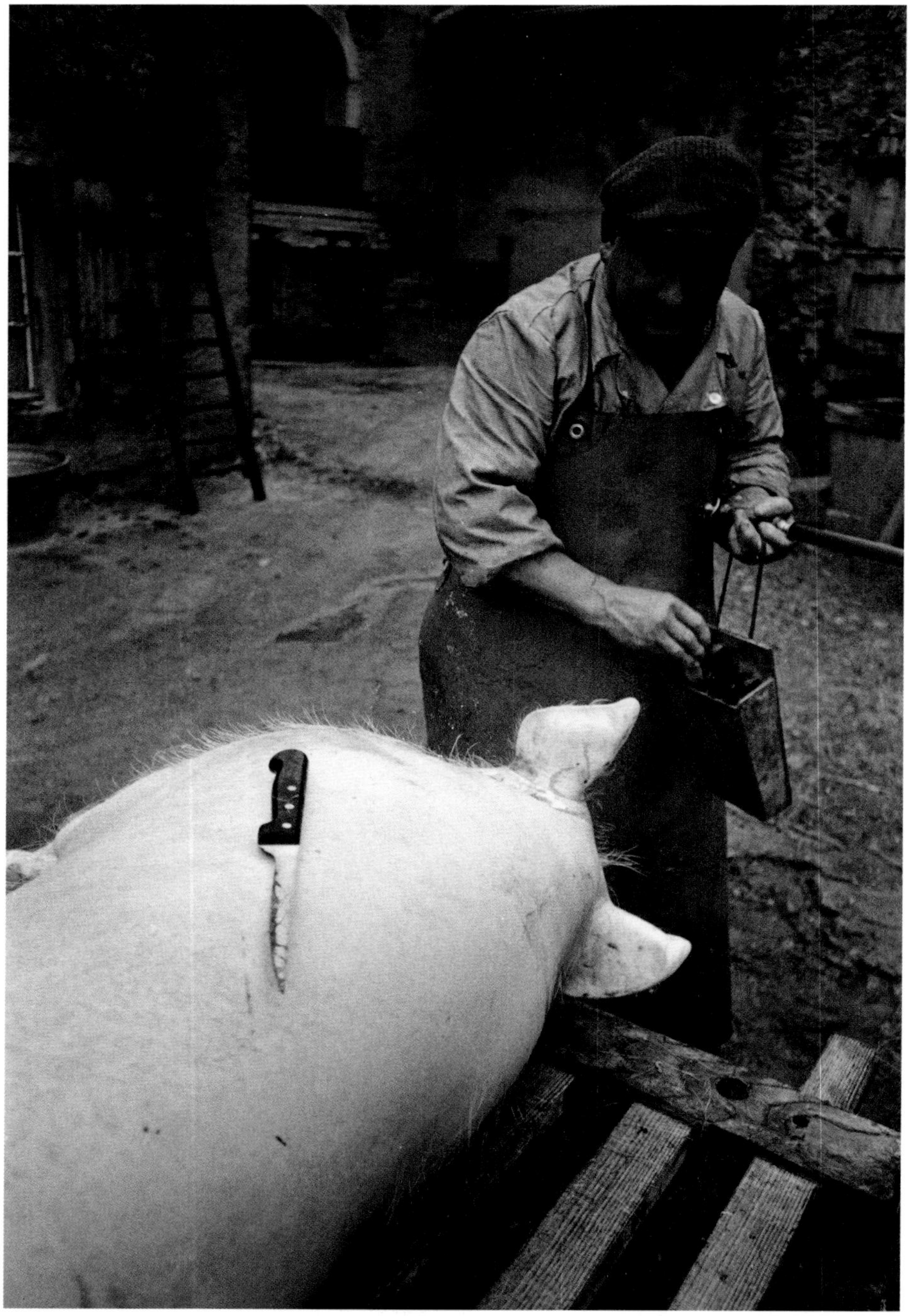

Lussy-sur-Morges, Switzerland. Slaughtering day, 1969.

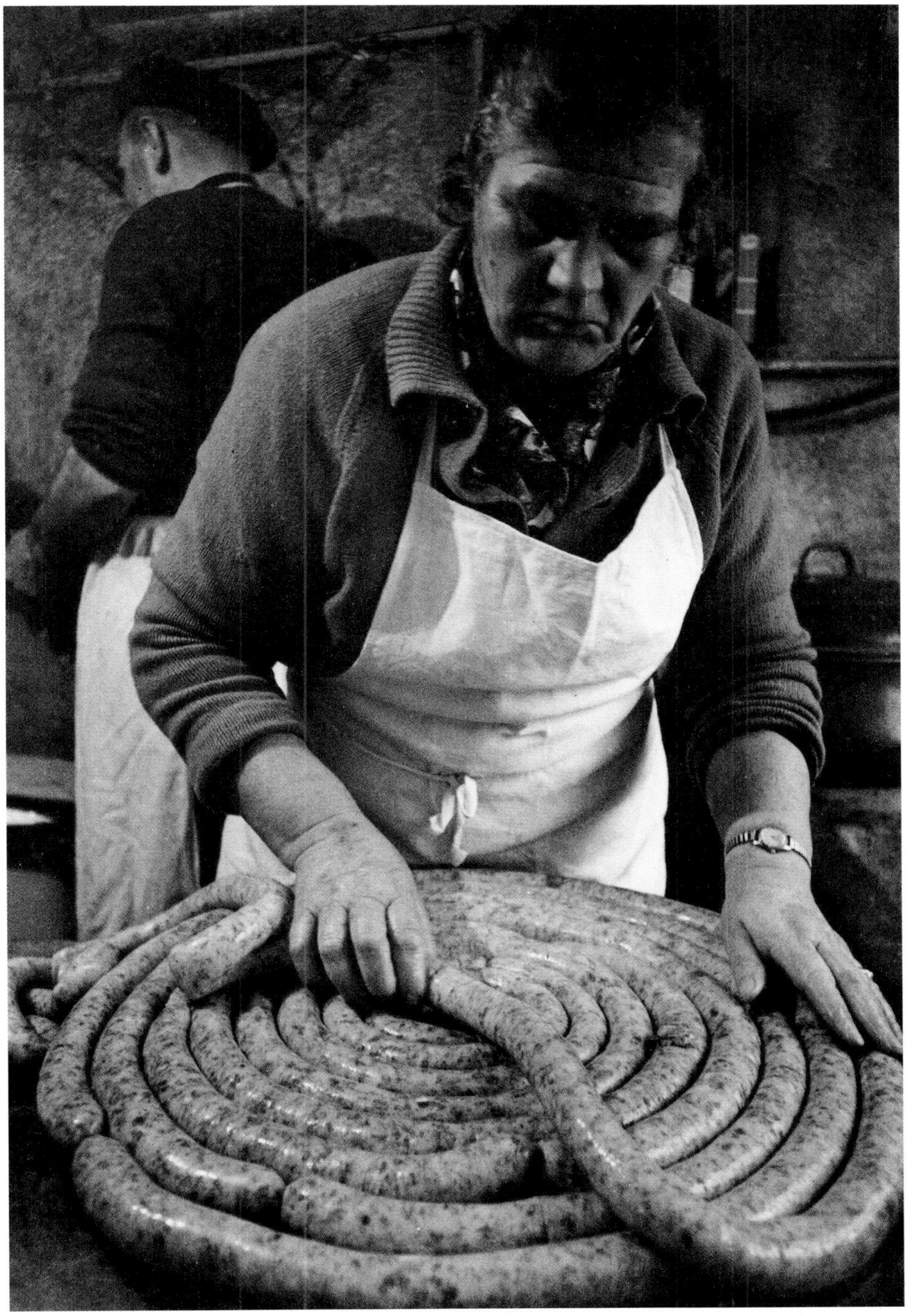

Lussy-sur-Morges, Switzerland. Slaughtering day, 1969.

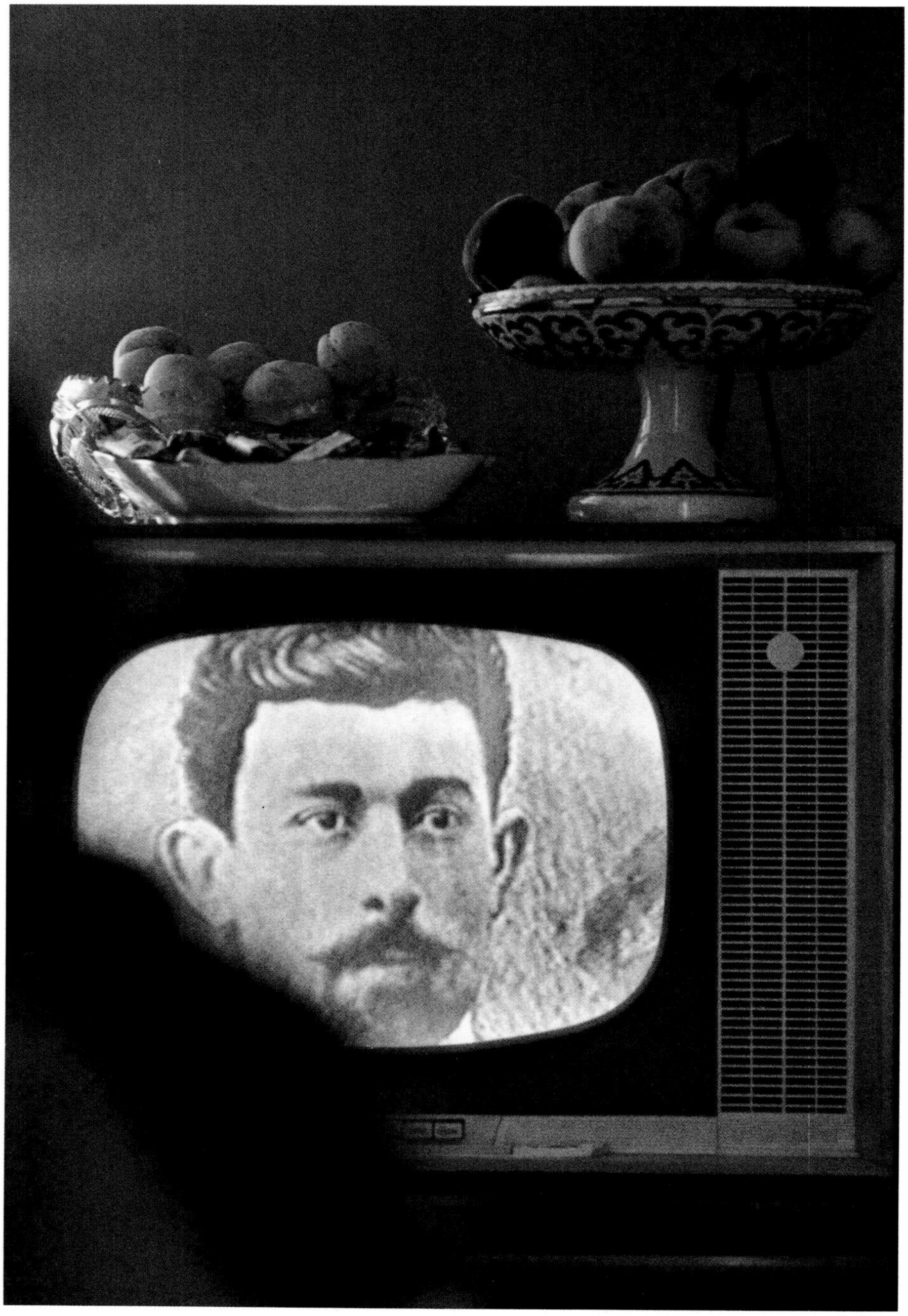

Tbilissi. Soviet television. Young Stalin, 1967.

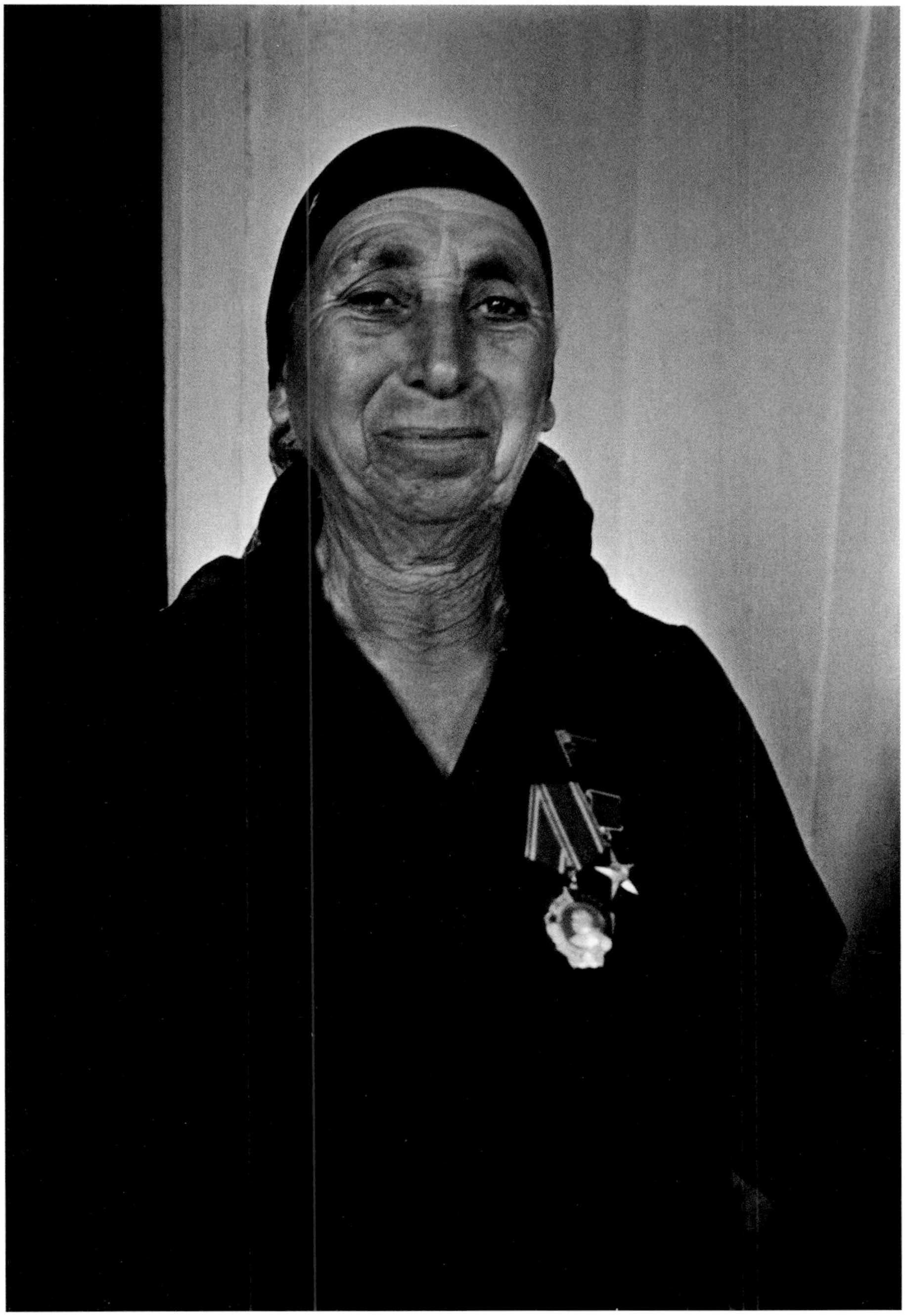

"Worker heroine": a tea picker in Soviet Georgia, 1967.

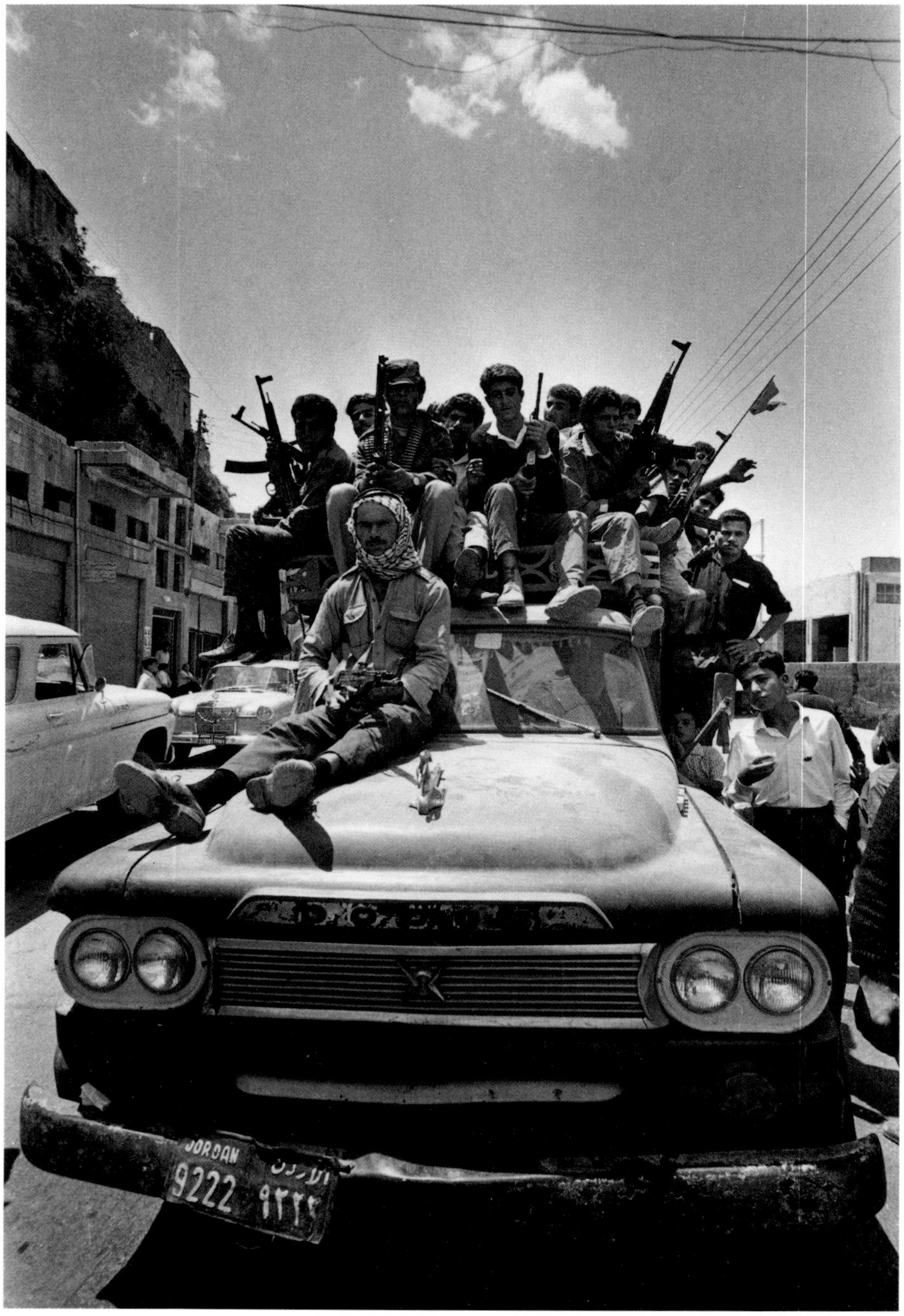

Amman, Jordan. May 1, 1970.

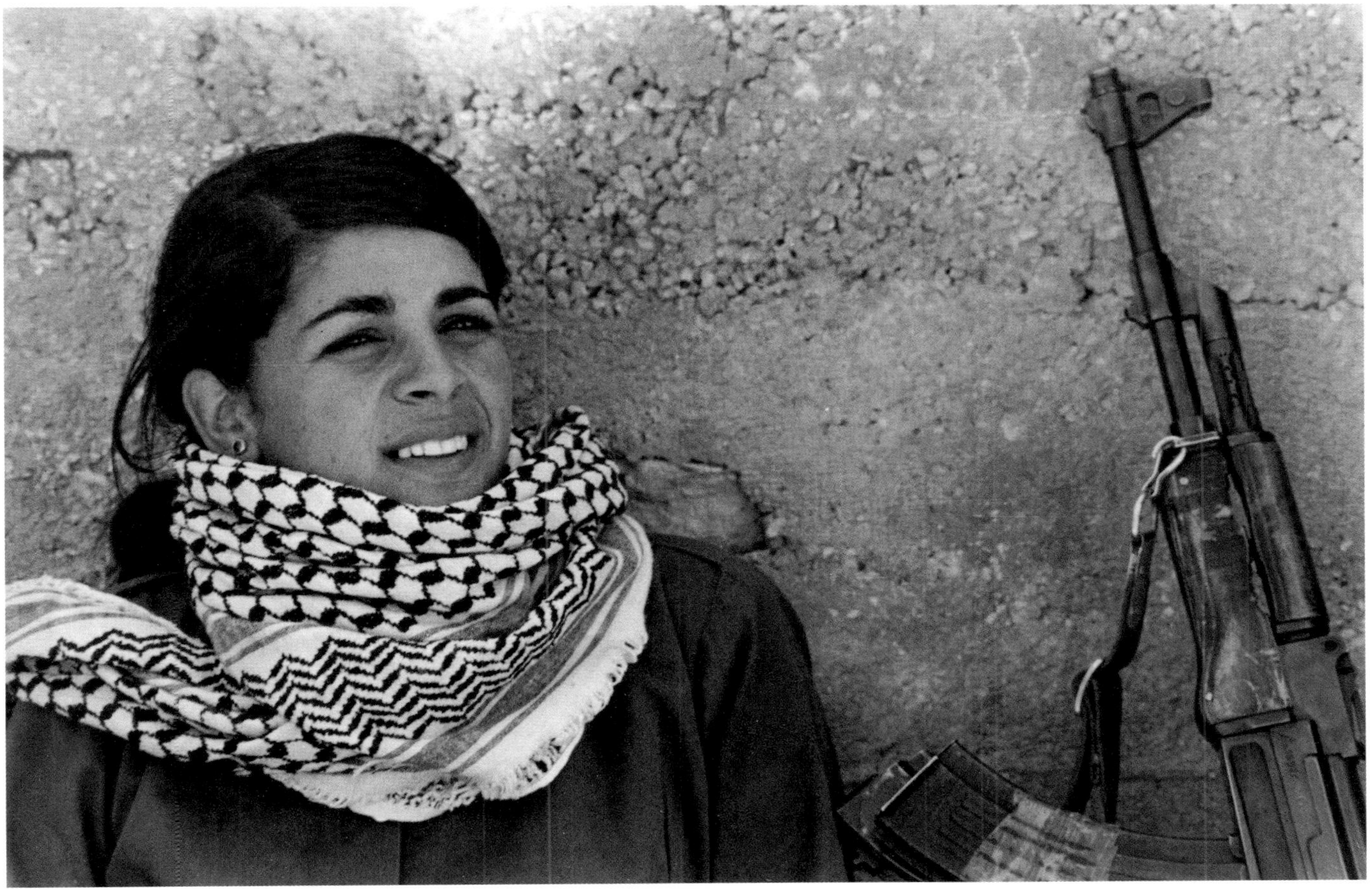

Amman, Jordan. Militant with her first kalachnikof, 1970.

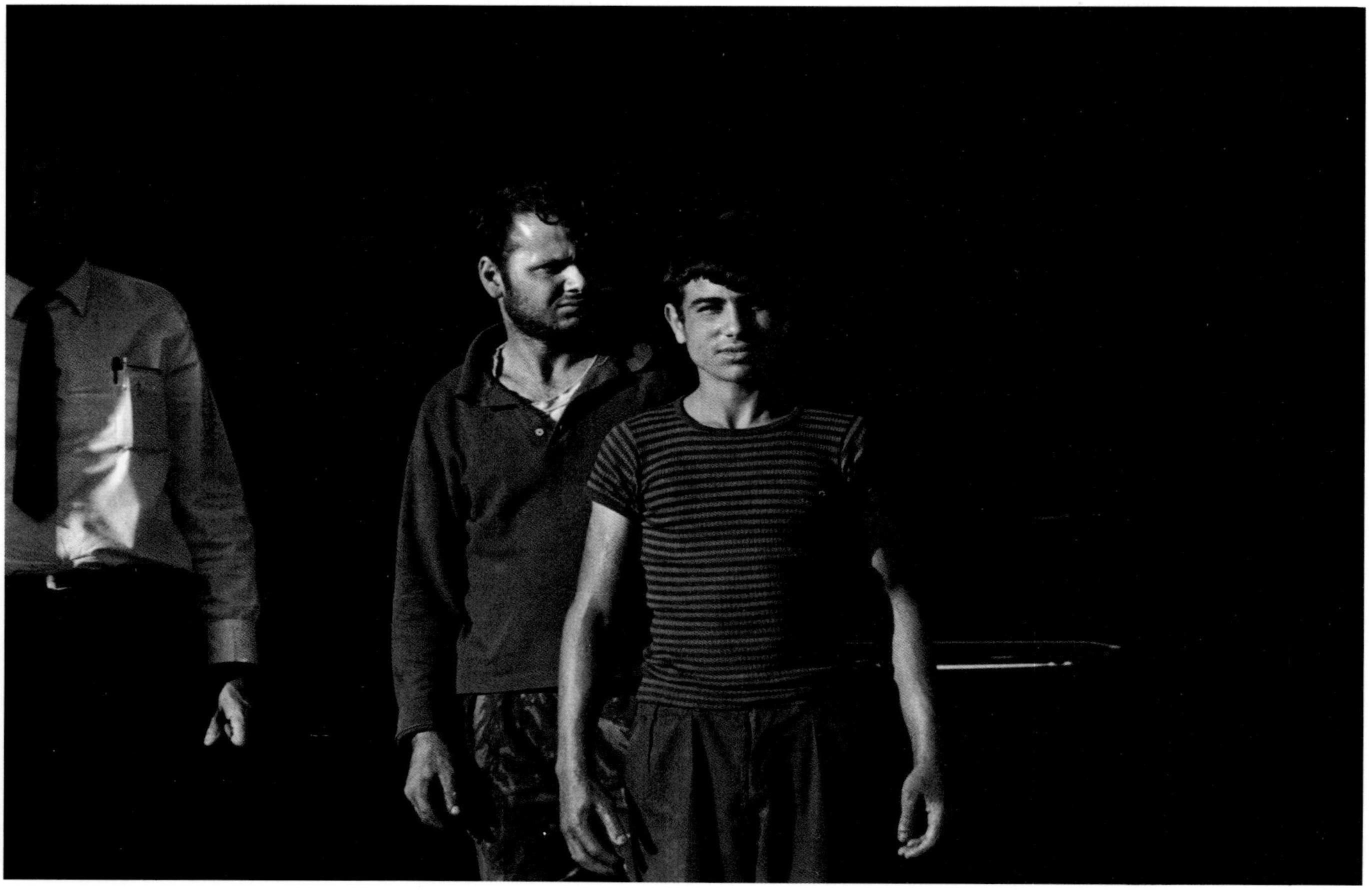

Jordan. Burial of a martyr in the streets of Amman, 1970.

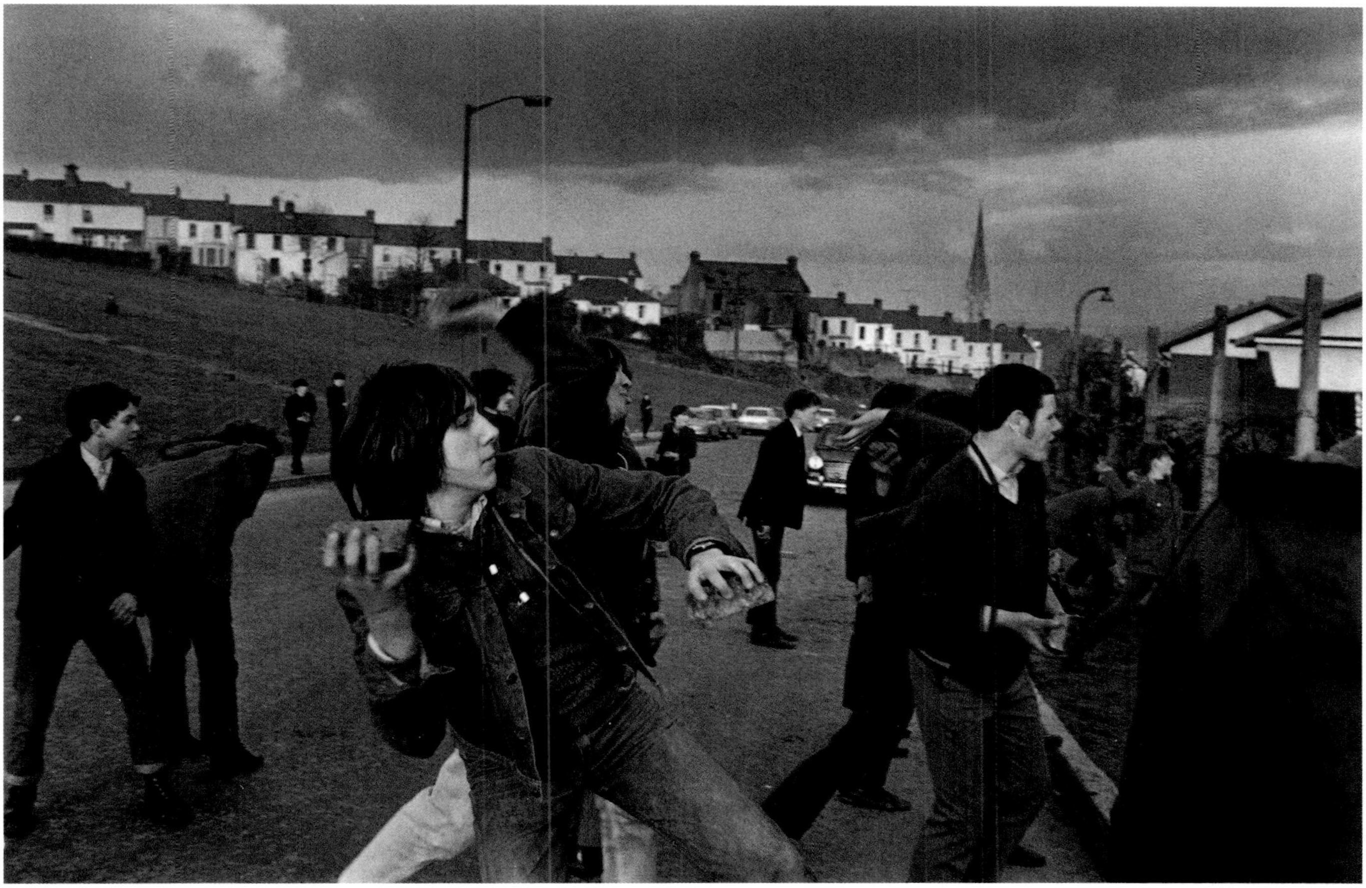

Northern Ireland. Explosion and children throwing stones at British soldiers in the streets of Londonderry, 1970.

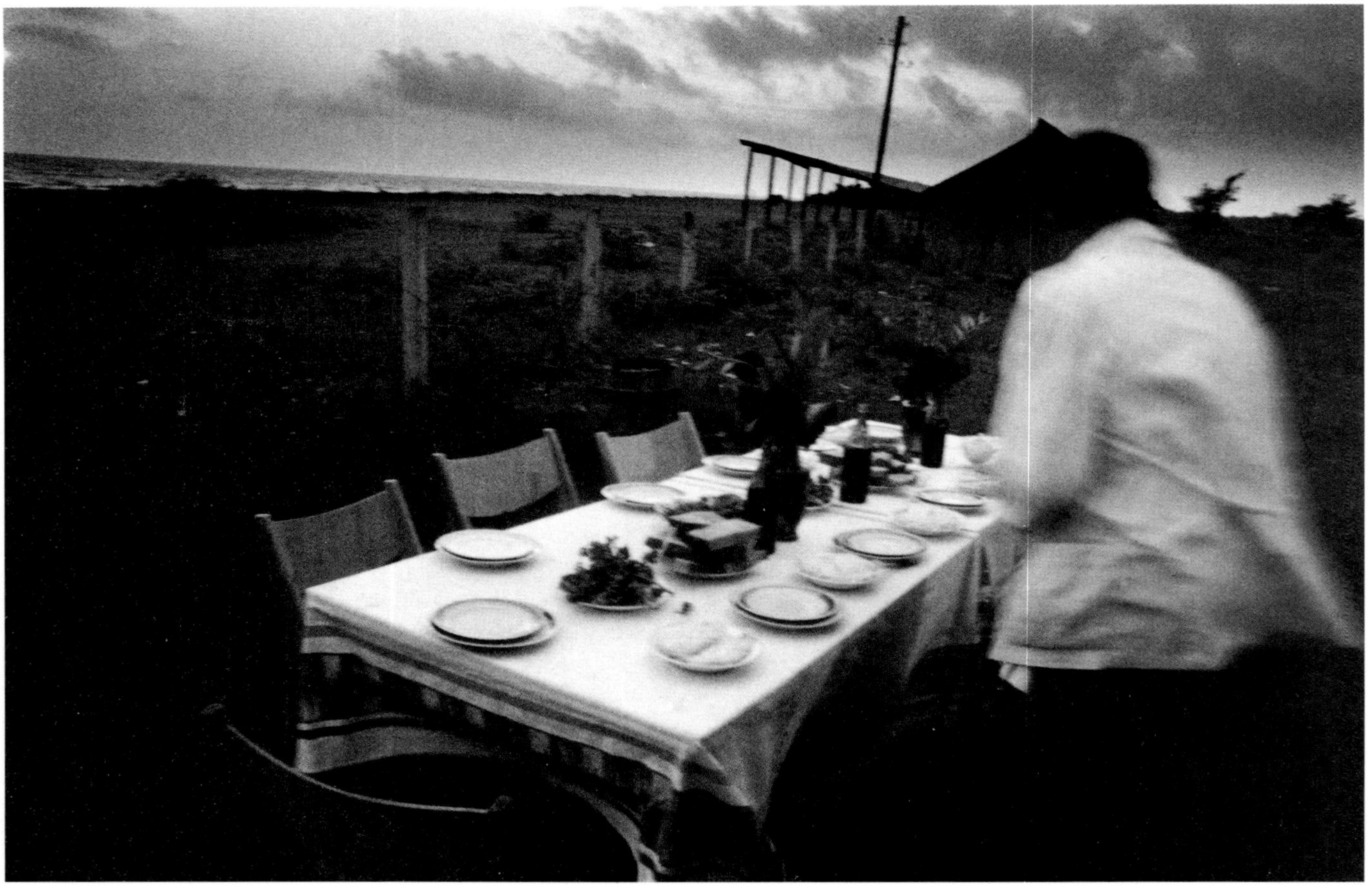

Black Sea coast, USSR. Table set for a picnic, 1967.

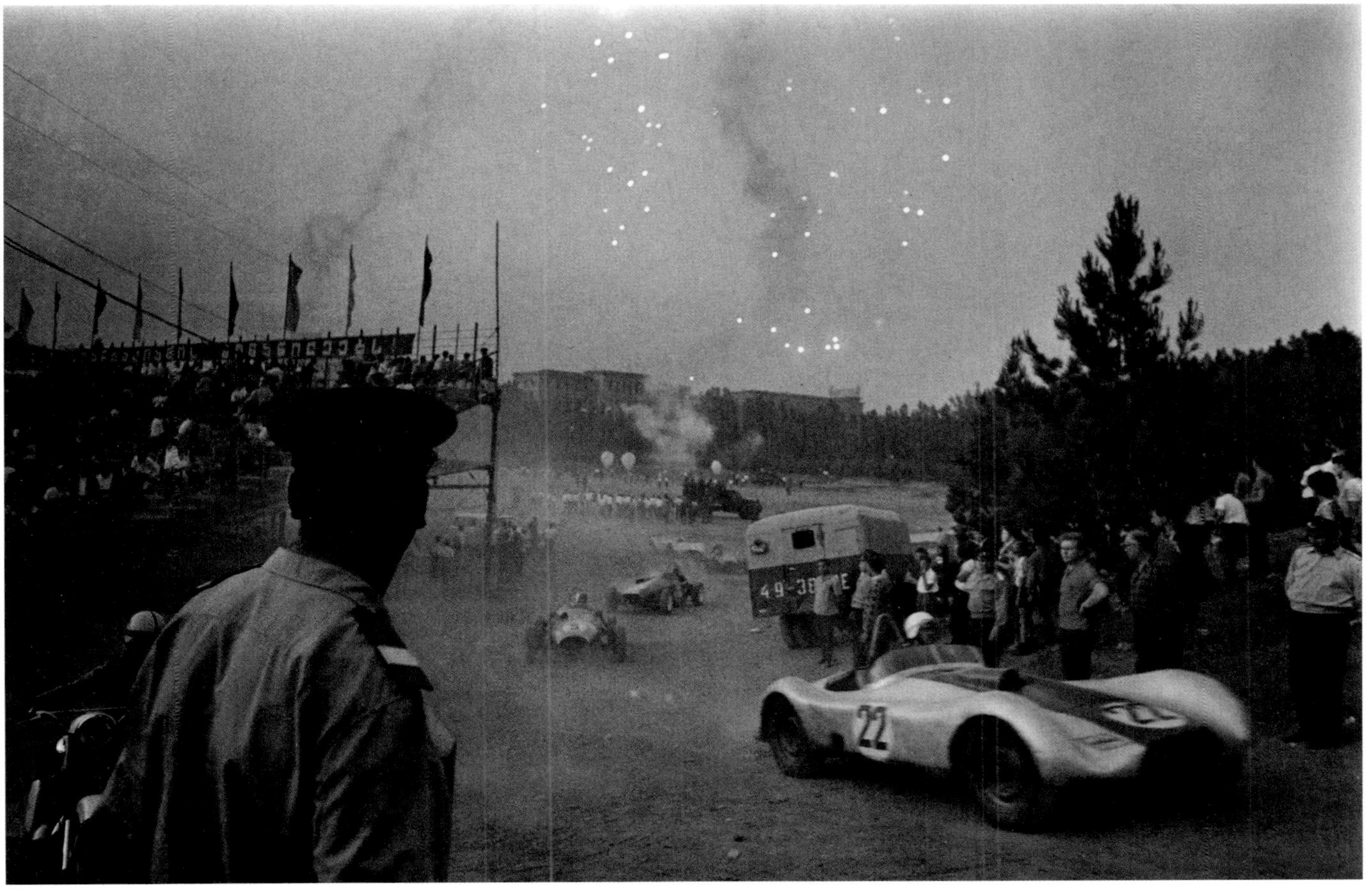

Tbilissi, USSR. Spartakiades, a festival celebrating graduation and the beginning of summer, 1967.

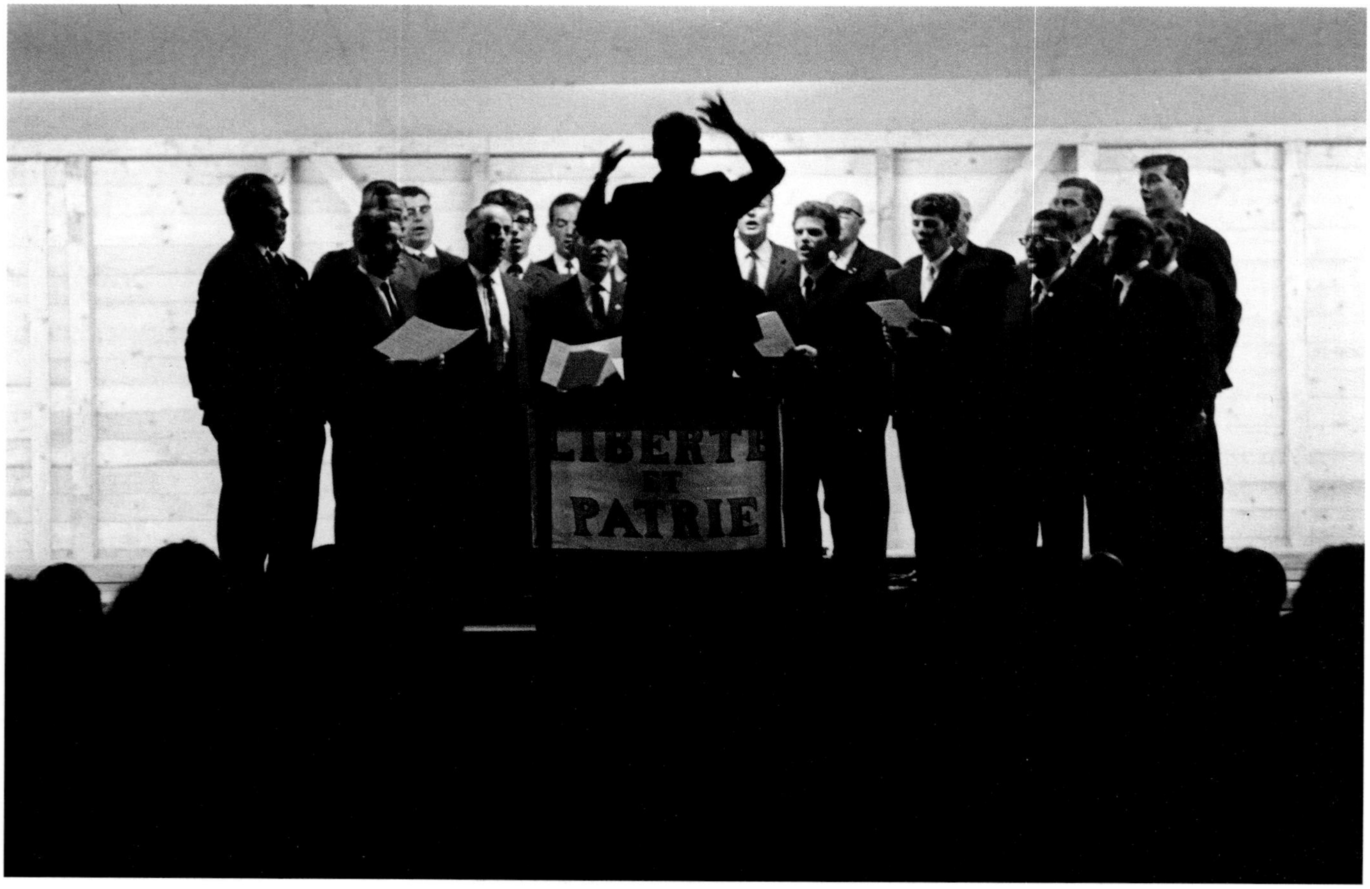

Orbe, Switzerland. Music Society band, 1968.

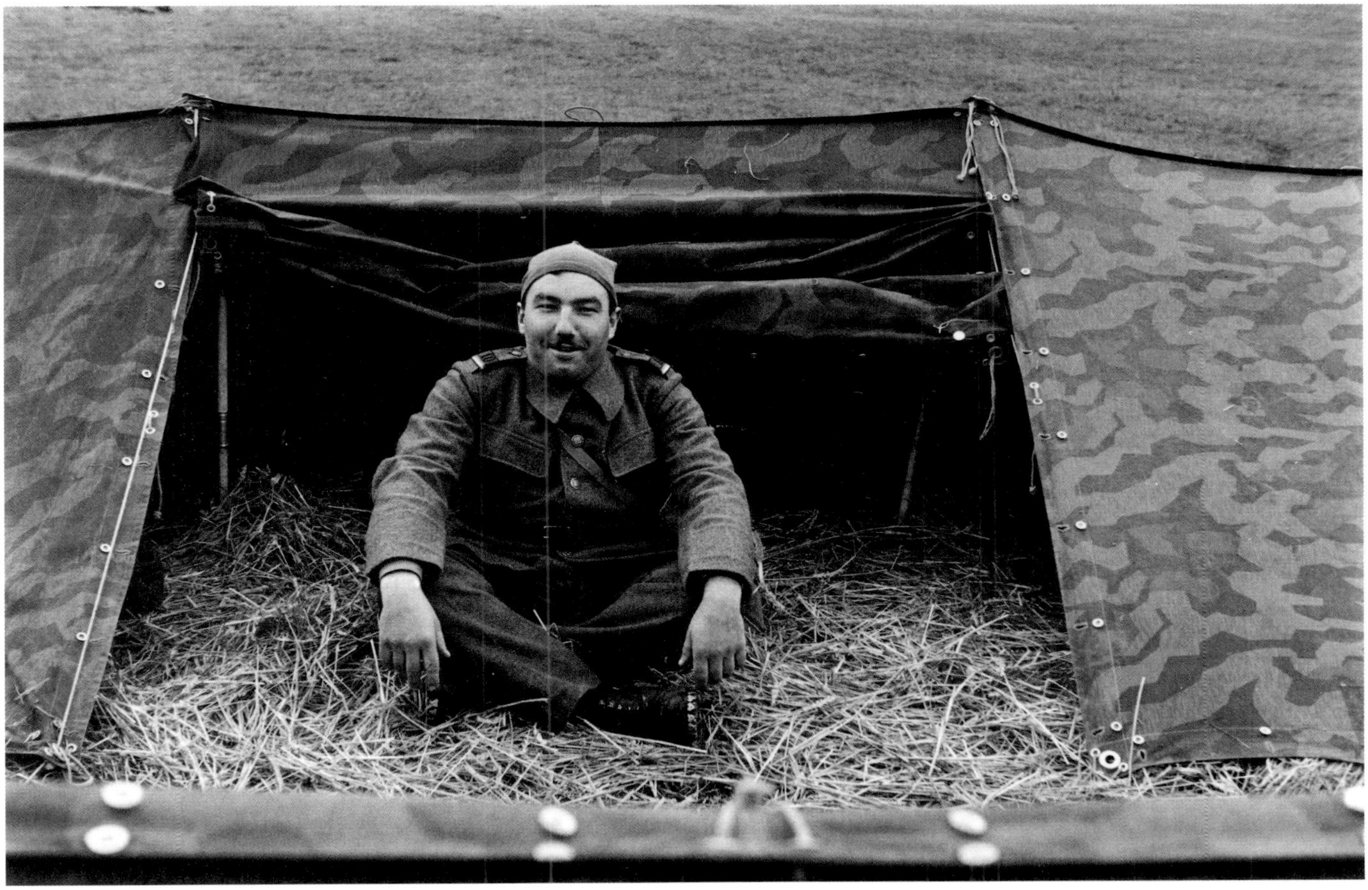

Vernayaz, Switzerland. Mountain medical corps 10, 1963.

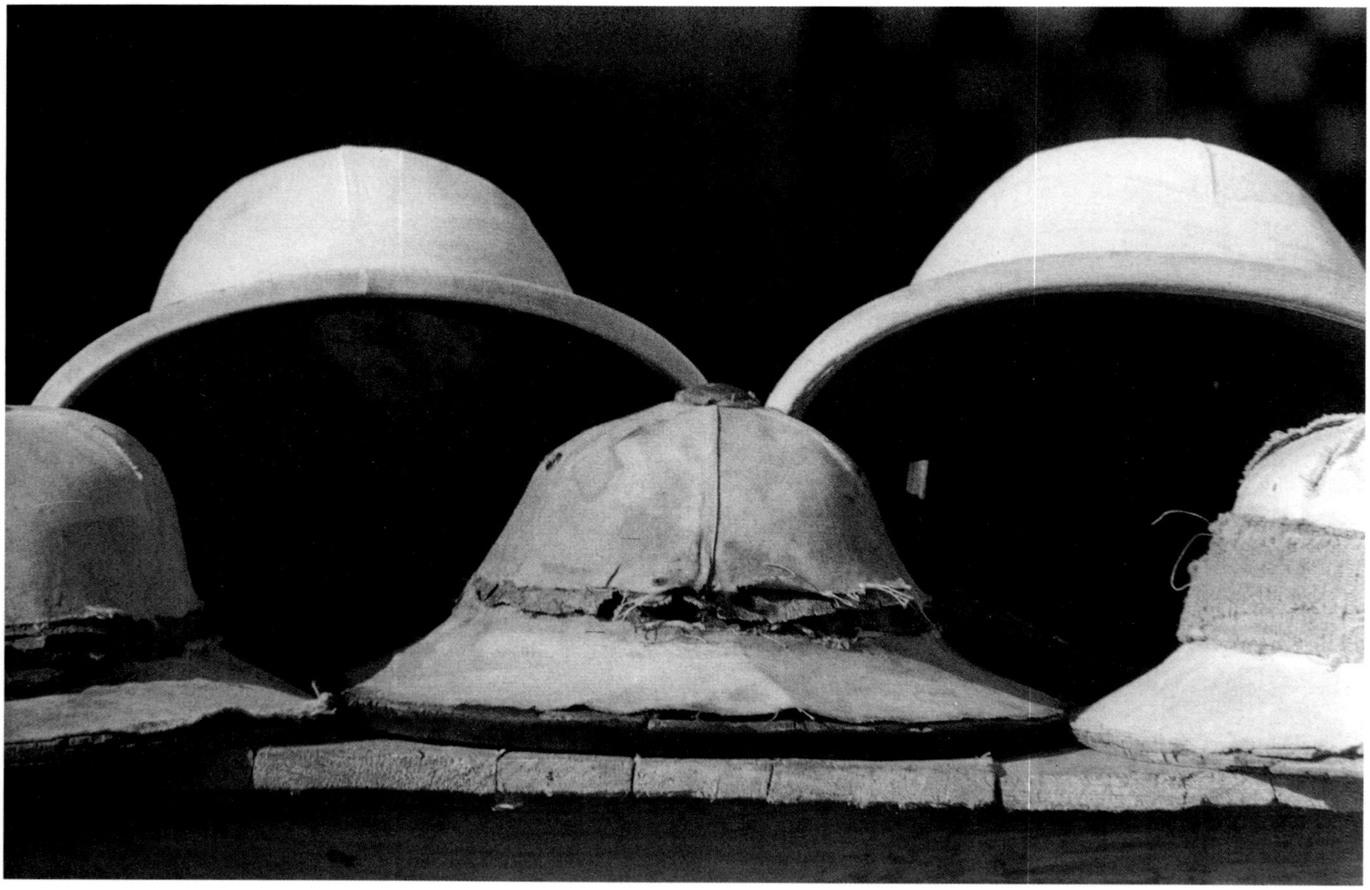

Senegal. Colonial helmets in the Diourbel market, 1965.

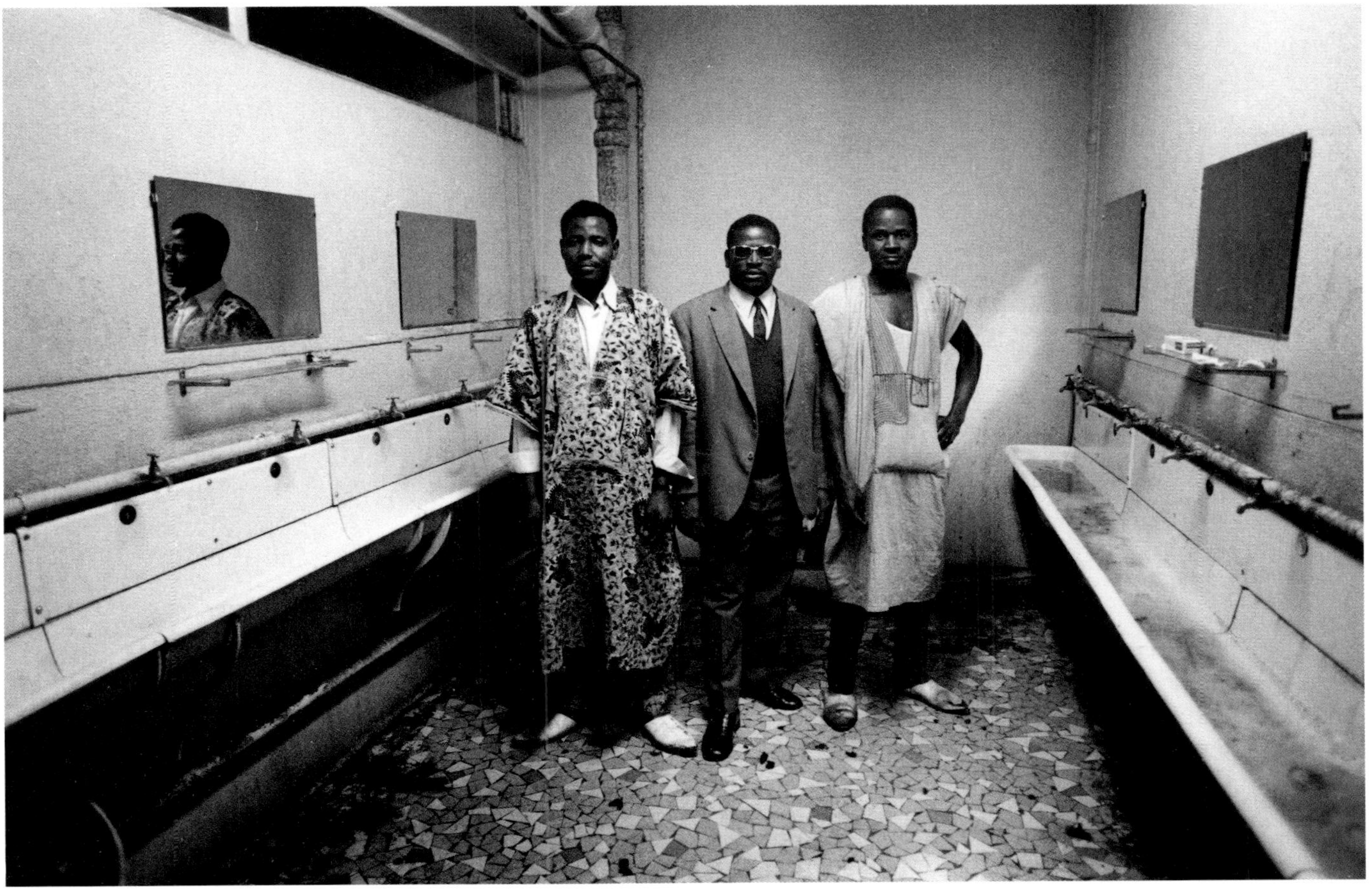

Senegalese workers in Paris, France. Showers in the Billancourt residence, 1969.

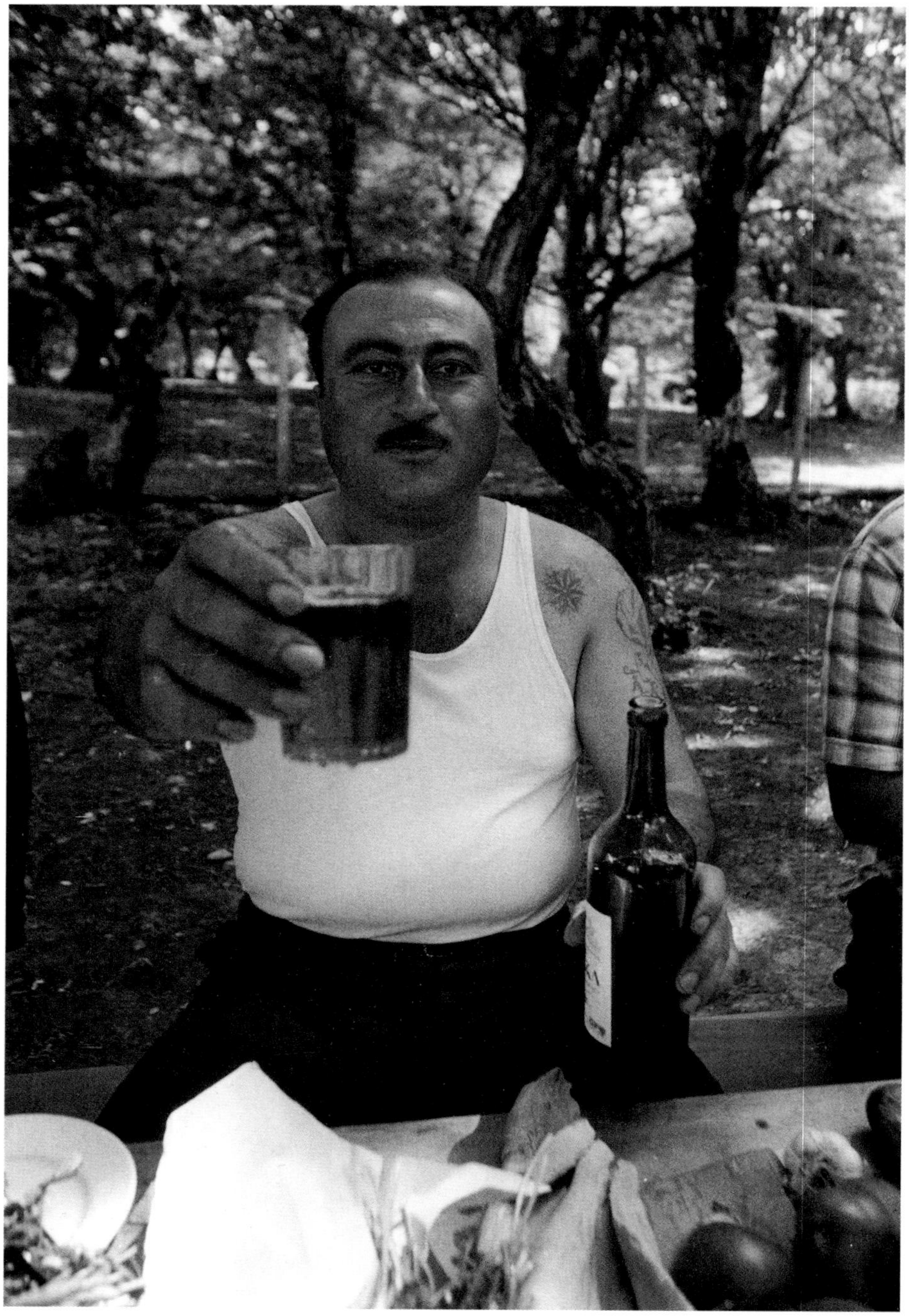

Karetie Valley, USSR. A toast to the assembled guests, 1967.

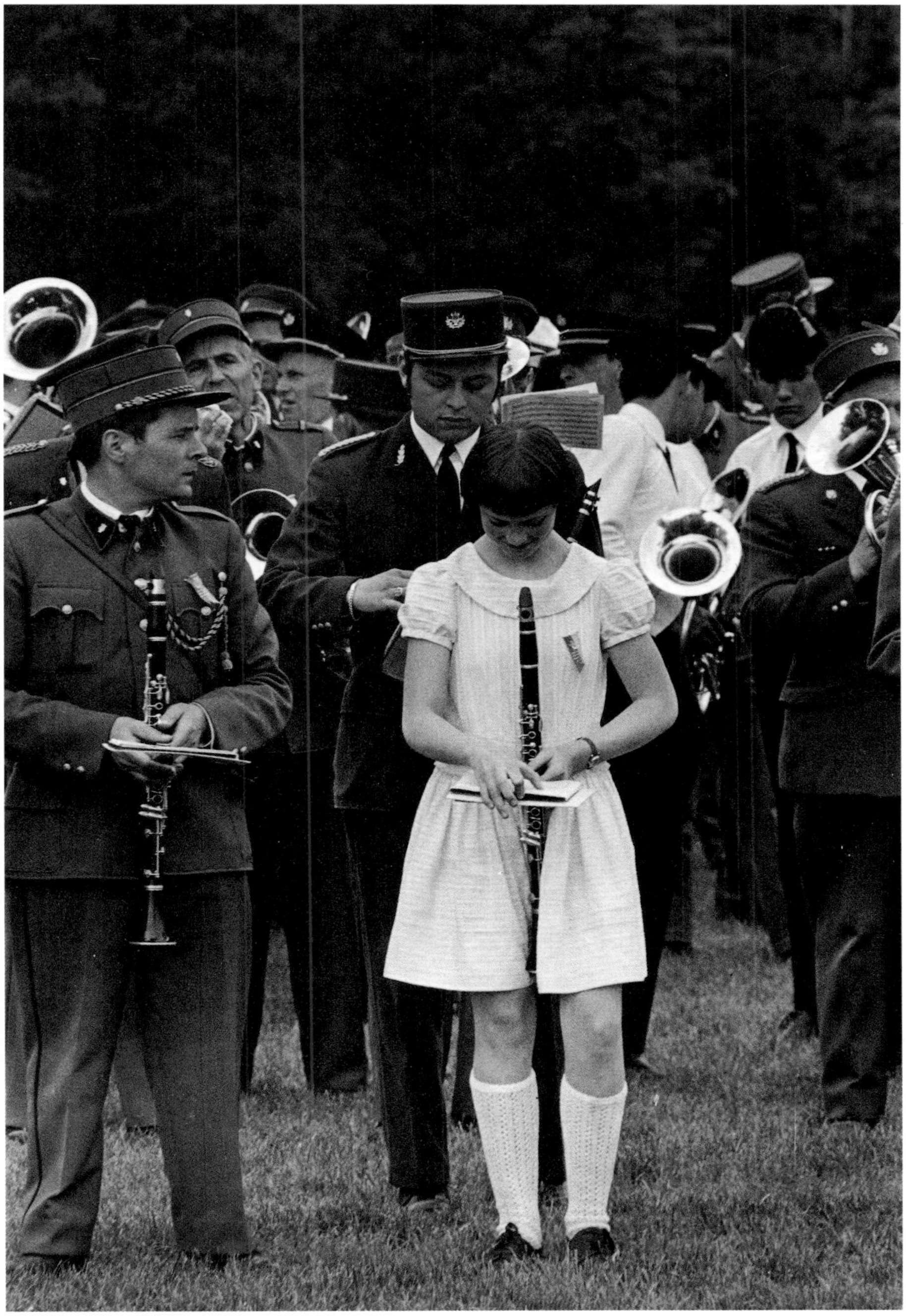

Orbe, Switzerland. Music Society band. 1968.

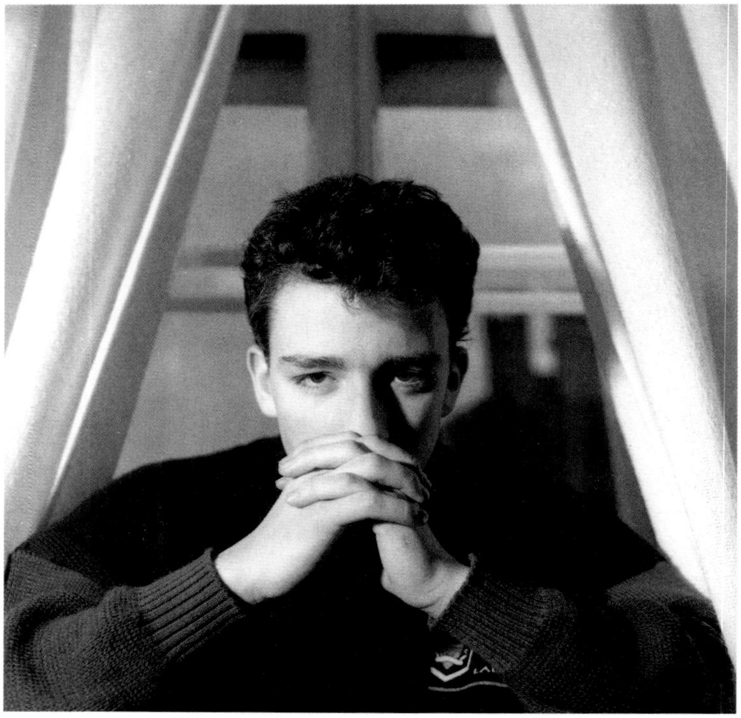

Lionel Deriaz

Born on May 27, 1969, and represents the fifth consecutive generation of the Deriaz family in photography. His name would appear to signify a break with the tradition of Alphonses and Armands. He is a Deriaz nonetheless, and prints from his family's glass plate negatives with sensitivity and skill. He is also a photographer with a keen eye, having studied photography with his father and at l'Ecole de Photographie d'Yverdon-les-Bains.

Lionel Deriaz. Photograph by Kathy Borgeaud, 1988.

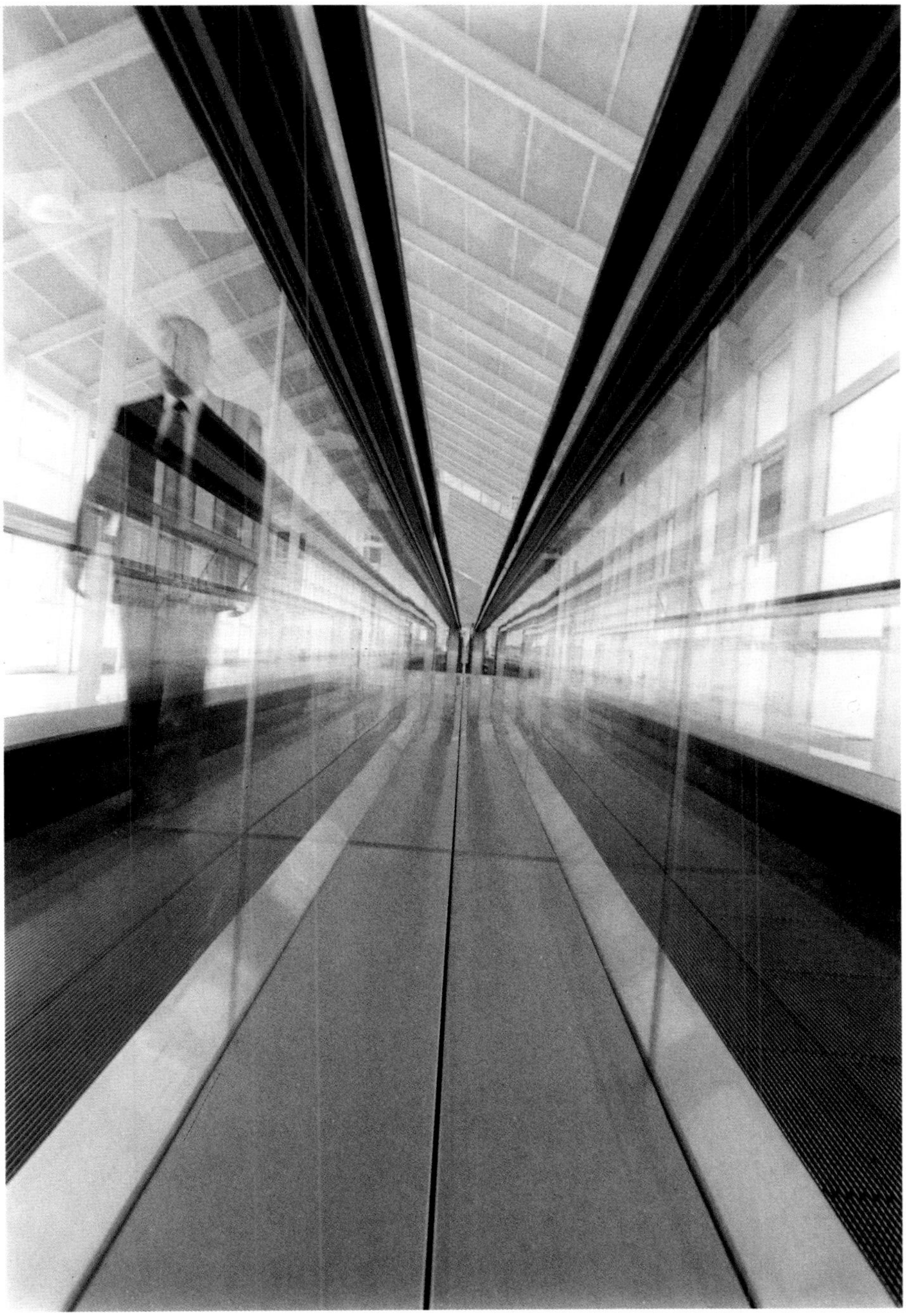

Frankfurt, Germany. Via Mobile, 1987.

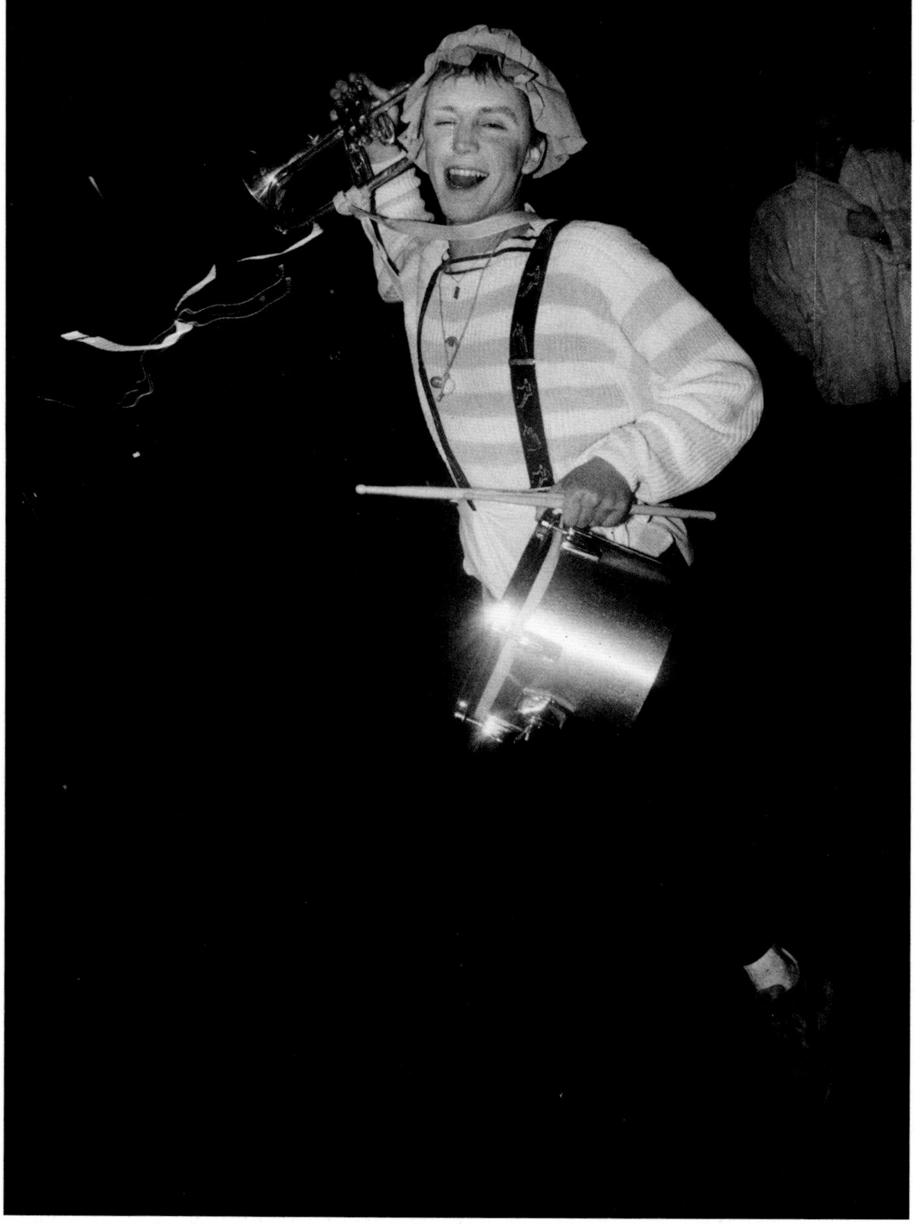

Baulmes. Alain, New Year's festival, 1988.

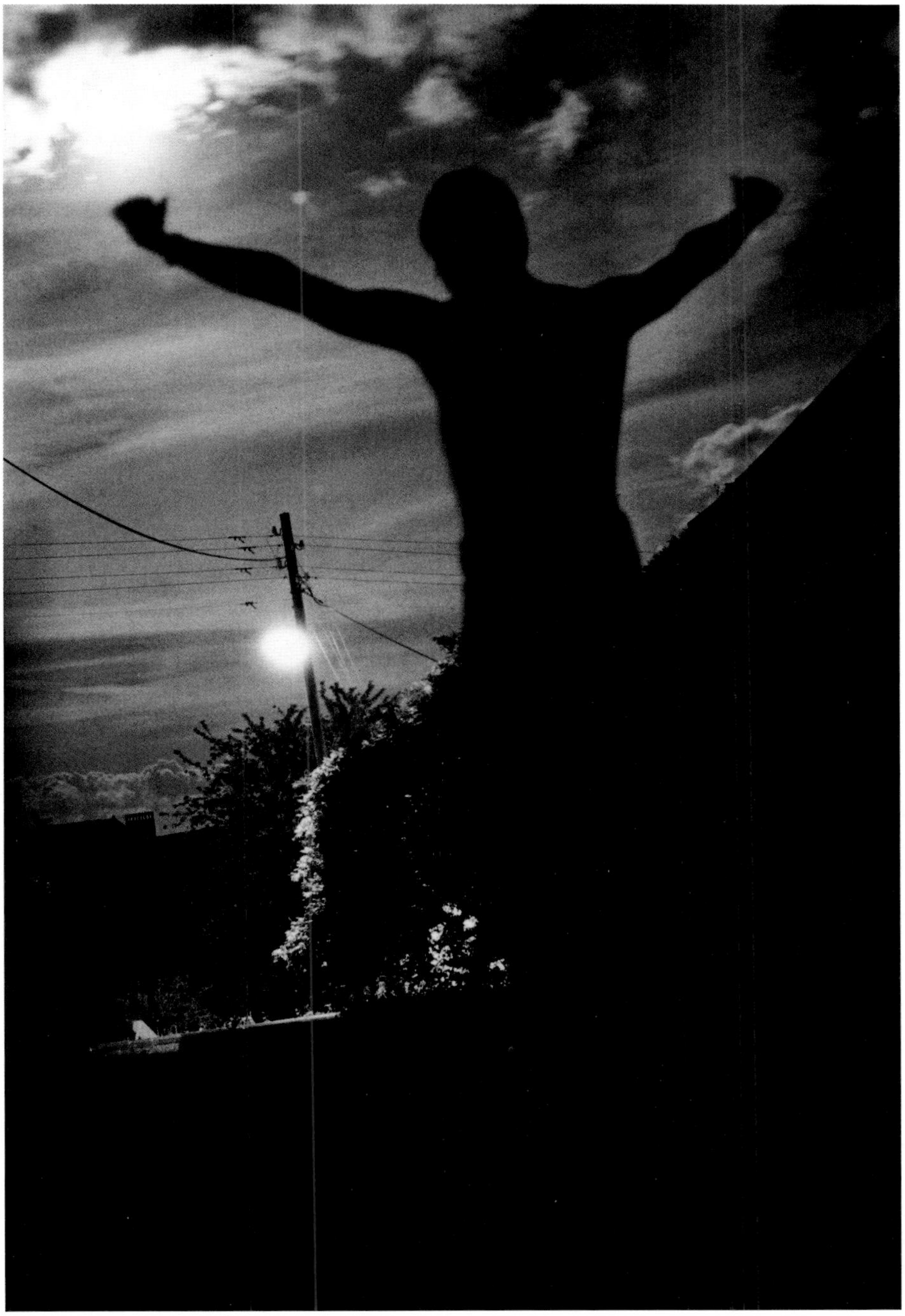

Baulmes. Self-portrait, 1987.

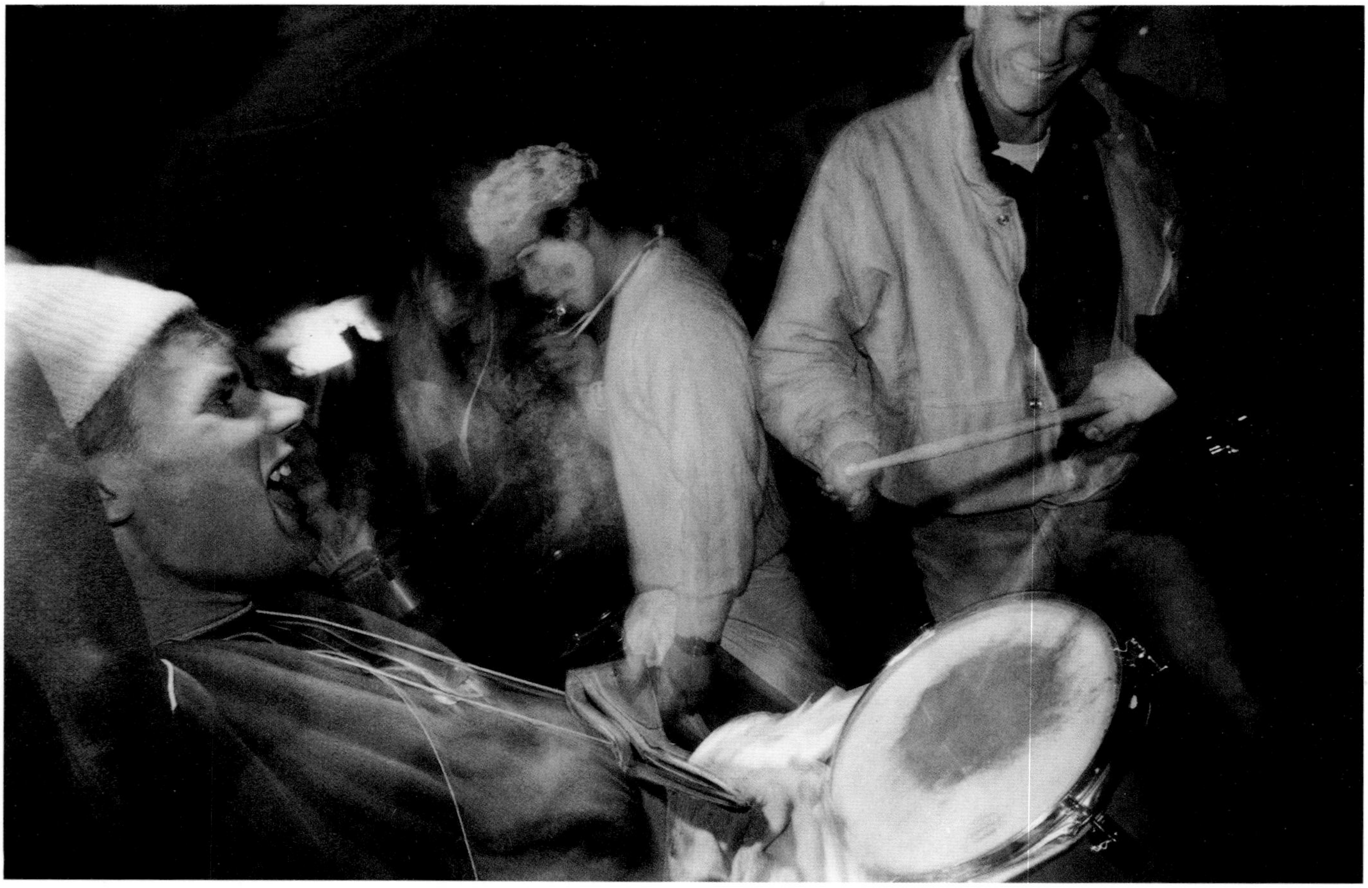

Baulmes. Didier and Pascal, New Year's festival, 1988.

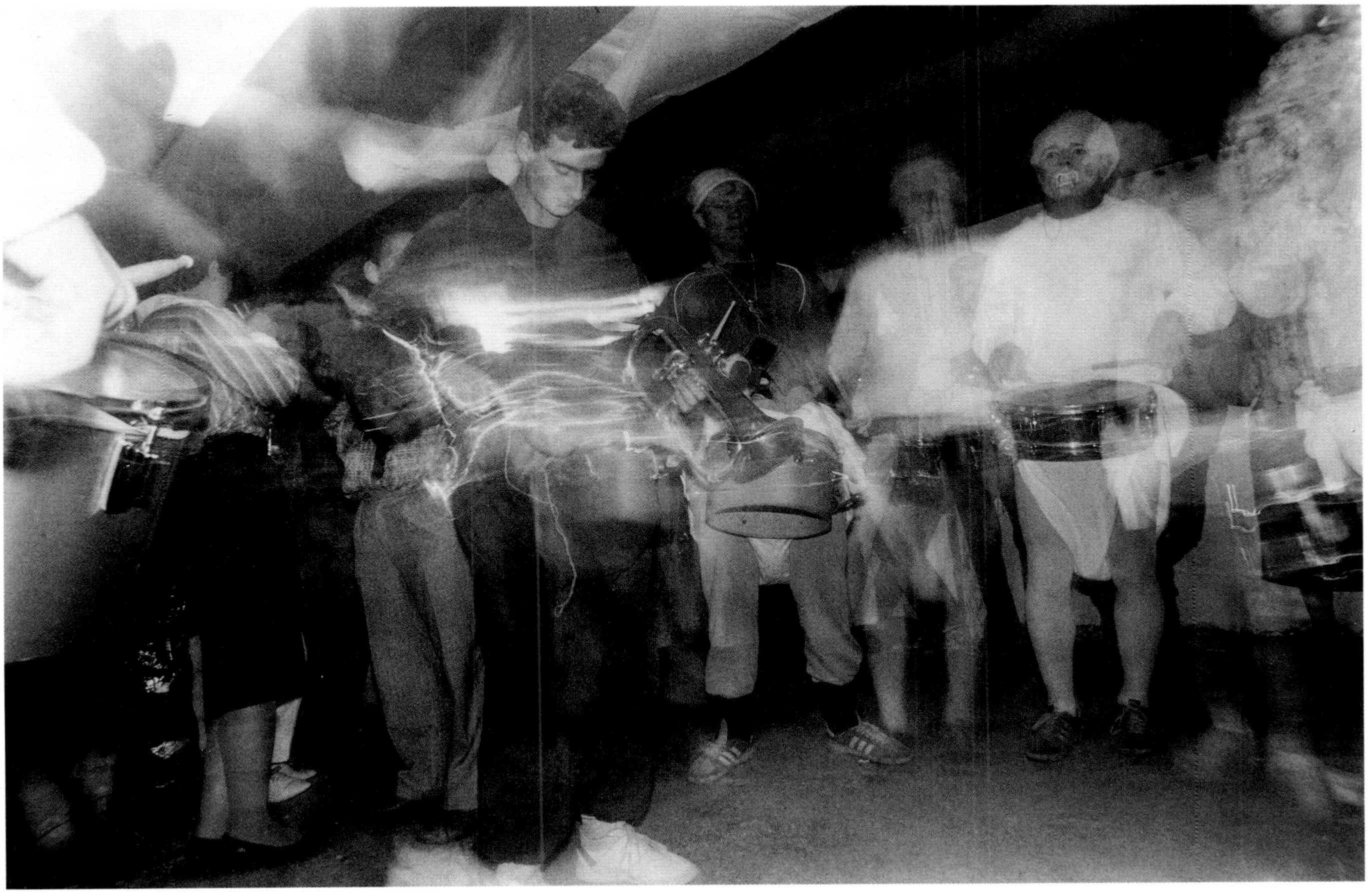

Baulmes. Sylvain and Gerald, New Year's festival, 1988.

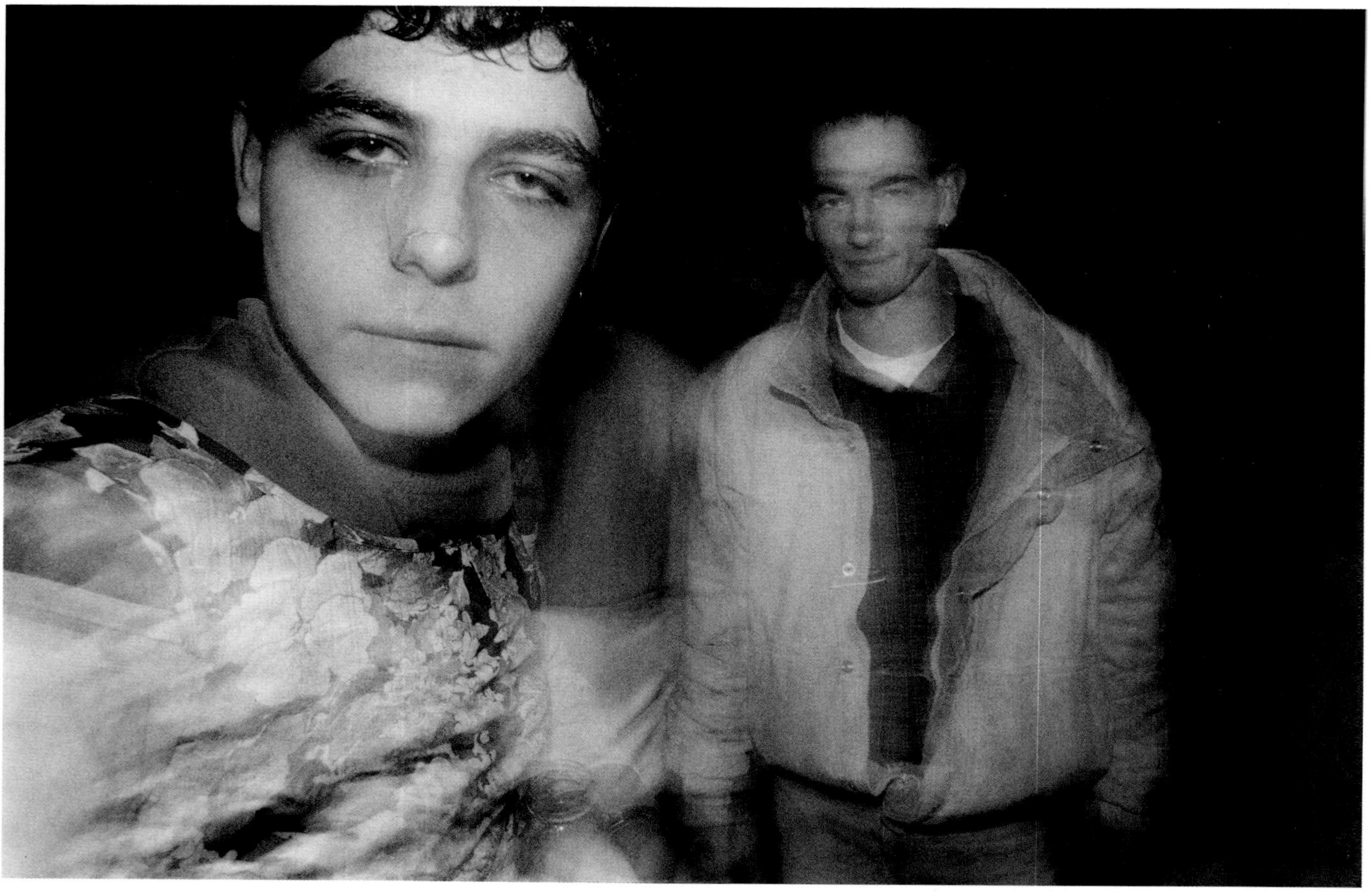

Baulmes. Flavio and Didier, New Year's festival, 1988.

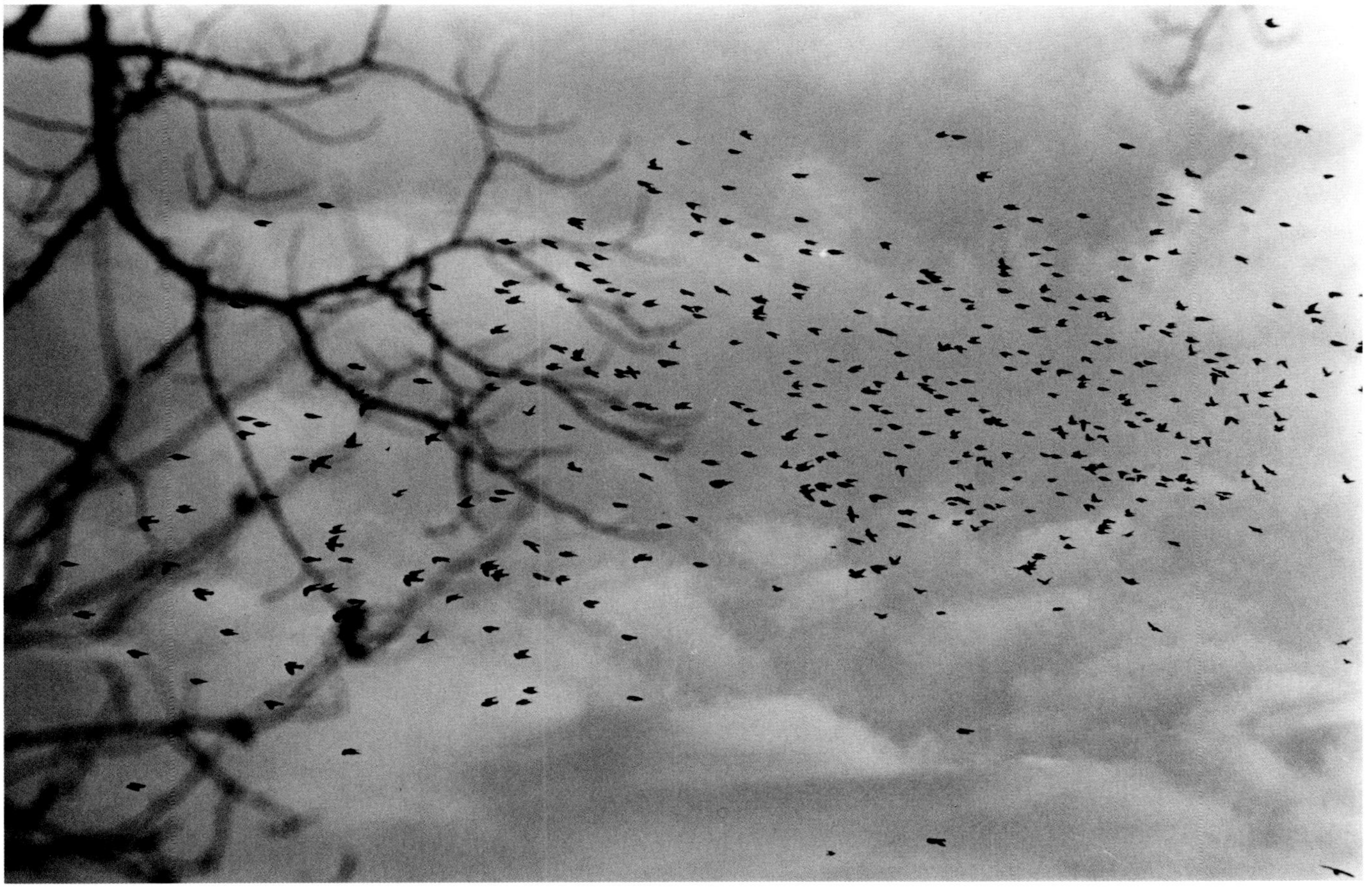

Yverdon, Switzerland, 1986.

Art Direction: Peter Wassermann
Layout: Andrea Hostettler
Production: Peter Renn
Photolithos: Lithorama by Gianetto, I-Torino
Type setting and printing: Meier + Cie AG, CH-8201 Schaffhausen
Binding: Eibert AG, CH-8733 Eschenbach

The production of this book was supported by the Swiss Cultural Institute
Pro Helvetia and the "Migros-Genossenschafts-Bund".

ISBN 3-7231-0387-1